The Hoover Presidency

The Hoover Presidency

A Reappraisal

Martin L. Fausold, Editor
George T. Mazuzan, Associate Editor

State University of New York Press   Albany 1974

For

JOHN E. MAZUZAN

A Vermont Editor

SAMUEL FAUSOLD

A Pennsylvania Educator

Published by State University of New York Press

99 Washington Avenue, Albany, New York 12210

© 1974 State University of New York

Printed in the United States of America

Library of Congress Cataloging in Publication Data

Main entry under title:

The Hoover Presidency: A Reappraisal

    Papers presented at a conference held Apr. 27–28,
1973 at State University College at Geneseo.

    Bibliography: p.

    1. United States—Politics and government—1929–
1933—Congresses. 2. Hoover, Herbert Clark, Pres.
U.S., 1874–1964—Congresses.   I. Fausold, Martin L.,
ed. II. Mazuzan, George T., ed.

E801.H68   973.91'6'0924   74–13876

ISBN 0–87395–280–4

ISBN 0–87395–281–2 (microfiche)

Contents

Preface   vii

Introduction   3

I. Before the Crash

  1. Donald R. McCoy, To the White House: Herbert
     Hoover, August 1927–March 1929   29

  2. David B. Burner, Before the Crash: Hoover's First
     Eight Months in the Presidency   50

II. Antidepression Efforts

  1. Albert U. Romasco, Herbert Hoover's Policies for
     Dealing with the Great Depression: The End of
     the Old Order or the Beginning of the New?   69

  2. Jordan A. Schwarz, Hoover and Congress: Politics,
     Personality, and Perspective in the Presidency   87

  3. Ellis W. Hawley, Herbert Hoover and American
     Corporatism, 1929–1933   101

III. The Interregnum

  1. Alfred B. Rollins, The View From the State House: FDR 123

  2. Frank Freidel, The Interregnum Struggle Between
     Hoover and Roosevelt   134

IV.   Foreign Policy

1. Selig Adler, Hoover's Foreign Policy and
the New Left   153

2. Joan Hoff Wilson, A Reevaluation of
Herbert Hoover's Foreign Policy   164

Bibliographical Note   189
Textual Notes   193

Preface

This book is a direct consequence of the State University of New York's Conversations in Disciplines program, an endeavor to promote conferences on specialized topics. On 27 and 28 April 1973, most of the nation's scholars of the Herbert Hoover period and presidency met at the State University College at Geneseo to reappraise the thirty-first President's years in the White House.

Prior to the Conversation all papers were read by the authors, who also served as the principal critics throughout the conference. At the sessions, the authors summarized their papers for some eighty attending participants. This allowed time for an invigorating dialogue among all who attended. Moreover, it cemented the papers into a composite and reappraised view of the Hoover presidency. Ultimately, the revised papers resulted in this volume of original essays.

We wish to express our appreciation to the central office of the State University of New York for the development and support of the Conversations in the Disciplines programs; the administration of the State University College at Geneseo for supporting this Conversation and this manuscript with financial assistance; and President Robert MacVittie and our colleagues in the history department at Geneseo for their cooperation and for providing hospitality at the Conversation.

Two people among many played major behind-the-scene roles: Harold F. Peterson, Distinguished Professor Emeritus of History at the State University College at Buffalo, shared ideas, raised important questions, and offered sage advice. In addition to presenting one of the conference papers, Donald R. McCoy, Professor of History at the University of Kansas, provided intellectual stimulation, criticism, and encouragement in the development of this project. Finally, our debt cannot be adequately expressed to many scholars and friends who participated in the conference and offered suggestions on the endeavor, but our thanks are warmly extended.

Martin L. Fausold
George T. Mazuzan

Geneseo, New York

Introduction

By Martin L. Fausold

and George T. Mazuzan

Historians at long last are beginning to comprehend Herbert Hoover's presidency in all of its complexity.* Much of their perspective, like that of the American public, was colored by the tinseled surface of the "roaring twenties" and by the increasing ill effects of the Great Depression. With the passage of time and current research on the Hoover presidency, especially since the opening of the Hoover papers in the mid-1960s, a truer perspective is emerging.† To start with, the election of 1928 is now viewed with a proper emphasis on the winner and not the loser. For decades Americans have been hearing about the role of Alfred E. Smith's Catholicism in that campaign and how his defeat presaged the rise of the coalition which elected Franklin Roosevelt president four times. The emphasis now is on Herbert Hoover's near perfect campaigns for nomination and election, the political weakness of the opposing party and its presidential candidate, Hoover's almost universal image as a brilliant engineer, humanitarian, industrial statesman, and extremely active and able secretary of commerce, and the prevailing belief in Republican prosperity.[1]

Although inexperienced in and unhappy with electoral politics, Hoover showed political mettle in 1927 by maintaining a low presidential-seeking profile at the time of Calvin Coolidge's famous "I do not choose to run" statement. Having subtly inquired of Coolidge about his real intent, the secretary of commerce and his aides, who strained to make their "chief" president, didn't make a public move until Coolidge finally asked: "Why not?" Hoover was ready; he brushed aside such contenders as Charles Curtis, Charles Gates Dawes, Charles Evans Hughes, and Frank Lowden and he won primaries in the states of New York, Oregon, California, Maryland, Massachusetts, and Michigan. It was an easy first ballot victory in the 1928 Republican Convention. Little did the public know how Hoover had neutralized such opposition as the Old Guard, who, as Donald McCoy notes, were bought off with nominal leadership jobs in the campaign. (See I-1)

Explanations for Hoover's election in 1928 are emerging as clearly as those for his nomination. Aside from having massive Republican support—including that of the disgruntled Old Guard—Hoover impressed many progressives. Such Democratic stalwarts as Louis Brandeis and Franklin Roosevelt had praised Hoover too recently for his image to be turned conservative. Add to their plau-

* The domestic area of this introduction was written by the editor; the foreign policy section was composed by the associate editor.

† See Bibliographical Note preceding the Introduction end/notes, pp. 189–91.

dits Hoover's own public relations as secretary of commerce (and as a presidential candidate) and one can understand America's opinion of him.[2] When in seven campaign addresses he ponderously called for cooperative approaches to depressed agriculture, a reasonably protective tariff to enhance business and labor, "fair play" to all Americans, including his Catholic opponent, government non-interference in business, the right of labor to organize, the enforcement of prohibition, and even public works to spur business and employment, he seemed to be advancing a surefire plan for continued prosperity.

There is no gainsaying, however, that much of Hoover's success in 1928 was attributable to the state of the Democratic party and its candidate, Alfred E. Smith. For one thing, the Democratic party was still dangerously schizophrenic, although less intensely than in 1924, when contending regional and ethnic elements fought to the death. Unfortunately for the Democrats, America's rural-urban, Protestant-Catholic, wet-dry dichotomies were concentrated in their party, the more national of the two major political organizations. And Alfred Smith's candidacy was particularly suited to exacerbate the divisions of 1924. Yet, the New Yorker was so outstanding a political figure that his fellow Democrats could not deny him the prize of presidential nomination four years later. In naming him, they accentuated the American division both in and out of their party. While many southern Democrats temporarily abandoned the party of their fathers, irresponsible Republicans like Assistant Attorney General Mabel Willebrandt spread hate and more respectable ones like William Allen White saw in Smith's candidacy at least a "threat . . . to puritan civilization." Sadly, the humane and sensitive Hoover did little to curb his followers' exploitation of these dichotomies. Smith proudly, and foolishly, deepened the split by accentuating his Catholicism, his Tammany association, and his East-side mannerisms.[3]

So Hoover won because of his well-organized campaign and his image, because of "Republican prosperity," and because of the state of the Democratic party. Ideological considerations were not significant, for the two candidates had similar positions. Yet in Smith's defeat there was some consolation, for in 122 GOP counties, the nation's twelve largest cities, and some northeastern states he made significant inroads which were a portent of things to come. For the moment, however, the Republican candidate gloried in his overwhelming triumph.

Few presidents-elect have been viewed as favorably as was Herbert

Hoover on inaugural eve, perhaps, as *The New York Times* reported, because he became president not by the ordinary political route but "by paths laid by his energy, personal ability and sterling character." His March 1929 inaugural address seemed to prove the accolade. In less than 3,500 words he called for the enhancement of self-government, economic and social justice, equality of opportunity, integrity in government, freedom of public opinion, religious spirit, the home, and peace. More specifically, he committed his presidency to noninterference in business, relief to agriculture, limited changes in the tariff, and full employment for all the people.[4]

To launch what Hoover called his "New Day," he gathered about him a cabinet of efficient administrators, who generally, like him, were short on partisan politics and were not inordinately pro-business.[5] Their selection was revealing of the president. For the first portfolio, State, Hoover approached Charles Evans Hughes, William Borah, and Frank Kellogg before turning to Henry L. Stimson, who would emerge as the strongest member of the cabinet—perhaps the only truly strong member. Andrew Mellon and James J. Davis continued as secretaries of the treasury and labor and manifested Hoover's ties to the previous administration. William D. Mitchell, Coolidge's competent solicitor general, and James W. Good, Hoover's midwestern political leader, became respectively the attorney general and the secretary of war. Hoover considered William J. "Wild Bill" Donovan, Coolidge's assistant attorney general, for one or the other of the two positions and raised such a public hue and cry by not appointing him to the cabinet that he filed in his papers a handwritten rationale for his actions. The public then, and historians subsequently, thought the president in large part bowed to anti-Catholic pressures, when in fact, Hoover questioned Donovan's commitment to antitrust enforcement and his "dictatorial tone." [6] Upon Good's early death, swashbuckling Patrick J. Hurley was appointed secretary of war. Automobile dealer and former Missouri Governor Arthur M. Hyde became secretary of agriculture and left the president free to make policy in an area of preeminent importance to him. Charles Francis Adams, the descendent of presidents, became secretary of the navy. Robert P. Lamont, a fellow engineer who was active in business, was appointed secretary of commerce. Walter F. Brown, a former Ohio political boss and a very early Hoover supporter, became the postmaster general. Except for James Good, Brown was just about Hoover's only nod to partisan politics in appointing his cabinet. Ray Lyman Wilbur, president of Stanford University and a close Hoover confidant of long standing, became the secretary of the interior.

The cabinet, unlike Coolidge's more independent one, was indeed Hoover's, especially regarding important policy areas. In Agriculture, for example, the president would make policy. In Interior, his alter ego, Raymond Wilbur, would reflect the president's wishes. In Treasury, Hoover would rely more on Undersecretary Ogden Mills than on Mellon. In Commerce, Lamont would keep Hoover's public relations and statistical apparatus available for presidential use. Only Secretary of State Stimson would at times manifest independence of the president, but he, of course, was always properly deferential. Though by normal standards the cabinet was adequate, it soon proved unable to meet the depression crises, and though Hoover used his cabinet, he frequently relied more on intimates outside of it for advice.

Following the inaugural ceremonies, the president vigorously and grimly set about carrying out his "New Day"—making as few political gestures as he had in appointing his cabinet. An intimate friend from California, M. L. Requa, worried on two political scores: "There seems to be a broad feeling that he is too much a machine . . . ; the great weakness of the President is that he is over the heads of most of the people, that he has no time for small talk and petty politics; that he has not the ability to slap people on the back and tell them that he has done a good job." [7]

In the eight months before the great October stock market crash, the president moved on a multiplicity of fronts. While many of his programs did not surface until after the crash, and so were overshadowed by it and subsequent conditions, David Burner catalogues some actions not overshadowed by the Great Depression (see I-2): publishing tax refunds, listing the political backers of judicial appointees, prohibiting leasing of naval oil reserves, releasing political prisoners, removing Mabel Willebrandt from the Justice Department, accepting peaceful picketing of the White House, permitting direct quotation of the president at White House press conferences, resolving a threatened railroad strike, entertaining a black congressman's wife at the White House, and increasing appropriations for Howard University.

Profound changes took place in the various departments, frequently under the auspices of presidentially sponsored or appointed conferences and committees. No American president has so efficiently organized the study of great problems by leading experts. Hoover felt that the findings of such conferences and committees could be the basis for proposing to Congress and other governmental and philanthropic bodies programs so logically constructed that favorable legislative or other action would be inevitable. That such results were not the case reflected the president's inability to understand and deal with bodies outside of the executive branch, especially the Congress.

Not surprisingly, Hoover's greatest efforts at change were attempted in those departments where the president had the most interest and exercised the most control, particularly the Interior and Agriculture departments. Very early in the administration, Hoover and Interior Secretary Wilbur initiated conference studies of child welfare, social waste, housing, public land policy, oil conservation, and federal involvement in public education. These conferences of course, frequently involved other departments, as the child welfare conference illustrates. Within four months of his inauguration, the president appointed twenty-seven recognized leaders in the field of child welfare to prepare a White House conference for November of 1930. The planning committee in turn called upon 1,200 experts, who worked on nearly 150 different committees that were divided into four sections: medical science, public health, education and training, and the handicapped. At the conference itself, 3,000 delegates produced publications which constituted the first significant encyclopedia on child health and protection. Consistent with Hoover's faith in the spirit of cooperativism and voluntarism, the $500,000 cost of the conference came from private sources. Within the Interior Department considerable interest was shown toward conservation (the area of National Parks and Monuments was increased by 40 percent) and the Indian service (by a doubling of its appropriations). Of course, prominent among these programs the Interior Department sponsored were the highly publicized activities of the Wickersham Commission on Law Enforcement and two important committee studies, those of the Committee on Recent Social Trends and the Committee on Recent Economic Trends.[8]

Burner finds manifestations of Progressivism in the combined expertise and voluntarism of many of these programs. Ellis W. Hawley covers the precrash months, but with different emphasis. (See II-3) He stresses the president's continued commitment to the antitrust laws and his sponsorship of the 1929 Agricultural Marketing Act. Both efforts emerged from Hoover's attempt "to blend liberal values with a type of corporatist thought that envisioned a decentralized, organic, interdependent social order, organized around and regulated by specialized functional groupings, yet held together and stabilized by responsible leadership, established principles of social equity and efficiency, and institutionalization of a 'natural' mutuality of interest." [9] Thus, while the president encouraged trade associations to engage in cooperative programs, he still believed in a healthy competition and enforcement of the antitrust laws and in the Agricultural Marketing Act he tried to institutionalize this same blend of corporatism and individualism for agriculture.

The Agricultural Marketing Act, passed in June 1929 by the special session of Congress which Hoover had promised to convene to relieve agriculture, was completely the president's handiwork and did indeed manifest his corporate ideals of cooperativism and voluntarism. While major farm organizations showed little enthusiasm for the bill, they tolerated its aims of controlling speculation, eliminating wasteful distribution, organizing cooperative associations, and minimizing surpluses. The Farm Bureau and the Grange were far more interested in stronger medicine, i.e., McNary-Haugenism or an export debenture program. [10]

The heart of the Agricultural Marketing Act was a $500 million revolving fund for making loans to cooperatives to merchandise farm commodities, expand cooperatives, and make advances to growers. Unfortunately, the program was intended to be a long-range one and was not suited to the crisis economic conditions following the crash. For the moment, however, Hoover was pleased with his farm bill. Tariff revision, also intended as an aid to agriculture, emanated from the same special session of Congress, but was extremely displeasing to the president. While supporting reasonable protection, Hoover soon became alarmed by the log rolling which tariff revisionism conjured up. The president, consistent with his belief in the constitutional separation of powers, hopelessly watched the Congress adjourn on 22 November 1929 without having passed a reasonable tariff bill. His distress was not abated when the highly protective Smoot-Hawley tariff was passed in June of the following year.

During the early months of Hoover's presidency, the period of "Forgotten Progress," there lurked ominous signs of economic recession. Automobile production reached its peak in June of 1929 and industrial production generally began to decline a month later. [11] More worrisome to the new administration and watchers of the economy was the speculative boom in the stock market. The market boom, financed by easy credit, paradoxically had encouraged advanced production and sale of certain goods and services at a time when their sale was reaching a saturation point. Hoover and the Federal Reserve Board watched anxiously the rise of the market in the spring of 1929, yet vetoed a New York Federal Reserve Bank cooling proposal to increase their discount rate by 1 percent, for fear that legitimate and nonspeculative borrowers might be denied credit. Washington favored persuasion as a means of discouraging New York banks from lending to speculators. When persuasion and an unnerving of the market by secret daily meetings of the Federal Reserve Board broke the market, Charles E. Mitchell, the head of the National City Bank and a director of the New York Federal Reserve Bank, blew the whistle on the tight-money policy, pushing money for speculation again. The Federal Reserve Board, as John Kenneth Galbraith has indicated, "retired from the field." That speculation continued on Wall Street throughout 1929—with a slight break in early September—to the Great Crash in early October is well known.[12]

Contrary to conventional wisdom, the stock-market crash did not cause, but rather precipitated the Great Depression, which had evolved to such startling proportions by the time Hoover left office. Internationally, political instability following World War I, intergovernmental debts and reparations, and an unstable balance of payments and international trade explain the depression. Aggravations on the national scene include the lack of an adequately planned conversion from war to peace, the pressure of sick industries, maldistribution of income, weak labor organizations, technological unemployment, and an inordinately probusiness attitude in Washington.

Hoover responded to the crash and the pending depression positively and vigorously. With little precedent for such efforts, he became anticyclical and brushed aside Mellon's admonition that the economy be purged through the liquidation process.[13] Typically ignoring the Congress, he resorted to a semicorporatist approach, convening in Washington meetings of leaders of labor unions and great industries such as banking, construction, and railroads. These conferences voluntarily agreed to industrial peace, wage stabilization, and expanded construction, thus making the president's blend of government initiative and private organization successful. For additional government action Hoover urged all the state governors to attack the coming depression either by public works or other state and local expenditures. After all, the state governments cumulatively encompassed far more of the gross national product than did the federal government. Almost to a man, the governors, including Roosevelt of New York, reacted positively. Secretary of Commerce Lamont wrote to the president on 3 January 1930 that the governors of twenty-nine states reported public works construction by their state and local governments would be at $3 billion during 1930, a figure even higher than that spent in 1929.[14] In addition, the president launched his own public works that would result in an expenditure of more than $2 billion on nonproductive (and non-self-liquidating) public works during his presidency.[15]

For all of Hoover's efforts at employment and wage stabilization, disquiet soon was apparent. Lewis Strauss, his faithful follower, called the White House to urge that the president get off the front page so that his efforts wouldn't look "futile" should a depression come.[16] Labor Secretary James Davis was equally candid. Although expressing the people's gratitude for the "stimulating effects of the various conferences," he noted that "the slump . . . is very much more serious than we anticipated" and encouraged expeditious action to "furnish work for those who are so unfortunate as to be unemployed." [17] Except for certain, albeit substantial, measures requested of the Congress—banking reform, railroad consolidation, economy in government, merchant marine subsidies, public health services, and government reorganization—Hoover would not go beyond his effort to organize private and local stabilizers in providing for relief.

Misgivings within the president's circle were contained by the White House, but such was not the case with the Congress. Although the Senate was hardly known for its progressive measures—except for occasional legislation proposed by western Republicans—Democratic Senator Robert Wagner of New York in early January of 1930 introduced three bills, calling for public works planning, a governmental statistics-gathering capability, and a federal-state employment service. The president was annoyed by Wagner's intrusion but half-heartedly supported the first two measures. The employment service bill he vetoed outright, fearing that it might become a vast organization largely dispensing political patronage.[18]

Hoover propagandized his various stabilization efforts and displayed confidence during the first half of 1930,[19] expressing relief when Congress adjourned in early July. Although giving the president little that he asked for, except certain public works authorizations, at least the legislators had not gone the dole route. Yet the president's assurance was ambivalent—at times a front to aid restoration, at times sincerely believed. While some insiders, like Commerce Secretary Lamont, exuded hopefulness, others, like Lamont's principal statistician, continued to warn against optimism.[20] By October of 1930 the president publicly recognized the depression, but not without stressing its worldwide character. As the depression got worse, he reacted by pushing his voluntary corporate approach harder, this time appointing the President's Emergency Committee for Employment, headed by Arthur Woods, an official of the Rockefeller Foundation. Edward T. Clark, Coolidge's former secretary and his informant in Washington during the years 1929–1932, reported that the president established PECE to "offset appropriations for direct relief." [21] Woods, while loyal to the president's voluntary efforts, in fact favored the large public works appropriations which he apparently had been appointed to foil.[22]

By the midterm election, the American people spoke regarding Hoover's voluntary and cooperative antidepression policies. Even considering the midterm tradition of increased opposition to the incumbent party, the election was a debacle for the Republicans. The GOP suffered a net loss of five governors, eight senators and over fifty congressmen. The Democrats would organize the House of Representatives. Edward T. Clark was inclined to blame Hoover, largely because of the vague impression he presented to the country.[23] *The New York Times* more fairly attributed the defeat to Republican bumbling generally, noting particularly the Smoot-Hawley tariff.[24] The act, initially introduced in the special session of the previous year as an agricultural relief measure, was logrolled into an all-time high tariff. The president, hesitant to interfere with the business of the Congress, protested the petty politics played out in the bill's passage. However, seeing in it aid to agriculture and an important flexible provision that enabled the president to change rates, Hoover ignored multiple demands to veto it and signed it in June of 1930, in time for the people to react at the polls in November.

The embodiment of Hoover corporatism was the Agricultural Marketing Act and its implementing agency, the Federal Farm Board. Throughout 1929 the Board organized local and state cooperatives for the major farm commodities into regional and national marketing associations. Then in 1929 and 1930 it advanced money from its revolving fund to cooperatives, mainly enabling them to support at higher prices their members' commodities. In wheat and cotton, where prices were most depressed, the Farm Board established stabilization corporations to shore up prices by buying directly on the market. But such machinery was intended to even out seasonal variations in deliveries and not to stem the downward price trend caused by worsening economic conditions. The Farm Board was dogged by criticism. From the beginning, the great farm organizations were skeptical. Private grain exporters, particularly Julius Barnes, former president of the Chamber of Commerce and a close friend of Hoover, fiercely opposed the Board's stabilization efforts.[25] Farmers themselves looked back on the good old Coolidge days, causing Farm Board Chairman Alexander Legge to remind them that the former president's solution for distressed farmers was that they should "take up religion." [26]

For all the criticism of the Farm Board's programs, Hoover and Board Chairman Legge tenaciously fought for its retention, at times implementing its programs in a way almost foreign to the act's corporate ideal. Wheat and cotton stabilization corporations were obviously in the business of price-fixing, even though Legge contended that they were not, that in the interest of producers, processors, and consumers, the corporations only prohibited extremely low and high prices. And Chairman Legge encouraged production controls—voluntary ones—in the program.[27] At one point, the president seemed to go beyond voluntary production controls, asking the chairman about the desirability of giving farmers an option on wheat in consideration of reduced acreage. The Farm Board finally decided that it would be unwise to do so.[28] As farm prices deteriorated and the Farm Board's revolving fund reached depletion, Hoover queried the attorney general about authority to finance loans from the newly formed Reconstruction Finance Corporation to the Farm Board. The attorney general said it could not be done.[29] By mid-1932 the president sadly recognized the Farm Board's impossible task and witnessed its demise. His response then to the agriculture situation, as communicated to the governor of Iowa, was to aid farmers by pulling up the "whole fabric of the society." [30]

The Agricultural Market Act was in microcosm Hoover's concept of a democratic and Americanized corporatism. The blending of government, individuals, and groups found in the relationship of the Farm Board to the hierarchy of cooperatives understandably excited the president. It was government assisting farmers to help themselves cooperatively. The pathos of its failure is only comprehensible in retrospect. Its failure in cooperative marketing, voluntary production controls, and stabilization purchases was inevitable given the horrendous agriculture depression. In another time it might have worked. Like much Hoover did, it seemed a necessary transition to the more aggressive measures of the next administration.

In early 1931 Hoover appeared defensive; he stressed worldwide conditions as the principal cause of America's economic ills, chided Congress for considering relief measures that would have totaled $4.5 billion, and generally opposed the lame-duck Congress, which was beginning to seriously challenge his leadership. He vetoed a dozen congressional measures considered too statist or too expensive, including a bonus bill that would permit veterans to borrow up to 50 percent of the face value of their paid-up government-issued life insurance policy, a resolution to create a Muscle Shoals corporation, and a federal employment service bill. The bonus was passed over a White House veto. The president unenthusiastically signed Wagner's federal employment stabilization act but with little apparent thought at seriously implementing it. Although he supported the Senate's special committee to study unemployment insurance, he saw to it that Wagner, its driving force, was not appointed as its chairman.[31] Strained at best, Hoover's relationship with Congress seemed to deteriorate in the spring of 1931. He was understandably saddened when his mainstay in the House, Nicholas Longworth, died in April.

In the early months of 1931, Hoover felt he did not really need the Congress. He believed his cooperative system was working. Industrial and farm production, employment and payrolls were holding their own. And he wasn't just relying on state and local governments and charities. The federal government was doing its equal share. Federal public works were up nearly 50 percent over 1930. One economist, Herbert Stein, goes so far as to view Hoover as a prerevolutionary fiscalist. Stein is persuaded that the "stimulating effect of federal fiscal policy was larger in 1931 than in any other year in the 1930s except 1934, 1935, and 1936." [32]

By the late spring of 1931 the president's confidence regarding the economy was truly weakening. The economy took a decided downturn, exacerbated particularly, Hoover believed, by the collapse of Austria's largest bank, *Kreditanstalt*. This failure, caused by French pressure on Germany and Austria, who had formed a common tariff union, affected most of the nations of Europe. Europeans sought relief by cashing many of their American stocks and bonds, creditors stopped payment of many of their loans to Americans, American exports to Europe dropped significantly, and world indebtedness precluded Americans collecting on many of their investments abroad. Although the momentum of federal fiscal efforts in the United States accelerated in 1931, private construction fell off rapidly and big industry was strained to maintain the wage and employment pledges made to the president in the late fall of 1929. In his April 1931 Gridiron address the president admitted the existence of a serious depression.

Hoover responded to worsening conditions in mid-1931 by attempting to stabilize the European economies with a one-year moratorium regarding intergovernment indebtedness and a "stand-still agreement" whereby short-term bills would not be presented for payment until February 1932. Before announcing the moratorium Hoover wisely secured the support of congressional leaders, for not a few members of Congress wanted the president to convene a special session of Congress to consider the moratorium and a gamut of relief measures. Hoover, of course, would not agree to convening the Congress, since he believed their statist relief measures would only worsen the depression.

Although President Hoover's economic thought regarding the depression was quite sophisticated, his attempts at monetary policy-making failed. He could not match the bold world-stabilizing moratorium with an active program to shore up credit at home. In the summer and fall of 1931, Hoover expressed interest in bringing all banks under the Federal Reserve System through the guaranteeing of a certain percentage of bank deposits,[33] and he pleaded with the Federal Reserve Board to assume a more active monetary role generally. Practically all of the president's October eight-point program for the forthcoming Congress dealt with credit—more capital for federal land banks, the Reconstruction Finance Corporation, Home Loan Discount Banks, flexible discount regulations for the Federal Reserve System, aid to depositors, the reform of banking laws, economy in government, and the strengthening of the nation's railroads. Of course, as Lester Chandler points out, monetary policy in a macrocosmic sense was unknown during the depression years. The liquidationist attitude of Andrew Mellon still prevailed in the Federal Reserve System. Besides, power in the Federal Reserve System was largely decentralized, which precluded vigorous action by the Federal Reserve Board itself. Most importantly, when England went off the gold standard in September and gold was withdrawn from American banks—in anticipation of a possible bimetallic standard here—the Federal Reserve System tightened credit to protect the nation's gold reserves.

Of the several recommendations in Hoover's program to the new Seventy-Second Congress, none was as significant as the Reconstruction Finance Corporation. The president recommended it reluctantly. In October of 1931, consistent with his concept of an Ameri-

can corporatism, he called together the nation's leading bankers—
at Andrew Mellon's residence in Washington—to encourage them
to form a national credit association for the voluntary relief of ailing
banks, most of which were intermediate city and country banks.
The parent banks were to put $500 million of their reserves into an
instrumentality of their making, the National Credit Association.
The president was appalled at the bankers' reluctance and only
succeeded eventually in establishing the Association by promising to
ask the Congress for the Reconstruction Finance Corporation in
case the Association was not successful. The Association eventually
funneled some $40 million into ailing banks. When established in
the spring of 1932, the Reconstruction Finance Corporation provided for capitalization of $500 million and an authority to borrow
an additional $1.5 billion.

The president had political trepidations about the forthcoming
Seventy-Second Congress, which were frequently more addressed to
Republicans than to Democrats. In the House of Representatives
Nicholas Longworth was gone, leaving liberal Republicans like
Fiorello LaGuardia freer to roam about the chamber demanding
more direct relief. The House, however, was Democratic, so that
the president could blame the opposition party if things went
wrong. In the Senate, which remained Republican, Hoover lacked
political communication with both wings of his own party, the
conservatives because they resented the president suggesting that
they let the Democrats organize the narrowly divided body, and
the liberals because they, like LaGuardia, wanted more direct relief. When the Congress convened, Hoover seemed better off with
the Democratic leadership. Although he was somewhat suspicious
of Senate Democratic Leader Joseph Robinson's White House am-
bitions, the momentum of good White House-Robinson relations
continued. And Speaker John Nance Garner's conservatism would
bode well for the president in the House of Representatives.

For all the president's disdain for the Congress, the new Seventy-
Second Congress proved docile. Jordan Schwarz, in his book *The
Interregnum of Despair* and his essay (see II-2), describes how
Hoover's control over this Congress enabled him to get what he
wanted during his "One Hundred Days" from December of 1931
to March of 1932. Hoover still wanted no direct federal relief.
Doggedly he stuck to his voluntary cooperative approach. After all,
only in October of 1931 did Big Steel break its agreement to maintain 1929 wages. And if stabilization overseas and credit expansion
at home could be achieved, the curse of the dole—as Hoover viewed

direct relief—could be avoided. The president had not developed his ideas of American corporatism to see them go up in smoke with large federal relief programs. True to his belief, the president not only denied the states direct relief, he denied the coal industry a large government stabilization program and corporations relief from antitrust prosecution.

Credit was foremost in the president's mind, so he pushed for and got, early in the Congress, the moratorium to ease Europe's credit plight; the Reconstruction Finance Corporation to provide credit, in the form of loans to banks, railroads, and certain other industries; and the Glass-Steagall Act, which permitted the Federal Reserve System to use United States government obligations as backing of Federal Reserve notes, taking the pressure off gold as collateral. By early spring 1931, the Congress had agreed to much of the president's programs and then proceeded to give the president increased taxes—the Congress wanted new taxes to balance the budget, while the president wanted a new tax structure in order to avoid government borrowing that might make credit even tighter.[34] "The kissing bee," as Jordan Schwarz called the "One Hundred Days", came to an end on the method of raising tax levels.

If Hoover's first "One Hundred Days" of congressional support is to be likened to FDR's, his second "One Hundred Days" in the late spring of 1932 was truly the converse. The Congress gave the president revenue, relief, and antilabor injunction legislation,[35] which he didn't want, and denied him banking reform, some public power and stock market regulation, and reduction of federal expenditures, which he did want. The revenue measure triggered the turnabout in relations between the president and Congress. When first considered in late February and early March, there seemed unanimity on a $2\frac{1}{4}$ percent manufacturer's sales tax (plus increased income, estate, corporate, and miscellaneous taxes) that the House Ways and Means Committee had introduced. Ogden Mills and Hoover were delighted, feeling that the sales tax would be less likely to freeze capital. Ways and Means Chairman Robert L. Doughton thought otherwise and joined some middle western Republicans and Fiorello LaGuardia in fighting it. The House defeated the tax by a 236 to 160 margin on 1 April. It then passed a bill which used several other means to increase revenue. Speaker Garner's reputation (and presidential hopes) were diminished by the defeat. Senate Democratic leader Joseph Robinson learned from Garner's experience and followed his Democratic ranks in opposing the sales tax and accepted much of the House revision. On 6 June the president signed the Revenue Act of 1932, which had in it about every kind of tax except sales—excise, luxury, gift, mail, estate, corporation, and income—and which raised taxation to approximately the World War I level.

Hoover's bane in the late spring of 1932 was the accelerating demand for direct federal relief to ease the ever-increasing unemployment. The President's Organization on Unemployment Relief, which in August of 1931 replaced his Emergency Committee on Employment, continued to push the increasingly ineffective voluntary and cooperative approach, while members of Congress and other interested agencies called for direct employment relief. The American Society of Civil Engineers, an organization close to the president's heart, suggested to Hoover a large issue of federal government bonds to support a "huge expansion of public works construction as the most plausible solution to the unemployment problem." The president's response manifested his continued preference for corporatist over statist approaches. "The back of the depression," he wrote, "cannot be broken by any single government undertaking. That can only be done with the cooperation of business, banking, industry, and agriculture in conjunction with the government." He then reiterated the necessary federal government contributions —a balanced budget, the Reconstruction Finance Corporation, a loan program to credit institutions, the expansion of credit by the Federal Reserve banks, the strengthening of agriculture (although the Farm Board was moribund), self-liquidating public works, Home Loan Discount Banks, and, as a last resort, RFC aid to states. The society's proposal regarding large public works, Hoover predicted, would fail, for its indebtedness would destroy confidence in government securities, the proposals would be non-self-liquidating, few of the unemployed across the nation would be helped, and increased taxes would result. At best it would be only transitory relief.[36] The president, of course, was not averse to announcing that the administration was spending inordinately for public works—a planned $700 million expenditure in 1932 as compared to $250 million per annum prior to the depression. But by late July, with extremely high unemployment and a forthcoming presidential election, that was not enough. After considerable dickering with the Congress—Hoover insisted that any federal appropriation to states for relief and construction purposes be loans and not grants—he signed the Wagner-Rainey Relief Bill. This omnibus bill provided $300 million to states for direct relief (to be recovered beginning in 1935 by reducing federal highway aid to states), $1.5

billion for loans to states, municipalities, and public agencies for self-liquidating public works, $322 million for specified public works, and $200 million to aid closed banks in their liquidation.

At adjournment time in August of 1932, Hoover's relationship with the Congress had deteriorated to its lowest point. Jordan Schwarz blames much of the situation on Hoover, accusing the president of treating Congress callously and purposely attempting to lower its credit with an already disgruntled public. (See II-2) Many factors, of course, produced the ill-will between Congress and the president in the late summer—the deepening of the depression, the imminent presidential election, the president's handling of the bonus march, the increasing vociferousness of Congressional liberals, the president's rigid adherence to corporatist solutions, and the president's distrust of congressional broker politics. The last two elements are profoundly important to understanding the Hoover presidency. By the late summer of 1932 Hoover's noncongressional and nonpolitical programs of cooperativeness and voluntarism met ultimate resistance from a Congress which substituted direct federal relief for voluntarism and in so doing manifested the electoral and broker politics which the president found so distasteful. Hoover's elaborate economic and political thought could not square with the economic and political realities of the time.

Six months prior to the election, Presidential Secretary Walter Newton could write somewhat confidently across one of Harold Ickes's missent "Pinchot for President" letters: "The chief is gaining every day." [37] And six months prior to that New York National Committeeman Charles D. Hilles could catalog a list of issues on which the president might capitalize.[38] But by August of 1932 when the Republican Convention nominated Herbert Hoover, the public attitude, like that of the Congress, had changed so precipitately that gloom dominated the proceedings. However, the Democratic Convention, as Alfred Rollins notes, was the opposite and exuberantly nominated Hoover's friendly enemy, Franklin D. Roosevelt. (See III-1) Rollins comments that although Roosevelt and Hoover had indeed been warm associates in the Wilson administration, by 1928 FDR was "locked in on Hoover" and thereafter ran for the presidency himself rather than react positively to the president's leadership. Hoover had become Roosevelt's "moving foil." [39]

Although ideological distinctions between Hoover and Roosevelt were minimal in the 1932 campaign, differences could be perceived. The Republican platform basically encompassed Hoover's cooperative and corporatist approach: local government and private aid to relief, sound money, economy in government, cooperative efforts in agriculture and industry, a protective tariff, and world cooperation. While echoing many similar points, the Democratic platform contained more statist planks: lower tariffs, public works, relief to states, a reduced work week, farm price supports. Although Franklin D. Roosevelt possessed many New Day ideas and paid homage to sound currency, balanced budgets, and economy in government, he, albeit ambiguously, talked about such statist programs as a domestic allotment program in agriculture and regulation of public utilities. In his San Francisco Commonwealth Club speech he affirmed a political liberalism that prophetically separated him from Hoover. Ideological distinctions aside, by election time Hoover's defeat was as inevitable as Smith's had been four years previously. Nothing could save the president. Even the implausible though ingenious idea of having the hero Charles Lindbergh fly him about the country to campaign would have had no impact. The president had lost what he tried hardest to maintain, the confidence of the people. His vaguely understood plan for salvation through a cooperatively organized corporatism, at first supported, then tolerated, now met no approval at all.[40] In the midst of the nation's greatest domestic crisis since the Civil War the cold logic of his philosophy was resented. Only 39.7 percent of the voters supported Hoover as opposed to a whopping 57.4 percent for FDR.

Both Hoover and FDR had campaigned as Wilsonians committed to the idealism and limited statism of the New Freedom. The glimmer of distinction manifested during the campaign, however, was accentuated during the interregnum period. In a reflection of his nonpolitical stance (in an electoral and broker sense), Hoover ignored the election returns and continued his efforts to organize, assist, and protect enlightened action by private groups. Roosevelt, showing his political sense, read a mandate into the election returns and started his open-option trek to the New Deal. Hoover's solutions—a balanced budget, a gold standard, a restoration of credit, banking reform, administrative reorganization, and world stability—while the incoming president did not particularly oppose them, were nevertheless not established in Roosevelt's priority of things. At a 22 November meeting with Hoover he was understandably leary about possibly committing his incoming administration by cooperating in political discussions with England regarding the foreign debt question. And when Hoover and Henry L. Stimson, at a 20 January 1933 meeting, strove to tie the debt question to the forthcoming World Economic Conference, FDR refused outright, seeing in the proposal an emphasis on world rather than domestic solutions to the American depression. Roosevelt also saw possible domestic consequences in the world conference, like a gold standard, which might preclude options as yet undecided by him and his brain trust.

As inauguration day approached, unemployment grew to almost one-fourth of the labor force and banks across the country were failing by the thousands. Hoover clung to the stabilization of currencies and a restoration of confidence in the national and international economies as bedrock solutions. Much of the problem at home, he abrasively asserted, stemmed from a loss of confidence caused by the Democratic election, which could be corrected by Roosevelt's assurance that "there would be no tampering or inflation of the currency; that the budget would be unquestionably balanced even if further taxation is necessary; that government credit will be maintained by refusal to exhaust it in an issue of securities." [41] Roosevelt demurred. Frank Friedel, in assessing the interregnum (see III-2), supports Roosevelt's refusal to be entrapped by Hoover's suggestions. Yet Friedel believes that Roosevelt should have cooperated with Hoover to save the banks instead of being guided by visions of bankers as moneychangers being driven from the temple.[42]

A debt is owed to the New Left historians who are largely responsible for initiating the reassessment of the Hoover presidency. Their writing at first emphasized Hoover's foreign policy, which in turn set the stage for a reappraisal of his domestic program by a gamut of historical schools. Hoover himself never separated foreign and domestic policy.

Hoover's approach to foreign policy can be distinguished by two broad features. First, he brought to the White House an economic foreign policy which showed his strong belief in self-sufficiency for the United States as well as a somewhat conflicting desire for an interdependent world economy managed by enlightened capitalists acting through multinational forms of cooperation. He hoped to implement more fully the program he formulated while secretary of commerce under Harding and Coolidge. Second, in political foreign policy, Hoover was adamant in utilizing peaceful measures, a policy best exemplified by his stance toward Latin America and his handling of the Manchurian crisis of 1931–32.

Hoover entered the presidency full of confidence in America's leadership as the new creditor nation of the world. His candidacy had included a promise of greater prosperity through foreign trade, and he viewed the post-World War I era as one when America had replaced Britain's domination of world trade and finance. After all, as secretary of commerce, Hoover helped accomplish this when he moved to implement a comprehensive plan for the nation's economic foreign policy. Joan Hoff Wilson's essay (see IV-2) elaborates on Hoover's four-point program, which included a more equitable trade balance, more direct government supervision over foreign loans, domestic monetary control, and an open-door policy among the industrial nations of the world (in which the United States would be the dominant nation). But by 1928 he had not achieved his goal due to opposition from elements in the business community as well as from the State Department.*

Hoover has been criticized by contemporaries and later historians for the course he followed in economic affairs after the depression struck.[43] However Hoover himself was confident his policies would work if vigorously followed. Note, for example, his view of the tariff. With certain reservations he had always supported high rates, however he always considered the tariff only one aspect of his total economic program. Although Joan Wilson emphasizes that Hoover believed high import rates would help achieve economic self-sufficiency for America (see IV-2), still he wanted some flexibility in the rates, an increase in the investigatory power of the Federal Tariff Commission, and the ability to expand American trade through negotiation of bilateral commercial treaties.

In this total context, it is difficult to call Hoover's high tariff economically isolationist. Those who charge this emphasize only his tariff position, but Hoover never viewed the tariff as an end in itself and he believed the nation could have both protection and trade. It must be remembered that Hoover thought the economic woes of the depression could be relieved through international cooperation, and he was convinced that the high rates would not harm world trade. Professor Wilson notes that once the United States ceased to export capital, the tariff became an obstacle to adjusting payments on debts to the United States and that the higher duties were "artificial restraints" of trade. But Hoover did not see it this way; he stuck by his belief in high rates and signed the Smoot-Hawley bill of 1930.

Government regulation of American loans abroad is another area in which Hoover has been subjected to criticism. As secretary of commerce, Hoover was not successful in achieving regulation, but

* See Bibliographic Note preceding the Introduction notes, pp. 191–92.

he hoped to do so in the presidency. Of course, the depression immediately curtailed any efforts in that area, nevertheless, his attempt to supervise loans substantiates the moral basis of his economic foreign policy. Hoover's criteria for approving loans were that they be economically sound, that they be used for productive purposes in the recipient countries, and that the recipient should not already have over-borrowed. He failed to have this policy instituted with the result that private American investment overseas became an "informal economic empire" with little concern for productivity and with very little coordination. Because Hoover believed American foreign loans were good for both the recipient and the United States, some scholars have mistakenly coupled him with this speculative, informal, economic empire. This charge is undeserved; on the contrary, Hoover should be credited with attempting to regulate the loans. Had his proposed policy been followed, a more stable, less speculative, foreign loan program might have developed.

Historians, however, have generally praised Hoover's Latin American policy.[44] From the beginning of his administration, he had high hopes for improved relations with America's southern neighbors. Immediately following his election, but before taking office, Hoover traveled throughout Central and South America (the only inhabited continent he had never toured), a trip which set a "good neighbor" tone for his future policy.

In December 1928, J. Reuben Clark, a State Department Latin American expert, submitted a long memorandum to lame duck Secretary of State Frank B. Kellogg that argued historically for the removal of the obnoxious Roosevelt Corollary from the Monroe Doctrine. When Hoover and Secretary of State Henry L. Stimson published this document in 1930, many took it to mean a formal renunciation of any intervention rights claimed under the 1904 Corollary. Hoover, it should be noted, intended just that, despite the reservations of certain government officials.

In addition to words, Hoover also acted. He moved to eliminate the remaining American military occupations in Haiti and Nicaragua,[45] and succeeded in reducing the number of American troops serving there. Further, he refused to use nonrecognition as a means of unseating Latin American governments. This set a policy that succeeding Washington administrations carried on, to a certain extent at least.

Hoover might have been more successful in Latin America, had not the depression intervened. With it came uprisings from the discontented masses in several South American countries, and American economic policies after 1929 could offer little substantive aid to these nations. Nonetheless, the policies Hoover did set had a general noncoercive basis, which was intended to change Latin America's image of its North American neighbor.

Hoover's political foreign policy has usually been judged in relation to his administration's handling of Japan's 1931 thrust into Manchuria.[46] Throughout the twenties, the United States had maintained a delicate political arrangement with the Japanese, and in the early years of the Hoover administration, Secretary Stimson endeavored to uphold the treaty structure in the Far East. When, for example, the 1929 war broke out between China and Russia along the Chinese Eastern Railway, Stimson made a vigorous though unsuccessful effort to procure a settlement under the Kellogg-Briand pact. This was not lost on Japan. The next year, Stimson emerged from the London Naval Conference with a new treaty, but in the process, allowed Japan a more favorable ratio in the construction of light cruisers.

But the civilian government in Japan, which accepted the London Treaty, came under increasing attack from the military, and the economic situation, which grew worse with the deepening world depression, strained the already tenuous Japanese-American relations. (Japan exported 40 percent of its goods to America in 1929; in 1931 it was reduced to 15 percent.) It became harder for the Japanese civilian government to argue against the military with any favorable American-Japanese economic facts. Stimson did not fully comprehend the Japanese domestic situation, and when their military forces moved into Manchuria in September 1931, Stimson believed he could appeal to the Japanese government to leash its generals. This did not succeed, so there followed in January 1932 the Hoover-inspired Stimson Doctrine, which brought into play, through nonrecognition of Japanese gains, all the moral force America had available. By this time, Stimson appeared willing to move beyond a mere moral sanction and condemn Japan out of hand, but Hoover had a more realistic assessment of the oriental situation and would not allow Stimson to go beyond the moral sanctions already imposed.[47]

Confusion over the roles Hoover and Stimson played in the Manchurian crisis has stimulated current historians to reevaluate Hoover foreign policy more in the context of his time. In 1931–32 Stimson knew his limits, but later he became a part of a more interventionist foreign policy. Hoover, meanwhile, consistently maintained a moral, nonintervention position. This has led some to read the positions of the two men in their later years back into their respective stands on the Manchurian crisis of 1931–32. It is only recently that Hoover has been credited for his consistency and any reevaluation of the man must underscore that significant characteristic.

The new interest of revisionist historians in Hoover foreign policy has stressed both the subtle, productive nature of his economic policies as well as the noncoercive aspect of his political policy. The essay of Joan Hoff Wilson (see IV-2) underscores both these features. Selig Adler also emphasizes revisionism by questioning the re-habilitative approach to Hoover found in the latest writings of William Appleman Williams. (See IV-1) Adler sees a paradox in the fact that the revisionist school had formerly assaulted "the very kind of informal American economic empire that the Secretary of Commerce did so much to promote." His provocative criticism goes to the heart of current revisionism. Thus both essays raise questions which should encourage further study in Hoover's foreign policy.

This volume includes several new interpretations of the Hoover presidency. Although inexperienced and unhappy about electoral politics, Herbert Hoover conducted a superb presidential campaign in 1928. His presidency prior to the crash was innovative; his policies were profoundly based on an ideology of American cor-poratism, which balanced statism, associationalism, and individual-ism. The Agriculture Marketing Act illustrates in microcosm Hoover's concept of this balance. The administration's response to the stock market crash was vigorous and prerevolutionary in its fiscal and monetary efforts. The president's program for the Seventy-Second Congress was well integrated and consistent with his ideo-logical vision. Furthermore, it was well received by the press and the Congress. But harmonious relations between Hoover and the Congress reversed completely during the second "One Hundred Days" in 1932. The deterioration of the president's national sup-port in the summer and the fall of 1932 was precipitous and un-precedented in recent American history. During the interregnum Hoover stolidly attempted to implement his concept of American corporatism, while Roosevelt, more flexible and more political than Hoover, started his trek toward the New Deal. He avoided entrap-ment in Hoover's ideological framework, as he believed the election returns demanded of him, and he considered how his administra-tion might effect necessary changes when he took office. Throughout his presidency, Hoover conceived of foreign policy as inseparable from domestic policy.

Two inimical themes dominated the Hoover presidency—a vision of an Americanized corporatism and a commitment to non-electoral politics. The corporatist vision (a term Ellis Hawley has given us) appears as continuous in Hoover's presidency as in his *American Individualism,* written in 1922, and *The Challenge To Liberty,* written in 1935. He always opposed statism, yet he was no advocate of laissez-faire, and he refused to abandon the notion that a proper blend of organized expertise, systematized associationalism, and enlightened individualism would provide the ideal blend of order and freedom. His thought and commitment, Alfred Rollins has aptly said, ran deep like a shaft, though narrow.

Hoover's corporatist vision was inimical to the statist politics required for a successful implementation. His Tocquevillian dream of a cooperative individualism could not be imposed from above, and, under depression conditions, Americans lacked faith in the notion that it could evolve naturally. Franklin D. Roosevelt, intellectually more shallow than Hoover, was more politically able. Unlike Hoover, he could lead from above by drawing support from below—from electors across the land, and specifically from the constituencies of members of congress. Yet, Hoover's failure as president may have been, in the perspective of history, his success. His goal and dream of American individualism, contemptuous of laissez-faire, and Sumnerian individualism, was perhaps as profoundly important to the American future as the leviathan politics of the New Deal. In considerable part, his corporatist struggle to blend the forces of government, capital, and labor was prophetic. Such a view of the Thirty-First President seems to be emerging among historians. Significantly, Frank Freidel, a definitive Roosevelt biographer, views Herbert Hoover as the most outstanding president of his party in the seven decades since Theodore Roosevelt occupied the White House.

I

Before the Crash

To the White House: Herbert Hoover, August 1927–March 1929

DONALD R. MCCOY

University of Kansas

*Donald McCoy was born in 1929, in Chicago, Illinois. He received
his B.A. degree from the University of Denver, his M.A. from the
University of Chicago, and his Ph.D. from American University.
He began his teaching career at the State University of New York
at Cortland in 1952 and in 1957 was appointed to the History
Department at the University of Kansas, where he is serving as
Professor of History. Professor McCoy has been a Fulbright
Professor at University of Bonn and currently is Director, Special
Research Project, Harry S. Truman Library. Among his publications
are* Angry Voices: Left-of-Center Movements in the New Deal Era
(Lawrence, Kansas: University of Kansas Press, 1958); Calvin
Coolidge, the Quiet President *(New York: Macmillan Co., 1967);*
Landon of Kansas *(Lincoln, Nebraska: University of Nebraska
Press, 1966). At present he is chairman of a committee directing a
series of presidential monographs that the University Press of
Kansas is publishing.*

*McCoy, the most recent Coolidge biographer, describes in the
following essay how Herbert Hoover prepared for the 1928
Republican nomination and then planned a highly effective
campaign. Hoover saw the personality of Alfred E. Smith and the
topic of prosperity as major issues. McCoy points out that the
campaign demonstrated Hoover's ability to build good public
relations, to organize the party while minimizing factionalism,
to present his views clearly, and to gain the strong support of the
popular incumbent, Calvin Coolidge. After such a successful
campaign and presidential start, McCoy thought it "bitterly
paradoxical" for Hoover and the nation that history's script
altered so drastically after the new president stepped onto the stage.*

It was about noon, the drizzly day of 2 August 1927, that the thirty
or so reporters in attendance upon Calvin Coolidge filed into the

mathematics classroom of the Rapid City (South Dakota) High School. President Coolidge was already there, and when the door was closed he told the newsmen that "the line forms on the left." As they passed by him, he handed each a slip of paper which read, "I do not choose to run for President in nineteen twenty-eight." [1]

Although some people interpreted Coolidge's statement as a crafty bid for a draft nomination, others concluded that he would not be a candidate in 1928. There is no absolute proof of what the president had in mind, though the weight of evidence favors the view that he was uninterested in running again. Regardless of Coolidge's meaning, the significance of his announcement was immediately seen by Senator Charles McNary's friend, Carl Smith, who wrote: "Whether Calvin meant it or not I believe he is fairly out of it. The country has in a large measure accepted the statement at face value, and the active candidates will occupy the field without much elbow room remaining." [2]

Carl Smith was right. There was soon a plethora of would-be Republican presidential nominees. Prominent among the early contenders were Senators Charles Curtis of Kansas, Guy D. Goff of West Virginia, George Norris of Nebraska, James Watson of Indiana, and Frank Willis of Ohio as well as Vice President Charles Dawes, former Secretary of State Charles Evans Hughes, and former Governor Frank O. Lowden of Illinois. Standing above all of them, however, was the Secretary of Commerce, Herbert Clark Hoover.[3]

Hoover's background was tailor-made for a presidential nominee in 1928. He had been born in 1874 in the Iowa farming village of West Branch. Orphaned at an early age, he worked his way to an engineering degree at Stanford University. He became a wealthy man before World War I, working as a mining engineer in various parts of the globe. Then came his years as chairman of the American Relief Committee in 1914, chairman of the Belgian Relief Commission in 1915, and the wartime United States Food Administrator. After the war, Hoover was the prime force behind economic relief to Europe and Russia and was prominently mentioned as an candidate for president by both Democrats and Republicans in 1920. In 1921 he was named secretary of commerce. In these and various other positions, he earned the reputation of being an innovative and productive public servant. Certainly, no one worked harder to come to grips with the many changes in the pace and quality of life during the postwar decade. And Hoover, along with many other Americans, thought that he was just the man to make the most intelligent use of knowledge and technology to combat society's problems for the good of all. In short, the commerce secretary was the Republican front-runner in 1928 because his name had become synonymous with prosperity, humanitarianism, efficiency, and resourcefulness. Moreover, he had astutely built up a broad network of political and business supporters.[4]

All of this did not mean that Hoover would not have to work for the nomination. His backers counted on getting Coolidge's support. As time passed, however, it became clear that the president was not going to endorse anyone for the Republican nomination, much to the disappointment of the Hoover forces.[5] His reasons for not endorsing Hoover's nomination are worth investigating. First, there was the possibility, however slim, that the Vermonter would decide to seek renomination in case of a national emergency or the threatened nomination of a political enemy, such as Dawes. Therefore, it would not do for Coolidge to be committed to another candidate. Second, he believed that the nominee should be the party's choice, not the president's. Third, it would not be helpful for him to take any step that would foster rancor in his administration or additional divisions in Congress when there were still matters of great public importance to be dealt with. Fourth, Coolidge was probably afflicted with that rare strain of Potomac fever that keeps a president from looking favorably upon the political maneuvering of his potential successors, all of whom he could consider callow. Fifth, Coolidge did not greatly admire his secretary of commerce.

This last point should be elaborated. Hoover had been one of President Harding's favorites, which allowed him to go a long way toward becoming "Secretary of Commerce and assistant secretary of everything else." Although his power and widespread influence were not significantly curtailed during the Coolidge years, it was plain that the new chief executive was not completely happy with Hoover. Personality differences were part of the situation. Hoover's drive and brilliance probably seemed a case of overreaching to Coolidge, who expected a man to do his job but not the work of other men as well. Hoover's fame at home and abroad undoubtedly was taken by Coolidge as challenging his own prominence. Then too, the president, who could accommodate ripples but not waves, was occasionally irritated with the extra work and controversy generated by his energetic secretary of commerce. Coolidge was certainly disturbed by Hoover's willingness for the government to assume additional tasks and even bear extra expense. This was seen in the president's coolness toward Hoover's farm-board plan and his ideas on the development of water resources, the tying of production controls to farm loans, and federal restrictions on banking and financial practices. All this, and perhaps more, led Coolidge to say of Hoover in May 1928, "That man has offered me unsolicited advice for six years, all of it bad!" [6] He nevertheless retained Hoover in his cabinet and allowed him wide-ranging activity, no doubt in recognition of the commerce secretary's signal contributions to the administration's success and popularity. Moreover, although Coolidge felt under no obligation to usher Hoover into the White House as his successor, he did not feel strongly enough to do anything to prevent him from becoming the next president.

Herbert Hoover's campaign for the 1928 Republican nomination had begun, for all practical purposes, in 1926. At that time he had engaged a veteran newsman, George Akerson, as his assistant, with responsibility for further developing political contacts and promoting publicity. Thus, when Coolidge made his Rapid City statement, the Hoover forces were ready. The commerce secretary, who was attending the annual Bohemian Grove encampment, wrote that "within an hour a hundred men—publishers, editors, public officials, and others from all over the country who were at the Grove—came to my camp demanding that I announce my candidacy. Telegrams poured in from all parts of the country. . . ." [7] If this was evidence of substantial grass-roots support for Hoover, it was also proof that his previous publicity and political efforts had been effective.

Hoover was, of course, aware of the president's sensibilities. In September he told Coolidge that although he had been deluged with "urgings" to indicate his position on seeking the nomination, he preferred that his chief run again for the presidency. Coolidge did not respond, so Hoover told the press that the Vermonter should be renominated. It was plain that the secretary of commerce did not intend to be caught off base. It was also clear that there was a strong Hoover campaign for the Republican presidential nomination, even if it was conducted by his friends and associates. There was a great deal of press speculation, most of it favorable, about Hoover as a possible nominee, and popular support for Hoover grew steadily. A measure of his success was the number of smears attempted by his opponents. Common was the one that he was an amateur in politics. He was also charged with being a pacifist, a thief, a desegregationist, an Anglophile, and with having been married by a Catholic priest. Far more dangerous was the sentiment among many conservative Republicans that he was neither a party regular nor safe on economic matters. This led Hoover to stress his unswerving fidelity to the party and especially to President Coolidge, the safest of the safe.[8]

Hoover's progress toward nomination was also forwarded by people outside his camp. In December 1927 Coolidge somewhat amplified his August statement, saying to the Republican National Committee that "my decision will be respected." Of course, some questioned what his decision had been, but the Hoover forces concluded that this was enough to justify intensification of their efforts. By the end of January 1928, they had completed plans to campaign for delegates in several states, the various Hoover clubs had been united into the Hoover-for-President Association, and Colonel Horace A. Mann and former Congressman James W. Good began organizing the South and the Middle West for Hoover. The Senate also entered the act. On 10 February, it adopted a resolution announcing that violation of the tradition of only two terms for a president would be "unwise, unpatriotic, and fraught with peril to our free institutions." [9] This opened the door wider for Republicans to declare for anyone except Coolidge.

What Hoover especially desired, and several times sought, was Coolidge's encouragement and preferably endorsement. For example, he inquired if Coolidge would run in the Ohio presidential primary election. After the president said he would not, Hoover asked if his own name should be on the ballot. Coolidge's simple response was, "Why not?" Although the president's answer was no endorsement, it did clear the way for Hoover to enter the primary elections. On 12 February, Hoover accepted an invitation to enter the Ohio primary, although he stated his conviction that he would "not strive for the nomination." He would instead continue to devote all his energies to being secretary of commerce. He added that if he were chosen it would be his "duty to carry forward the principles of the Republican party and the great objectives of President Coolidge's policies—all of which have brought to our country such a high degree of happiness, progress and security." [10]

In one stroke, Hoover had made clear much of his campaign strategy. He would be the candidate of "happiness, progress and security," which left little for his opponents to campaign upon. He would identify himself closely with the immensely popular incumbent president and with the Republican party. He would say as little as possible, obviously to avoid antagonizing his opponents and revealing his vulnerabilities. He would stick to his job, thus gaining credit for dependability, while others were on the hustings. He would present his name to the electorate in order to show that he had popular appeal.[11] He would do all this in ways that would demonstrate that the nomination was seeking him more than he was seeking it.

This strategy was successful, largely because the public was enthralled by Hoover's well-publicized accomplishments and dynamism as well as the promise he gave of better things to come. Furthermore, his combination of amateur, business, political, and press supporters gave him splendid service. In addition to publicity and organization, they raised $380,151 for his preconvention campaign, substantially more than the amount available to the other Republican candidates altogether.[12] The only weak spots in his campaign for nomination—and they were minor—were his inability to enlist Coolidge's support and the results of the presidential primary elections, in which Hoover was far from appearing the all-conquering hero. He won New Jersey, Oregon, and his home state of California without opposition. He could not, however, defeat his opponents in their home states. Frank O. Lowden humiliated the commerce secretary in Illinois, George Norris (who also took progressive Wisconsin) thrashed him in Nebraska, and Guy Goff and James Watson beat him in West Virginia and Indiana, respectively. Even Ohio's Frank Willis, who had died during the campaign, took twenty delegates in the Buckeye state. Hoover did win smashing victories in Maryland, Massachusetts, and Michigan, where there were no favorite sons on the ballot.[13] Therefore, despite occasional disappointments, Hoover's primary performances added to his stock of delegates and kept his name constantly before the public.

If the president refused either to back or to encourage Hoover, he did discourage efforts to nominate himself. In March Coolidge told his would-be supporters in Wyoming that he was unavailable, and in April he forbade the use of his name in the Massachusetts primary. Senator Watson wrote that he and New York National Committeeman Charles D. Hilles were reprimanded for working for the president's renomination in order to stop Hoover. As Coolidge declared, "You and Charley Hilles are bad boys, and I want you to behave yourselves. I have studied it all over and have finally concluded that I do not want that nomination." Coolidge's wish not to be a candidate was finally taken as irrevocable by all but the diehard anti-Hoover men when, soon before the convention, Treasury Secretary Andrew Mellon and National Committee Chairman William Butler told their home-state delegations from Pennsylvania and Massachusetts to vote for Hoover.[14] Therefore, Hoover went into competition at the national convention solidly holding the position of favorite. By June his associates assured him that he had 450 delegates, and, on the first day of the convention, James W. Good calculated that he would receive at least 673 votes on the first ballot.[15]

The Republican National Convention opened in Kansas City, Missouri, on 12 June. The proceedings were a desert of dullness. The usual invocations and committee reports were given, and roll calls taken. The few contests over the seating of delegates and the platform were polite debating exercises. The speeches were usually too long and contained nothing unexpected. The platform was adopted after the delegates listened unresponsively to the reading of Wisconsin's usual liberal alternative resolutions. The party went on record for continuing the policies of the Coolidge administration, in other words, efficiency, economy, tariff protection, amity with other nations, and a little bit better of something for every American so long as it would not cost much.[16]

Presidential nominating speeches took place on 14 June. Alabama yielded to California, and John L. McNab put Herbert Hoover's name before the delegates. McNab presented the commerce secretary as "engineer, practical scientist, minister of mercy to the hungry and the poor, administrator, executive, statesman, beneficent American, kindly neighbor, wholesome human being," the man whom the public believes "best represents the genius, pure and undefiled, of wholesome and forward-looking Americanism." Then followed other nominating speeches and a host of seconding talks. The delegates arrived at a decision on the first ballot, giving Hoover 837 of 1,089 votes, with the remainder being scattered among eight other men. Frank O. Lowden, who had withdrawn his name, came in a distant second with 74 votes. Then the permanent chairman, George H. Moses, declared Hoover's nomination unanimous. On 15 June, the convention chose Charles Curtis of Kansas to run for vice president.[17]

Before the balloting for the vice presidential nominee, Senator Moses read a telegram to the convention from Herbert Hoover. The new nominee pledged himself to stand upon the Republican platform, for "under its principles the victory of the party will assure national defense, maintain economy in the administration of government, protect American workmen, farmers and business men alike, from competition arising out of lower standards of living abroad, foster individual initiative, insure stability of business and employment, promote our foreign commerce, and develop our national resources." Hoover specifically committed himself to find a "sound solution" to the problems of agriculture. In short, he felt himself consecrated to "give the best within me to advance the moral and material welfare of all our people and uphold the traditions of the Republican party so effectively exemplified by Calvin Coolidge." [18]

There it was. The nominees were selected, the platform written, and an excellent forecast given of what the Republican campaign would be like. The party would stand on Coolidge's record, and Hoover would also stand on his own all-encompassing image as a man who could do everything and do it right. Even Coolidge immediately lent his support, now that the party had made its choice, in what was for him a warm endorsement. He wrote his heir apparent that "your great ability and your wide experience will enable you to serve our party and our country with marked distinction. I wish you all the success that your heart could desire. May God continue to bestow upon you the power to do your duty." [19]

In studying the 1928 election campaign, one is struck with the fact that historians have been chiefly concerned with the loser. There are many reasons for that. Alfred E. Smith conducted a vigorous campaign. He donned some liberal trappings while, paradoxically, trying to appropriate Hoover's prosperity and tranquility issues. More important, Smith himself became a central issue in 1928 because of his Catholic, Tammany, urban, antiprohibition, and immigrant-son identifications. Then too, historians, partly because of the liberal bias of many of them and partly as a matter of duty, have been much concerned with trying to find links between Smith's campaign and the Democratic victories of the 1930s. Therefore, Hoover's 1928 campaign has received little more than a sidelong glance from scholars.[20] It deserves more than that.

The important thing about Herbert Hoover's campaign is that it was almost perfect, given the time, the circumstances, and the nominee's background. In 1928 prosperity had reached a higher peak than ever before in America's history. Employment, wages, salaries, and profits were at record highs. Opportunity seemed greater than ever. Labor was well enough satisfied that the American Federation of Labor and the Railroad Brotherhoods opposed neither Hoover nor Smith. (It is not coincidental that Hoover during the 1928 campaign went on record favoring "curtailment of excessive use of the injunction in labor disputes.") [21] As for farmers, rising prices and Hoover's assurances that their problems merited special attention helped to keep them in line.

It is axiomatic that when the incumbent's policies are popular, the new leader stands on the record and generally promises more of the same. Hoover was not the man to flout that. Indeed, he did less than successors usually do to establish their own programs, partly because he was already intimately linked with the successes that the Republicans claimed and partly because he was neither an outstanding orator nor a man who liked campaigning. But Hoover had another problem. He was aware that President Coolidge was sharply sensitive to any statement that might reflect adversely upon his record. Therefore, although Hoover's brain teemed "with schemes of good and new for Titipu," he could not afford to vex the touchy American mikado. Neither could he risk introducing issues that might switch to himself the negative response of many Americans to Alfred E. Smith.

Smith and the Democrats had a surfeit of problems. The party had done little to ready itself for the campaign. Between 1924 and 1928, there had been virtually no national Democratic organization, and the party had developed neither new national leaders nor compelling issues. It was clear by the time that the Democrats met in convention in late June that only New York's Governor Smith could be nominated. He was fifty-four years old and was the urban counterpart of Hoover's poverty-to-success story. There was no doubt that Smith had the most outstanding record of public service and the most effective political organization in the Democratic party.[22]

The Democrats nominated Smith on the first ballot. If the Catholic, urban (though not urbane) son of immigrants was not elected president, it was a high accomplishment that he obtained a major party nomination. It was quite likely that he personally would become an important campaign issue because 1928 was dominated by Protestantism and nativism and there was widespread distrust of anybody associated with New York City and Tammany Hall. As though to insure that result, Smith sent a telegram to the convention accepting the nomination but vowing, in contradiction to the Democratic platform, to work for modification of prohibition. That unleashed the hounds of a dry heaven, both Democratic and Republican, against him. It probably also stiffened attacks against him on other grounds, for rum, Rome, Tammany, the city, and immigrants seemed interlocking and undesirable in the minds of many Americans. Thus, when Assistant Attorney General Mabel Walker Willebrandt assailed Smith before Protestant audiences for his stand on prohibition, it was plain that her listeners were usually thinking about all five of the issues simultaneously. Smith also played into his opponents' hands when he named John J. Raskob, a prominent Catholic businessman and wet, a recent Republican, and another New Yorker, as the chairman of the Democratic National Committee. Raskob would underline Smith's prosperity appeal and work wonders in raising funds, but his background otherwise only further antagonized prohibitionist, Protestant, and rural America.[23]

There were few issues separating the Democrats and Republicans in 1928. Not only was there no mention of Woodrow Wilson's League of Nations in the Democratic platform, but there was an essential sharing of Republican issues. The Democrats indicated that they would do better than the Republicans on debt and tax reduction, orderly farm marketing, a federal farm board, agricultural cooperatives, outlawry of war, improved transportation facilities, and labor injunctions. If there was a hint of something like McNary-Haugenism in the platform, there were also a commitment to maintain a high tariff, scant recognition that some unemployment remained, and only a suggestion that federal regulation might be useful in some areas. The Democrats basically had also become worshippers at the high altar of a permanent, all-pervasive, business-controlled prosperity. Moreover, there was no acceptable alternative available to the voters. The only things noteworthy about minor parties in 1928 were that the Communists, as the Workers party, ran a ticket for the first time in the United States and that the Socialists nominated Norman Thomas, who thus began his long career as their perennial presidential candidate. These and the lesser third parties had little appeal in America during the high tide of prosperity, and they received a total of less than 400,000 votes.[24]

What it meant was that the only significant issues left were prohibition and Alfred E. Smith. The Democratic nominee had, in his telegram to his party's convention, made prohibition a real issue. It seemed, however, a poor Democratic issue, for all indicators showed that repeal of prohibition ran contrary to majority national sentiment in 1928. Smith himself became an issue, in part because of his Lower East Side accent and the flaunting of his New York City background, neither of which large segments of the electorate could stomach.[25] Moreover, he was not just a professional politician, but a Tammany Hall politician, reputedly the most venal of all political organizations. To many Americans he also personified the frightening aspects of alien elements. He not only was Catholic, but opposed prohibition and championed immigrants and their children. Because of these factors and, it should be emphasized, because of the small difference between Republicans and Democrats on other issues in 1928, Smith and prohibition became the great issues.

Clearly, there was little need for Hoover to do more than stand on his and the Republican record. There was also great danger if he did more than that, both because he might split the Republicans and because he might display vulnerabilities to the voters and the Democrats. Hoover set up his campaign organization early. Secretary of the Interior Hubert Work was the new chairman of the Republican National Committee. Joseph R. Nutt, who had supported Hoover for president as early as 1920, became treasurer, James Good was named director of the national committee's western division, and Senator George H. Moses of New Hampshire headed the eastern division. Hoover closely supervised their operations, and the result was a record income of funds, extensive organization of political workers, and a vast outpouring of campaign materials through a variety of media, including film, print, and radio.[26]

All this seemed essential, for Hoover could not rely upon the party's progressives and Old Guard for adequate support, partly because of his starchiness in dealing with politicians whose interests and ways differed from his (a problem that would become great during the critical days of depression). He had to pick up enthusiastic support where he could, for example, from Senator William E. Borah of Idaho, to whom Hoover had made a special commitment on prohibition, from the duty-minded Charles Evans Hughes, from moderate and business-oriented Republicans like Dr. Work, whose pulses beat at one with the nominee's, and from those like former Governor Henry J. Allen of Kansas who looked for political preferment.[27]

The lukewarm attitudes of many Republican leaders also probably explain the eagerness of the Hoover forces to obtain maximum support from President Coolidge. National Chairman Work early tried to force Coolidge's hand, but the best news he could give the press after meeting with the chief executive was that "he will do what he can." The next chapter in the Hoover-Coolidge story came when Hoover indicated that he would resign from the administration, which brought from the president the response that he need not quit. Hoover did resign anyway, effective 14 July, to devote himself completely to the campaign. He soon visited Coolidge at the summer White House in Brule, Wisconsin, 16–17 July. Although there were no political statements to the press, the president did appear publicly with a weary-looking Hoover on a couple of

occasions, and he advised him to conserve his strength. That was
just the first of the nominee's several visits to Coolidge, none of
which yielded immediate endorsements from the president.[28]

Yet, if Hoover perhaps overdid the work of pursuing Coolidge's
favor, the White House did not interfere in the campaign and
some support for Hoover was forthcoming. The president wrote
him in August that his acceptance speech "ranks very high in
political discussion. I congratulate you upon it and upon the reception which has been given to it by the country." The occupant of
the White House was also reported satisfied that the West and
agriculture had lined up behind Hoover. More important was
Coolidge's 21 August statement that Hoover's service as secretary
of commerce "has been of great benefit to the commercial life of
the nation and has given a new impetus to our entire business
structure. You have gained a knowledge of the mechanics of business and government that is unsurpassed. It will always be a satisfaction to me to have had the benefit of your wise counsel in
meeting the problems which have arisen during my administration.
My best wishes will always attend you in the broader field to which
you have been called." In September it was reported after a conference between the two men that Coolidge was anxious to be
helpful and, a bit later, that the president was taking a keen interest
in the campaign. Toward the end of the month, Coolidge sent a
message to the Massachusetts Republican convention endorsing both
the Hoover-Curtis slate and the state ticket. The president's final
effort came the week before election when he telegraphed Hoover,
"You have shown your fitness to be President." Hoover's success at
the polls was assured, he continued, and it was plain that the
presidency would be in "competent hands." [29]

If this was a low level of support by the retiring president, it was
probably the most he had to offer, given his laconic ways. Those,
and they were many, who felt that Coolidge had let Hoover down
clearly did not know Coolidge or they would have understood
that he was temperamentally incapable of great ballyhoo, even for
himself. Yet, the idea that Coolidge did nothing for Hoover until
just before the election is belied by the record, and what the president did would have seemed stronger if it had not been for the
public complaints of Hoover's supporters that he was not doing
enough.[30]

Herbert Hoover characteristically threw himself into the campaign. It was an "eighteen-hour day" job for him. Addresses had to
be prepared, a chore not because he gave many, but because he was

the last president who did most of the work on his speeches. In Washington and far and wide over the land, he labored to unify the party behind him, and if some Republican leaders laid down on the job, there were few defections. He spent much time, and with considerable success, supervising the work of his campaign organization. His was a never-ending round of committee meetings, press conferences, public appearances, and speeches, as well as the preparations for all of these. Yet, Hoover did not particularly care for campaigning. He remembered well the monumental egos he was supposed to flatter and the huge number of autographs that had to be scratched out. Other chores he did not sound happy with included "the local committee at every depot must ride to the next station. Hundreds of thousands of people at train stops must have some sort of speech. Thousands of babies must be shaken by their plump fists." Then there was what Hoover called "campaign dirt." Although Governor Smith received most of this, Hoover was sensitive to what was thrown his way. There was the story that he had robbed a Chinese, and the nominee took some abuse because of his Quaker faith. There were also attempts to show that he was either hostile or overfriendly to racial minorities, that he was a British subject, and that he was a party to corruption in the Harding administration.[31]

Hoover's chief strategy on the way to victory was to run a campaign free from mistakes. He had to make some speeches, as he explained, to educate the people on the issues. He also needed the exposure. His main campaign goals were, therefore, to cement his identification with "Prosperity" and as the man who could do everything, or as one pamphlet put it, be "Ten Candidates in One." National Committee Chairman Work kicked off the campaign on 2 July by stressing that Hoover was a well-known man of remarkably varied accomplishments and background, probably the most versatile nominee ever. The campaign would be run, Work added, on the principles of prosperity, efficiency, and good government, with the Coolidge administration's record serving as the keynote. The campaign largely reiterated and elaborated upon these themes, although the Republican nominee countenanced subsidiary attacks against Tammany Hall and against Smith for his position on prohibition.[32]

Hoover's first major speech was his acceptance address on 11 August. Then 70,000 people in the Stanford University Stadium and millions by radio heard him extol the virtues of America, individualism, and the Republican administration. "Peace has been made.

. . . Commerce and industry have been revived. . . . We in America today are nearer to the final triumph over poverty than ever before in the history of any land." He then detailed what he stood for, and it was compendious. Most prominent was his famous statement that "given a chance to go forward with the policies of the last eight years, and we shall soon with the help of God be in sight of the day when poverty will be banished from this nation." In line what that, he went on record for "a job for every man," "larger comfort and greater participation in life and leisure" for workingmen, "the promotion of business," "equality of opportunity for all irrespective of faith and color," and the fostering of harmony and cooperation among government, business, and labor. He described "farm relief" as "most important," and proposed that it could be achieved through an "adequate tariff" and a farm board that would develop "stabilization corporations which will protect the farmer from the depressions and demoralizations of seasonal gluts and periodical surpluses." Among the other government actions he espoused were public works and the development of water resources, enforcement of prohibition, revision of the national origins basis for immigration restriction, and the promotion of child development. He inveighed against corruption and dishonesty by any party, saying that "it is treason to the state. It is destructive of self-government." Anticipating the introduction of religion into the campaign, he declared, "By blood and conviction I stand for religious tolerance both in act and spirit. The glory of our American ideals is the right of every man to worship God according to the dictates of his own conscience." [33]

The acceptance speech was an able homily to good works, materialism, and Americanism. Hoover's campaign was now in high gear and would roll forward relentlessly with press statements, public appearances in well-selected places, and speeches, long and short. Not once did Hoover mention his opponent's name, but instead talked of Republican unity and "a constructive progressive party." [34] His campaign was, in a nutshell, a triumphal procession by a nominee who exuded supreme confidence that the election would only serve to ratify the votes already cast in the minds and hearts of the voters.

The remainder of Hoover's major speeches, and there were six more, elaborated upon what he had said at Stanford. At his birth place, West Branch, Iowa, on 21 August, he marvelled at the virtues of small-town life and underscored the importance of gaining cooperative solutions to the farmers' problems. He also declared in favor of developing the St. Lawrence Seaway to improve foreign trade and stressed the importance of family life and the well-being of children. At Newark, on 17 September, he linked the tariff and increased foreign trade with prosperity and, especially, high wages for labor. He asserted that public works should be used to offset unemployment and that there should be increased use of mediation in labor-management disputes and restrictions on the use of labor injunctions. His creed was opportunity for all through the maximum employment of study, inventiveness, and self-reliance. Soon after his Newark address, he felt constrained to dissociate himself from the rising use of religion against Governor Smith. That, he stated, "does violence to every instinct that I possess. . . . Such an attitude is entirely opposed to every principle of the Republican party." [35]

Hoover gave his next major speech in the South, at Elizabethton, Tennessee, 6 October, to a crowd estimated at 50,000 and to a vast radio audience. There he appealed for "fair play" in the campaign. Otherwise he recited the various points in his program, laying emphasis on prohibition enforcement, humanized immigration regulations, a protective tariff, the expansion of foreign trade, and the establishment of a federal farm board and more agricultural cooperatives. The Republican leader also gave a nod to states' rights, though cautioning that the principle could not be followed so far as to make the control of monopolies impossible. On 15 October, in Boston, he declared that the tariff was the dominant issue of the campaign. The Republicans would make the necessary revisions to protect all Americans economically from unfair foreign competition, which, by implication, the Democrats could not be trusted to do.[36]

Hoover carried the battle to Smith's home town a week later. There, in New York City, he gave his most aggressive speech, indicating that the Democratic policies in agriculture, prohibition, and electric power added up to an espousal of state socialism. Such policies could only lead to the ruination of "free industry and free commerce," "political equality, free speech, free assembly, free press, and equality of opportunity." In contrast, the Republicans opposed unnecessary interference in business, standing instead for cooperation and responsible competition, which would assure the continuance of liberty, progress, and prosperity in the United States.[37] Thus was Smith severely caned for his flirtation with the ogres of McNary-Haugenism, public power, and prohibition modification. And Hoover's New York City address, however ridiculous it looks today, was politically effective. It kept the prohibitionists stirred up, cast additional doubt on Smith's grasp of or even interest in farm problems, and partly countered the Democrats' business and prosperity appeals.

The Republican nominee's last major speech was given on 2 November at St. Louis, where he extolled the advantages of his farm-board proposal as an effective cooperative way to help agriculture to solve its pressing problems. He reiterated the need for cooperation between labor and capital in reaping the highest material rewards for all Americans. Again he emphasized that the government's role would be to use public works to spur business growth and employment, to protect natural resources, and to promote education, health, and science.[38]

Election day was 6 November, and a record-breaking number of Americans went to the polls. In fact, 67.5 percent of the eligible voters—almost 11 percent higher than in 1924—cast their ballots. Hoover won a smashing victory, receiving 21,391,993 popular votes and 444 electoral ballots to 15,016,169 and 87, respectively, for Smith. The victor carried forty states, including five southern and four border states. Smith won in only eight states, though those included normally Republican Massachusetts and Rhode Island. He also did well in Connecticut and Illinois, and in a number of states the Democratic nominee apparently attracted the 1924 Progressive vote, which most observers thought would go Republican or stay at home.[39] Clearly, the Hoover-Smith contest had substantial effects on geographical voting patterns, as Hoover cracked the South and as Smith made significant inroads in the cities and the East.

The question was who would capitalize on these shifts in the future. One should not assume that the election turned on the religious, urban, and Tammany-Hall issues. Had they not been present, Hoover would still have been the winner, for prosperity was the nation's dominant concern. On this, Hoover was unassailable because of his record, reputation, sophistication, and campaign. He also had the prohibition issue on his side and, as he admitted, he was favored by the religious and Tammany questions in the South. In short, it was a paradoxical election. Smith and prohibition were the two major issues separating the Democratic and Republican parties, but they did not decide the election, however much they gave it color and fire. They did, however, bolster the conviction that Hoover was the man to forward prosperity. Thus, although both nominees championed business property and all that that entailed, Smith could not match Hoover in terms of the record, and his image was flawed by his background, his provincial personality, and his lack of versatility. It can therefore be said that the election boiled down to a question of whom most voters preferred to manage prosperity, and that was easily answered, given Smith's weaknesses. When other issues were added, they only swelled Hoover's and Smith's votes in roughly equal proportion. What Hoover gained were the votes of those many Americans who intensely disliked Smith. The New Yorker gained a larger turnout of urban and ethnic Democratic voters and the support of many independents and some Republicans, who once having voted Democratic would not find it difficult to do so again if the circumstances warranted.

One should not overlook that Hoover's presidential victory was accompanied by a substantial increase of Republicans in the House of Representatives and the Senate. The result was that they would possess 100 seats more than the Democrats in the lower house and 17 more in the upper chamber, which were comfortable margins under normal conditions.[40] Conditions, however, were not long to be normal. The Democrats consequently, could build on Smith's 1928 gains and Hoover's subsequent difficulties. Yet, the probability should not be ignored that Smith's gains would have been as transitory as Hoover's were if the latter had had a successful administration.

Herbert Hoover ran a remarkably able campaign for president in 1928. He deserves credit for that, whatever his political errors before and after. During the campaign, he established himself as what most Americans were looking for—he was a champion and expert technician of prosperity and progress, an idealist representing enlightened individualism, humanitarianism, harmony, liberty, moral rectitude, and tranquility, and a firm believer in honesty, efficiency, economy, peace, the home, and the family. He was also close enough to the dominant religious, ethnic, and rural or small-town backgrounds to draw support against Smith. Add Hoover's rise from rags to riches, from obscurity to international fame, and he was hard to resist. If anyone seemed a man for the times, it was Herbert Hoover. He knew what to do with his wealth of background and talents, at least under the conditions existent in 1928. His organization was superb in supporting him; he minimized factionalism within the party; his speeches contained what most citizens wanted to hear and offered few opportunities for his opponents to attack him; his statements buttressed his image as a wonder man above vicious partisanship. Then there was Hoover's ability to gain some backing from the very reticent incumbent president. What it all added up to was an almost flawless campaign, though one, it must be emphasized, that would tragically snap back at him when conditions changed drastically.

After the results were in, the question was how would Hoover prepare to assume the reins of government? It was obvious that something had to be done soon about farm policy and tariff revision. The president-elect also had his image to maintain. Yet, he could not move too fast or overtly because of the incumbent's sensitivity to poaching on his preserves. After all, the majesty and the power still resided in Calvin Coolidge. Hoover had to find approaches to the seat of power that were both dynamic and stealthy.

The president-elect rested after election day, although his relaxation was often punctuated with considerations of who should serve in the new administration and what that administration's policies and initial strategies should be. Commanding of attention almost immediately after election day was the announcement that Hoover would probably tour Latin America before his inauguration. His objective was to "dispel the suspicions and fears of the 'Colossus of the North' [and] win the respect of those nations" after the damage done there by United States's economic and military intervention. Reading between the lines, one must conclude that Hoover also wanted to expand the nation's trade in Latin America and put it on a healthier basis.[41] His Latin American visit was a dramatic, unprecedented action by a president-elect, and it was also a splendid way to keep him from colliding with Coolidge during the interregnum.

Hoover left the United States on 19 November on the U.S.S. *Maryland* and was gone until 6 January 1929, when he returned on the U.S.S. *Utah*. He visited with the leaders of eleven Latin American countries. He told the president and president-elect of Nicaragua, who were enemies, that the United States planned to end its military occupation there, a statement which Hoover liked to think postponed the possibility of civil war in Nicaragua. During the tour, Hoover made fourteen talks, which emphasized becoming "good neighbors" through cordial contacts, cooperation "for the common upbuilding of prosperity and of progress throughout the world," and a common dedication to freedom and democracy. He suggested increasing exchanges of students and professors and the development of inter-American aviation and laid the basis for the settlement of the Tacna-Arica dispute between Bolivia and Peru.

Other results of his tour were the continued withdrawal of United States' military forces from Latin America and attempts to improve diplomatic representation in countries to the south.[42] All in all, the journey was a success in contributing to better relations. It also offered Hoover opportunities to consider further his overall policies and appointments away from the immediate pressure of domestic concerns.

And those pressures were intense. Even before he left for Latin America, Hoover felt compelled to discuss, for example, the development of inland waterways with the chairman of the House Committee on Rivers and Harbors, Representative William E. Hull of Illinois. While the president-elect was away, he was also in constant touch with events at home. Yet, the Latin American trip was a refreshing break. Pressure for action developed in the meantime, however. When Hoover returned to the United States, he went directly to Washington where he stayed for two weeks, meeting with President Coolidge, congressmen, and prospective members of his own administration.[43]

One thing he had to deal with was patronage, but it was not too burdensome, for he decided that most of the incumbents were of sufficient quality to merit retention in office. The largest proportion of changes was made in the cabinet, in which he kept only James J. Davis as secretary of labor and Andrew Mellon as secretary of the treasury. Two of Hoover's closest campaign aides, Walter F. Brown and James W. Good, were appointed department heads, as postmaster general and secretary of war, respectively. Moreover, three of the new president's personal aides, Lawrence Richey, French Strother, and George Akerson, became central figures on the White House staff, and Hoover's long-time friend, Ray Lyman Wilbur of Stanford University, was named secretary of the interior.[44]

During his fortnight in Washington, Hoover made many decisions and promises, but either out of respect for Calvin Coolidge or the fear of offending him, the president-elect refused to announce his plans until he became chief executive in his own right. Nevertheless, other parties to Hoover's plans made it reasonably plain what he intended to do. The pressure to act on farm and tariff problems was especially strong, and Hoover decided to call Congress into special session to deal with these matters. He thereby assisted the Coolidge administration, for his firm promise of prompt farm relief pacified farm-bloc senators who had threatened to hold up ratification of the Kellogg-Briand war renunciation pact until something was done for agriculture. Word also leaked out that Hoover would appoint a nonpartisan commission to investigate the problems involved in prohibition enforcement.[45]

Hoover arrived in Florida on 22 January for a long vacation. There was, however, more work than relaxation for him there. Further consideration had to be given to appointments, policies, and strategies. Information about such things still found its way into print. For example, after a meeting between Hoover and Senator Reed Smoot of Utah, the press gathered that the president-elect remained unchanged in his opposition to McNary-Haugenism and in his wish to have only adjustments in selected duties instead of a completely new tariff.[46]

Inauguration day came 4 March. Almost silent companions, Coolidge and Hoover motored to the Capitol, where in the rain Hoover was inducted as the thirty-first president of the United States before a crowd estimated at 50,000. He unburdened himself of a long address, which was partly a homily on American virtues and partly a discourse on what his program would be. There were no surprises. He announced that he would appoint a commission to probe "the whole structure of our federal system of jurisprudence, to include the method of enforcement of the eighteenth amendment and the causes of abuse under it." That way solutions to America's problems of law enforcement, especially of prohibition, might be found. He reiterated his intention to encourage cooperative self-help in order to widen business and employment opportunities and to combat poverty. Education and public health would also be promoted, the first to broaden the base of leadership available to the nation and the second to reap "economic benefits . . . reduction of suffering and promotion of human happiness." The longest section of Hoover's address dealt with his profound concern for the maintenance of world peace. He endorsed arms limitation, the "creation of instrumentalities for peaceful settlement of controversies," the renunciation of war as a form of national policy, and American adherence, with suitable reservations, to the Permanent Court of International Justice. He also announced that he would call Congress into special session to provide farm relief and to make "limited changes in the tariff" in order to assist farmers, labor, and manufacturing. The new president dealt in summary fashion with other mandates he believed the voters had given him. These included "the maintenance of the integrity of the Constitution; the vigorous enforcement of the laws; the continuance of economy in public expenditure; the continued regulation of business to prevent domination in the community; the denial of ownership or operation of business by the government in competition with its citizens; the avoidance of policies which would involve us in the controversies of foreign nations; the more effective reorganization of the departments of the federal government; the expansion of public works; and the promotion of welfare activities affecting education and the home." [47] Obviously, the new president's goals were set high, matching the confidence of most Americans in him and in themselves.

The United States was thus launched on what unexpectedly turned out to be the most unhappy period in its twentieth-century history. Herbert Hoover had shown his mettle as engineer, business-man, humanitarian, statesman, and even politician before he became president. He was perfectly cast to take the lead in the story of prosperity and well prepared for the accompanying role of peace-keeper. It was bitterly paradoxical, for Hoover and the nation, that the script was drastically altered soon after he stepped on stage. The new part called for talents that few Americans at the time seemed to possess. Certainly, Hoover's stock of them was deficient. Scholars must, nevertheless, not overlook his earlier great successes, those which established him as an outstanding American and which include the remarkably successful campaigns that he undertook to secure nomination and election as president of the United States.

Before the Crash:
Hoover's First Eight Months
in the Presidency

DAVID B. BURNER

State University of New York at Stony Brook

*David Burner was born in 1937 and educated at Hamilton College
(B.A., 1958) and Columbia University (Ph.D., 1965). He taught at
Oakland University in Rochester, Michigan, the City College of
New York, Hunter College, and Colby College prior to coming to
the State University of New York at Stony Brook in 1967, where he
is currently Associate Professor of History. His major publication
is* The Politics of Provincialism: The Democratic Party in
Transition, 1918–1932 *(New York: Alfred A. Knopf, Inc., 1968). In
addition, he has written and edited numerous other works. At
present Professor Burner holds a Guggenheim Fellowship, which
is allowing him to complete a biography of Herbert Hoover.*

*Like Professor McCoy, David Burner also views Hoover as a
"marvelously attractive" figure in 1928. Burner describes Hoover
as a strong president and suggests that his tenure be viewed as part
of a larger effort dating back into his Commerce years. By
categorizing the needed reforms Hoover initiated prior to the crash,
Burner concludes that the president attempted to build "great
cooperative units that would receive energies from the bottom up
and their efficiency from the top downward." While he agrees that
Hoover's system did not work, he sees the effort as distantly
related to a "later (post-New Deal) joining of technical proficiency
to a diffusion of power."*

The Herbert Hoover of 1928 was a singularly attractive figure to his
fellow citizens. He was American in many ways his countrymen
liked to think archetypical of their nation: homespun, competent,
generous, successful, and also innovative in a manner that managed
to be respectful of the past. However, this simple figure can be

broken into contradictions which make him more interesting and suggest a more intriguing national temperament than Hoover's fairly self-satisfied electorate probably perceived by themselves. For the strain between nostalgia and expertise that the Hoover figure seemed so comfortably to resolve is a considerable one, and the compound of expertise and voluntarism for which Hoover spoke resolved the strain only precariously. Expertise, whether America deserves to claim a large measure of it or not, has been a traditional American tenet and the man who in 1928 represented it could expect therefore to awaken the most conservative instincts from his countrymen. Yet expertise is also profoundly antitraditional and for a psychological as well as a practical reason: it means a world of relentless analysis, of hard glittering facts with the comforts of memory and custom chilled out of it. Expertise also threatens to bring with it large-scale centralized organization that wars with American creeds and local arrangements. Here Hoover's voluntarism served as a nice counterpart to his technocratic side. His notion that reasonable men would spontaneously organize themselves around objectives suggested a way out of central dictation and brought also a sense of the fellowship and good will that can attend highly technical labors. Hoover's voluntarism also allied itself more directly to the idea of technocracy in a manner reminiscent of the Enlightenment and its confidence: it sustained the grand—and to our vision innocent—notion that a rational intellect, shown the rational thing to do, will do it without coercion. In this sense voluntarism made Hoover's brand of expertise all the more cheerful and gave it an even larger flavor of American tradition—and the Enlightenment or its kindly optimism about the instructed mind has been a gentle part of our tradition.

All this we can perceive beneath the surface image of Hoover— as any culture and its representative figures must hold contradiction beneath their partially composed surfaces. The Hoover of the late twenties, at any rate, embodied much of what was workmanlike and homegrown in his America. When the campaign is seen in this light, its exuberant naiveté becomes more understandable. Herbert Hoover waged his presidential campaign in the heady atmosphere of the late nineteen twenties, and he made his own contributions to the general buoyancy. The candidate boasted of the increase in real wages and the decline in hours of labor, the spiraling production of automobiles, radios, telephones, and electrical appliances, the rapid spread of secondary and higher education. When his Committee on Economic Trends reported that the nation's per capita produc-

tivity had increased by 35 percent in eight years, Hoover commented in 1928: "I do not claim the credit for this, but certainly
the [Commerce] Department helped." [1] In June the presidential
nominee rhetorically asked the Republican Convention: "Shall
prosperity be more thoroughly distributed?" [2] And in his August
Acceptance Address Hoover hymned the country's future: "We in
America today are nearer to the final triumph over poverty than
ever before in the history of any land. The poorhouse is vanishing
from among us. We have not yet reached the goal, but . . . we
shall soon with the help of God be in sight of the day when poverty
will be banished from this nation." [3]

Always vigilant against a hardening of social classes, Hoover
offered to lead in preserving his dearest ideal of equal opportunity.
His training and background gave him special powers to do anything; according to a dithyramb by a delegate who had nominated
him: "He sweeps the horizon of every subject. Nothing escapes his
view. . . ." [4] *The New York Times* grandly observed that Hoover's
decisions were based on a memory encompassing "all experience." [5]
Secretary of State Stimson was quoted as saying that Hoover's basic
objective was the abolition of poverty through technology.[6] A
popular belief that he was above politics added to his immense
prestige: an important figure in the Wilson administration, he
seemed to have had trouble deciding, almost a decade earlier, to
which political party he owed allegiance. In actuality, he had
joined the New York Republican Club in 1906 and contributed
$1,000 to Teddy Roosevelt's 1912 campaign. Kent Schofield sug-
gests that, like the aviator Charles Lindbergh, Hoover achieved
commanding stature both as a harbinger of the new technology
and as a symbol of the self-sufficient rural past: he combined per-
manence and change, nostalgia and confidence.[7] Under this shrewd
but benevolent man, his technocratic side softened by a famous
humanitarianism, Americans looked to a new day of material and
spiritual fulfillment.

All this, Hoover well knew, was a highly unrealistic portrait of
any mortal. On returning from a postelection good-will trip to
Latin America, he relaxed near Miami with an editor from the
Christian Science Monitor; before an open fire in J. C. Penney's
house on an island in Biscayne Bay, a pensive Hoover remarked:
"I have no dread of the ordinary work of the presidency. What I do
fear is the result of the exaggerated idea the people have conceived of me. They have a conviction that I am a sort of superman,
that no problem is beyond my capacity. . . . If some unprecedented

calamity should come upon this nation I would be sacrificed to the unreasoning disappointment of a people who had expected too much." [8]

An experienced and discerning businessman, the foresighted president knew that the future held a day of reckoning for the economy. Since the stock market began its unparalleled rise late in 1924 he had warned almost frantically of the consequences of easy credit and unrestrained speculation; on one occasion he burst in on Adolf Miller of the Federal Reserve Board, demanding to know why that institution was doing so little to restrain the market.[9] In these years Hoover and his admirers also experienced immense frustration under the small-spirited Calvin Coolidge, who blocked many of the commerce secretary's favorite schemes. In his *Memoirs* Hoover complained of Coolidge's reluctance "to undertake much that was new or cost money." [10] Hoover entered the White House with a sense of urgency. Some change was overdue and he wondered how long the economy could sustain its present condition.

Hoover brought to the presidency a belief in strong executive leadership, albeit this belief sometimes took curious form. "As adviser to the Congress," he later observed in the *Memoirs*, "the President must demonstrate constant leadership by proposing social and economic reforms made necessary by the increasing complexity of American life. He must be the conserver of natural resources, and he must carry forward the great public works in pace with public need. He must encourage all good causes. . . ." [11] Above all, accomplishment measured the effectiveness of any man's life; all else was grains of sand. Hoover said this many times in his lengthy career and repeatedly asked his assistants to compile lists of achievements.

As secretary of commerce, Hoover had several times urged strong government action. In the Mississippi flood of 1927 he asked for $10 million of government funds and secured legislation that made floods a federal responsibility. He also broached a plan of basic land reform to break up large southern plantations: under a land resettlement corporation, whites and blacks could purchase improved land, thereby striking out at the infamous farm-tenancy system.[12] The government would first appropriate $1 to $2 million, but he looked to private foundations for further expansion of the idea. Such acts distressed Wall Street and the Old Guard, who had long disliked Hoover for doing too much; way back in 1919, for instance, he had had the effrontery to call together some of the most important business leaders in the country and recommend that they establish "liaison" with the AFL. "The idea," one participant recalled, "got a very cold reception." [13]

All this is not to claim Hoover for modern liberalism. Like Frederic Winslow Taylor and other great technicians of his day, Hoover was a practitioner of industrial rationalization: in the twenties, as secretary of commerce, he had set out to harmonize the operations not of a single plant but of an entire technical economy. Closely allied was his peculiar concept of economic organization, in which he blended a taste for voluntarism and individual decision with a commitment to collective effort; and so he proceeded, always precariously close to contradicting himself, to nurture into existence great cooperative units that would receive their energies from the bottom up but their efficiency from the top downward. Hoover's desire to protect individualism usually made him reject out of hand any permanent governmental role; nonetheless, his world was aggressively modern: his ideas and programs for society arose from experience in engineering and international business.

Finally in possession of the highest national office, Hoover began to fire up the engines of Progressive reform. He had always worked at full throttle and did so in 1929. The plans and accomplishments of his months in office before the stock market crash have been overshadowed not only by that event, but also by memories of the long and rancorous special session of Congress that began in April. But while Congress debated over the Farm Board and the tariff—debates which are excluded from this account—important work got underway in the executive branch of government. Hoover's work in the months before the crash cannot be evaluated simply by a count of laws or a check of press releases. It must be viewed as part of a longer story beginning in the Commerce years. Perhaps most important, the downward curve of the economic cycle after 1929 prevented the full implementation of many of his early presidential efforts; solving problems of social justice or of conservation generally requires tax revenues. Yet any judgment of Hoover's term in the White House must first acknowledge that he organized the beginnings of "many reforms that were needed." [14] Some of these reforms came about during his term, some—delayed by the depression— came later, a few remain as points of discussion more than a generation later.

A series of dramatic announcements, many in the first weeks of his administration, indicated that Hoover would be an active and independent chief executive. Certainly no earlier president had done so much so quickly. Ten days after his inauguration Hoover ordered the publication of all large government refunds of income, estate, or gift taxes.[15] A longstanding goal of the progressives in Congress, the president's general, encompassing, and permanent action repudiated Secretary of the Treasury Andrew Mellon's earlier policy. Hoover publicly divulged the political backers of judicial appointments and vowed to end southern Republican patronage scandals.[16] Also in the early days of his administration, Hoover abolished the device of a presidential spokesman and sometimes allowed the press to quote from his biweekly conferences directly.[17] To promote oil conservation, on 12 March he forbade the sale or lease of government oil lands and canceled most permits then current—a "wise and farsighted policy," *The Nation* commented.[18] In the same month he intervened to head off a strike on the Texas and Pacific Railroad.[19] Later in the year, the president made it known that he would ask Congress to reduce taxes by one-fifth on high incomes, one-third on middle incomes, and two-thirds on lower incomes—and corporation taxes from 12 to 11 percent.[20]

Hoover earned a strong record in civil liberties during his early months in the White House. He slapped down a campaign by the right-wing periodical, *National Republic,* which claimed to have government backing for a fund to "fight the Reds." [21] A newspaper editorial elsewhere and petitions alleging "political prisoners" had disturbed Hoover; he requested that Attorney General William D. Mitchell provide their names and offenses. Later he could reply to Jane Addams that all such prisoners had been released years before and pardons had been granted to all who applied.[22] Hoover even inquired into the case of the labor martyr Thomas J. Mooney but was rebuffed by Mitchell on jurisdictional grounds.[23] The president also secured the resignation in May of the fanatical prohibitionist Mabel Walker Willebrandt as assistant attorney general; he disliked her dramatic methods of entrapping liquor-law violators, which included sending female spies into houses of prostitution and other espionage agents into prisons to check on administrators. Mrs. Willebrandt had appealed to 2600 Protestant ministers in an Ohio speech during the presidential campaign, asking them to work against Smith on religious grounds.[24] Hubert Work, the Republican National chairman, who supervised Mrs. Willebrandt and ran the 1928 campaign, resigned in June. Mrs. Hoover served tea at the White House to a black congressman's wife in June despite formal protests from southerners who had been courted during the campaign; Mrs. de Priest was the first formal Negro guest at the executive mansion since Booker T. Washington lunched with

Teddy Roosevelt.[25] In the same month, the president demanded a greatly increased budget for Howard University, which enabled the School of Law to attain accreditation.[26] And the first sentence the president commuted was that of a Negro for the murder of a woman: no eyewitness was present and conviction had depended on a confession "signed in the presence of police officers." [27] Late in the year Hoover refused to interrupt the peaceful picketing of Communists in front of the White House.[28] His attitudes in 1929 squared with his unruffled demeanor during the Red scare a decade before; there was no surer road to radicalism than by repression, Hoover had told an unappreciative Boston Chamber of Commerce in 1920.[29]

When a riot broke out at Leavenworth prison early in August 1929, Hoover had already begun to prepare a vast program of federal penal reform. To relieve overcrowded prisons, Attorney General Mitchell earlier had urged the setting up of prison camps on public lands for road and traintrack building, but national park personnel feared their presence would alarm vacationers.[30] The internationally recognized Sanford Bates, innovative head of the Massachusetts prisons, was chosen to undertake prison reforms. Little more than a decade earlier the two federal prisons at Leavenworth and Atlanta had held scarcely 2000 men. But new federal crimes—traffic in drugs, prohibition violations, car theft—resulted in desperate overcrowding. Bates found the federal prisons a nightmare: a single doctor, for instance, covered each institution; unskilled inmates provided nighttime medical care. The Seventy-First Congress passed eight costly prison-reform bills drafted by the Bureau of Prisons in mid-1929. A new penitentiary, graced by an architecturally notable library and chapel, soon rose on a thousand-acre stretch of the beautiful Susquehanna Valley near Lewisburg, Pennsylvania. Designed as a place for the rehabilitation of prisoners as well as their safekeeping, Lewisburg marked a fresh start in federal incarceration. In a new El Paso reformatory prisoners worked on the irrigation and reclamation of dry lands; in Chillicothe they learned industrial skills (although with some irony prison officials boasted of a five-day week and a seven-hour day). A full medical and educational staff was provided at the major centers. Probationary periods under close supervision became extremely common: by 1932 fully 5200 prisoners were released on parole as against 1200 in 1928.[31]

The further story of these first months in office lies in quieter unpublicized activities. The record reveals no slapdash run for

change, and some areas are disappointing. One question is especially pertinent: if Hoover wished to institute reforms, why did he
choose such a bland cabinet? Apparently he favored a brand of
men he called administrators, akin to Veblen's impersonal engineers. Many of the new cabinet members seemed remarkably
able to take the public point of view, notably Interior Secretary
Ray Wilbur, Attorney General Mitchell, and Navy Secretary Charles
Francis Adams, Jr. Secretary of State Henry L. Stimson was an able
man of internationalist leanings. The president also had a political
purpose behind his appointments: the Republican Old Guard and
a sizeable segment of the business world distrusted him; a cabinet
generously peopled with millionaires could do him no harm.
Hoover believed necessary reforms could come about best under
men who would make reasonable change acceptable to the dominant
element in the Republican party—and by extension to the nation
at large.

To a surprising degree Hoover's domestic reform activities cen-
tered in the Interior Department—the traditional home or "frontier" department; he worked through his trusted old friend, Ray
Lyman Wilbur, on leave from the presidency of Stanford. The work
of the department during 1929, and the work of the various commissions and committees it instituted, represent Hoover's brand of
social activism, with its balance of governmental initiatives and
restraint, its preference for voluntarism stimulated by publicity
from Washington and organized on a vast scale.[32] Publicity—that
was the heart of it. Publicity, requiring the pooling of expertise
and the gathering of precise data, spoke to Hoover's technocratic
tastes. It accorded well with the timber of his morality, which liked
the call to duty muted by the appeal to fact. Publicity evokes and
aids organization, but does not compel.

Hoover's favorite method of attacking a social problem, then,
would begin with the appointment of a fact-finding body. In 1926
Hoover's commerce assistant, Edward E. Hunt (a former socialist),
labeled the method "one of the most important by which public
and private policy is determined." [33] Always the government would
apply pressure after the conference to insure the continuation of its
spirit. Hoover's first such "economic reconnaissance" was a study of
the social waste in industry for the Federated American Engineering
Societies, which he had served as president in 1920. Then he held to
this approach in 1929 as he moved forward in child health, housing,
oil conservation, public-land policy, and the role of the federal government in public education. Theodore Joslin, his secretary from

1926 to 1933, observed that Hoover "left nothing to chance" in calling these conferences; and he employed quantitative data to impress and persuade.[34] Usually, the groups he appointed came back with positions remarkably like the president's and they gave these ideas considerable publicity. The next step was for states and municipalities to hold similar smaller conferences; the process resembled that of Hoover's earlier idol, Theodore Roosevelt. The real test of the approach is the extent to which all the publicity brought either voluntary reform or legislative action on the state and local levels. In fact, considerable legislation had already resulted from the various conferences Hoover had initiated between 1921–28.[35]

As early as the second day of his presidency, child health received Hoover's attention. In response to Senator James Couzzens's desire to do something for crippled children, the president wrote, "I would like to discuss the children question with you . . . as I have a notion that we might develop something of rather broad character." [36] On 2 July the famous humanitarian who had fed millions of European children during and after the World War called for a White House conference on the health and protection of children. Financed by a half-million dollar grant from the American Relief Association (the repository of surplus contributions for Belgium relief), the conference was composed of representatives of the great voluntary organizations, together with the federal, state, and municipal authorities interested in these questions. Its purpose, according to Secretary Wilbur, was "to find facts, to define standards, to recommend changes." [37] It was indeed to be far broader than similar conferences under Presidents Roosevelt and Wilson; here as elsewhere Hoover was extending the Progressive tradition.

In the fall of 1929 more than 2500 delegates worked out the most exhaustive report on child welfare ever put together. Published in thirty-five volumes, it was for many years the handbook and Bible of social workers. Hoover, who had told the gathering that 8 million children needed professional attention, later applauded the widely publicized set of standards and conclusions, the state and municipal conferences, the legislative actions and heightened sense of public and individual responsibility. The *Memphis Commercial Appeal* termed the conference more important than the tariff or farm-relief measures.[38] "I would be obliged," Hoover wrote his budget director on 16 October 1929, "if you would treat with as liberal a hand as possible the applications of . . . the Children's and Women's Bureaus. I have great sympathy with the tasks they are undertaking." [39]

Another major conference, concerned with housing conditions
and practices and also financed by the ARA, went into planning
stages in mid-1929. Housing was intimately related to health and
public welfare. Already, while head of the Better Homes movement
in the 1920s, Hoover had called for a "radical departure in house
construction and economics," so that the average person could own
a four-bedroom home.[40] Again, fact-finding committees—twenty-
five of them—applied microscopes to their subjects. Similarly,
Hoover depended on a multi-volume research program and the
power of publicity to fulfill the conference's aim: "to define what
housing ought to be and to outline broadly the programs necessary
to make it so." [41] Once more it was observed that the effects of an
undertaking of this sort are largely intangible.

The report preferred voluntary action to coercive legislation on
the national level, but the resulting enactment of hundreds of state
and local laws on housing and zoning pleased the president. Where
voluntarism generated inadequate controls on waste or social in-
justice—here as in child labor and elsewhere—he favored federal
legislation. The Home Loan Bank system passed by Congress in
1932, designed to help small homeowners with mortgage payments,
was one recommendation of the housing conference. It also recommended nonprofit and limited-dividend companies to provide low-
cost housing, cooperative apartments for congested areas, careful
attention to lot and street layout as well as construction of individual houses. Other legislative suggestions included reduction of
safety hazards through more building codes; licensing of real-estate
brokers; smoke-abatement regulations; and restrictions on the ad-
vertising of homes. Hoover described the eradication of slums as
the next pressing order of business: each city or community should
have a master building plan; slums arose because of a lack of
planning.[42]

Hoover had yet another priority item, a National Advisory Committee on Education, which Secretary Wilbur appointed in May
1929. It included a dozen Roman Catholic and three Negro members. Hoover and Wilbur asked for a definition of the proper role
of the federal government in education; the fifty-two-member panel
came up with a controversial report as well as a solid book of facts
relating to education. Noting that the federal government was already engaged extensively in education, the committee called for
an end to wasteful duplication of effort and a more centralized
control. While abjuring federal dictation of the curriculum, the
educators endorsed using the federal tax system to give financial

aid to the states for education. The most controversial recommendation, passed by a heavy majority and opposed by Wilbur, who simply elevated the existing bureau to "Office" status, was "that a Department of Education with a Secretary of Education at its head be established in the Federal Government. . . ."[43] Its departmental status would permit it to present its programs forcibly to Congress. Wilbur himself in 1930 suggested a new name for his department: Conservation, Education, and Health. Hoover, who warmly commended the committee members, had taken a similar stand for a separate cabinet-level Department of Health, Education, and Welfare.[44] Congress ignored the recommendation to create a new cabinet office, but in 1930 it did set up another agency, the National Institute of Health, that had Hoover's early and strong support.

The president used with the Indians the same methods of research and publicity he brought to other problems. There were strong personal reasons for Hoover's special interest in Indian rights. Laban Miles, an Indian agent on the Osage Reservation and Herbert Hoover's uncle, frequently visited the president during his White House years. Another uncle, Dr. Henry Minthorn, had cared for the young Hoover in Oregon and had also worked as an Indian agent. Added to Hoover's natural interest in the West and his awareness of the Quaker tradition of fair treatment to Indians, this perhaps accounts for his care in selecting a Quaker, Charles J. Rhoads, to replace the racist Hubert Work, who described Indians as "primitive, nomadic people without . . . social or political entity. . . ."[45] Rhoads, who for years served as treasurer of the Indian Rights Association, and his new assistant, J. Henry Scattergood, were Philadelphia bankers noted for their leadership in charitable work; both gave up high salaries to come to Washington.

The government adhered to no simple plan of assimilation, which could have indicated contempt for Indian culture, nor to the reservation plan, which could spell permanent segregation. The two kinds of thinking coexisted, probably unaware of their conflict. The Advisory Committee on Education advocated a program for the preserving of a separate Indian culture. The problem of Indian learning, it insisted, "should not . . . be spoken of as one of Americanization or assimilation," and it argued against boarding schools or even the transfer of an ordinary elementary school to an Indian reserve. This recommendation accorded with the findings of the Brookings Institution Meriam Report of 1928. Lewis Meriam welcomed Hoover's choice of Rhoads as Indian Commissioner, and one of Rhoads's first orders was the elimination of boarding schools.

Under Rhoads and Scattergood the Indian Bureau held to the traditional Jeffersonian-Progressive goal of assimilating the Indians into
American society. But Hoover in 1930 wanted to "blend them as
a self-supporting people into the nation as a whole" without sacrificing the unique Indian culture.[46] Wilbur himself had expressed
similar views in a letter to *The Forum* as early as 1924: "The Indian
cannot be saved on the asylum basis. . . . Plans for the future
should . . . be based upon retaining, if possible, the best qualities
of the Indians and the best opportunities for the development of
the young Indian boys and girls. I appreciate the high sentiment
of those who desire to perpetuate what is good in Indian culture.
This can only be done in my opinion by having the Indian bring
this to the rest of the population." [47] In a letter to Secretary Work,
Wilbur observed that Indians should be given title to their lands
so they would be economically self-sufficient; he added that they
should attend public instead of reservation schools.[48]

The Indian Bureau under Hoover actually ended up with a
mixture of the two philosophies. It encouraged native arts and
crafts, along with modern skills such as auto mechanics. Hoover
even wanted a permanent record made of Indian sign languages.[49]
Rhoads and Scattergood, astute conservationists, worried about the
loss or corruption of traditional skills even as they embraced the
melting-pot ideal. They were essentially transition figures. Under
Rhoads permanent employment of Indians by the Bureau increased
substantially. Interested in preserving the Indian family, Rhoads
endorsed Senator McNary's Klamatt tribal incorporation bill, which
in John Collier's words "marked a great historical change in Indian
policy." [50] But Rhoads shrank from a general application of this
principle; he still wanted to force the white man's culture on the
Indian. The Bureau, incidentally, showed Hoover's and Wilbur's
propensity for enlisting academics in government service: W. Carson
Ryan of Swarthmore and Earl A. Bates of Cornell assisted in Indian
educational work.

Perhaps the most creditable accomplishment for Indians in the
Hoover administration came in simple budgetary terms. In spite of
the increase in appropriations throughout the decade, the Interior
Department report of 1927 entitled one section "The Poverty of the
Indian Service." Between 1929 and 1932 Indian expenditures almost doubled, rising from $15,968,000 to $27,020,000. This increase
—an initial $3 million additional request and a deficiency appro-
priation settled on in 1929 and a 30 percent increase effective in
the next fiscal year—escaped the fierce economizing after the crash

because Hoover knew Indian conditions to be deplorable.[51] Most of the funds went for schools and hospitals, better food and clothing for Indian children. Adult Indians continued ill-nourished and receptive to disease, but between 1929 and 1932 the percentage with trachoma declined by 50 percent and the capacity of sanatoriums increased by 15 percent.[52]

The need to preserve Indian culture was only part of the president's wider work in conservation. Donald Swain, author of a study of federal conservation policies in the period, terms Hoover "the first conservationist President since Theodore Roosevelt." [53] Wilbur and Hoover began a program of moving millions of acres of forest land into the national preserve—some two million in four years— while they increased the area of national parks and monuments by 40 percent. The Park Service budget itself shot up 46 percent in Hoover's first three years. Both outdoorsmen, the president and his secretary responded to pleas to save endangered species or places of national beauty; Wilbur was particularly interested in protecting southwestern desert lands as game preserves.[54] Both Californians, in 1929 they set aside "redwood groves and coastal lands" in the Northwest.[55] Wilbur mentioned waterpower and irrigation projects as two threats to the national parks. At the urging of the newly appointed National Parks Commissioner Horace Albright, Wilbur worked hard in 1929 to prevent the building by the Insull power interests of a dam above the beautiful Cumberland Falls in Kentucky. A member of the Federal Power Commission, he regretted the agency's limited powers to forestall such power projects and helped persuade the president to ask Congress for expanded supervisory regulations.[56]

A most curious effort came in two commissions appointed in 1929. The first, a followup to the generally well-received presidential order restricting oil drilling, culminated in a politically inept and unproductive conference of western governors in Colorado Springs.[57] The second was the Commission on the Conservation and Administration of the Public Domain appointed in April and composed chiefly of outstanding conservationists; it was asked to determine land and conservation policies for the Far West. This Garfield Commission, named after its chairman, the secretary of interior under Theodore Roosevelt, brought back exactly what Hoover had hoped for: recommendations for enlarged reserves of oil and mineral lands, national parks and forests, wildlife refuges. Following Hoover, the commission also suggested that the surface rights to land of use only for grazing should be returned to the states for more effective conservation. When criticism came from some conservationists, Hoover reaffirmed that the idea was "tentative." [58] The Congress, as so often under Hoover, ignored his commission.

From the early twenties Hoover was active in the expansion of inland waterways and waterpower facilities. The June 1929 Boulder Canyon Project Act, resulting in Boulder—now Hoover—Dam, was to an extent Hoover's accomplishment.[59] Seventy-five percent of its waterpower went to publicly owned corporations in California.[60] That fall the *New Republic* editorialized: "Secretary Wilbur's plans for the distribution of Boulder Dam power are so much better than his earlier announcements that the advocates of public ownership may well congratulate him." [61] In August an important survey of the upper Mississippi began. And in September Hoover demanded a St. Lawrence Seaway (in 1932 the Senate failed to ratify by one vote a treaty for the seaway that Hoover negotiated with Canada), a Great Lakes to Gulf waterway, and canalization of the Ohio River. The Columbia River, the Tennessee, the Missouri, the Illinois, the Allegheny—all received Hoover's attention.

In spite of his domestic achievements in 1929, Hoover devoted most of his energies to foreign policy. It was a "dazzling" eight months in foreign affairs, according to the New York *World*.[62] Already he had completed a pre-Inaugural good-will trip to Latin America, after which he resolved to appoint diplomats familiar with the languages and customs of the particular country. After taking office, the president began to withdraw marines from Nicaragua and Haiti, replacing military commissions there with diplomatic representatives. The Clark Memorandum of 1929 formally renounced interventionist policies in the western hemisphere, and Hoover laid the basis for the Tacna-Arica dispute between Chile and Peru, which involved many other countries.

The theme of the administration's foreign policies was distinctly antimilitarist. Preparations moved ahead for the London Naval Conference of 1930. The president hoped to use savings on naval-armament appropriations for social programs at home: "nothing could be a finer or more vivid conversion of swords to plowshares," observed the president.[63] He shut down some naval construction the day the Kellogg Pact was proclaimed, 24 July 1929. That summer he also appointed a commission of the Army general staff to survey the entire military establishment with a view to eliminating positions not essential to the national defense. In addition, certain obsolete army and navy posts were abandoned. With monies saved

Hoover demanded and got an increase in appropriations for the diplomatic service. In July Hoover even told an industrial and banking audience, whose representatives were going to the Soviet Union, that he was considering recognition. The president feared losing America's $100 million of exports to the Soviets and was unaffected by the fears of Bolshevism that Secretaries of State Hughes and Kellogg had exhibited. The president was said to be impressed by Ramsay MacDonald's practical approach to recognition, and he feared competition from German and British trade. The popular journalist Mark Sullivan had voted for Al Smith, but he praised Hoover toward the end of 1929:

> Hoover is making enemies right and left—especially right. Higher-tariff barons, jingoes, brass hats, big navyites, Prohibition fanatics, patronage hounds, and in general those who dread change— for each of these multifarious enemies he rises higher in the estimation of us small fry.[64]

A prominent group of social scientists, appointed by Hoover in 1929 to study social trends, reported three years later that they had found an increase in planning and centralization everywhere—and recommended more of it. Hoover had given this Research Committee on Social Trends a free hand: it recommended a leveling of income, unemployment payments to be financed by working people, and price-fixing on thousands of commodities. Many of the things it recommended would soon come into practice, for the idea of social management was becoming a reality. And with its fulfillment Hoover's own philosophy was both realized and contradicted. Expertise, benevolently applied, the expertise for which Hoover's own career had been an argument, was fixing itself in institutions of social control rather than in the voluntary associations for which the president had spoken. Perhaps it was destined to do so; perhaps his balance of voluntarism and technical proficiency had been inherently too fragile to sustain itself; or perhaps the weakness lay in the impatience of the American people, as Hoover once testily remarked. But if voluntarism could not exist in its purity, defenses still existed within the American social and political process against the corruption of expertise into coercion. These defenses consisted of America's normal democratic practices and the looseness and fragility of power throughout American society.

The New Deal maintained these defenses, so much so that one of the major impressions it leaves is not of disciplined centralization but of patchworks and mixtures: loose political alliances, partial schemes, and the further complication of America into such things as labor unions and local federal projects. In all this, the joining of technical proficiency to a diffusion of power, Hoover's ideal found at least a distant and alien equivalent.

II

Antidepression Efforts

Herbert Hoover's Policies for Dealing with the Great Depression: The End of the Old Order or the Beginning of the New?

ALBERT U. ROMASCO

New York University

Albert Romasco received his B.A. degree from the University of Massachusetts in 1953 and his M.A. and Ph.D. from the University of Chicago. He was born in Pittsfield, Massachusetts in 1930. He has taught at Illinois Institute of Technology and the University of California at Berkeley. Currently, he is an Associate Professor of History at New York University. Professor Romasco's major publication, The Poverty of Abundance: Hoover, the Nation, the Depression *(New York: Oxford University Press, 1965) is a standard work on the Hoover presidency.*

Romasco's essay takes a more conservative view of Hoover. After synthesizing the conflicting interpretations which have been advanced to explain Hoover's antidepression policies, Romasco suggests that all have agreed that Hoover's depression program represented "unprecedented innovation when compared to the tradition of prior recession presidents, who, in effect, waited passively for recovery." But Romasco differs with that consensus as he sees considerable precedence for Hoover's policies in the responses Theodore Roosevelt, Woodrow Wilson and Warren Harding made to recessions.

President Herbert Hoover has travelled a long historical road since his decisive defeat in November 1932. By the time that he left the White House to his successor, Franklin D. Roosevelt, in March 1933, the Great Depression had sunk to its lowest depth. And, in turn, his presidential reputation reached rock bottom. Politically portrayed as a do-nothing president, he was emphatically rejected at the polls because he failed to make good his repeated promise to restore prosperity. His fellow citizens judged Hoover pragmatically and without equivocation; seemingly, the historical case against him was closed. But, to paraphrase Charles A. Beard somewhat freely, no historical judgment is ever final or conclusive when it is viewed from different time perspectives.[1] Americans, indeed, have a propensity for revising and reinterpreting the past. But even though each generation rethinks the past within the context of its own present, there is no unassailable assurance that it perceives intellectually and politically either its present or the past in one single fashion. Certainly, Hoover's historical journey since 1933 lends support to the observation that each generation often harbors several, conflicting assessments of past episodes and figures, even if one judgment may be professionally more in vogue than others.

My purpose here is to explore briefly the various major historiographic modes of perceiving Hoover as a depression president and the attendant evaluations given to his policies for resolving economic stagnation. I shall also attempt to show how the intellectual and political viewpoints and values of historians influenced the judgments they rendered. Finally, I will state my own estimate of the historical significance of Hoover's policies for dealing with the depression.

Hoover's presidential career, or more specifically his handling of the Great Depression, has provided politicians, political commentators, and historians with a rich text for political sermons. The significance ascribed this tale, however, has been variously interpreted, largely depending upon the personal and political convictions of the particular chronicler. For our present purposes, the various interpretations may be conveniently subsumed under three broad, general heads: the right, center, and left, or, if you will, the conservative, liberal, and revisionist viewpoints of President Hoover.

The conservative defense of Hoover's executive tenure owes much to the indefatigable and protracted labors of Hoover himself. He had no intention of awaiting history's judgment; he instead set himself busily at work to shape his own vindication: let history follow. Actually, this historical venture began very early indeed, while Hoover was still in office, largely as a matter of immediate necessity. He was, after all, running for reelection in 1932, and it was essential that he defend not only his record, his analysis of the depression, but also his remedial policies as well. Most pressing of all, however, it was imperative that Hoover explain convincingly why his policies had not as yet worked. He desperately needed time for his program to take effect; that is, to turn the economy around the celebrated corner that he had looked for so fervently and spoken of so often. It was equally urgent, in Hoover's mind at least, that he warn the electorate in unmistakable terms about his rival, Franklin Roosevelt, whom he regarded as irresponsibly beguiling the people with dangerous schemes and proposals.

"This campaign," Hoover declared on 31 October 1932, in his famous Madison Square Garden speech, "is more than a contest between two men. It is more than a contest between two parties. It is a contest between two philosophies of government." [2] It meant, Hoover explained, that the American people must choose either the old tried-and-tested American system or the delusive promises of "a new deal." The American system, as Hoover defined it, encompassed the best traditions of our past: a concern for and preservation of personal freedom and liberties; a regard for high incentives, which could be promoted by equality of opportunity; and the unique value of a decentralized government, which could foster cooperative, voluntary action through group initiative and leadership. It was a system, he contended, that had served the people well, even during the severe economic crisis of the past three years. This entire heritage was now in jeopardy, threatened by Roosevelt's proposed changes in the governmental, economic, and social systems of the nation. Hoover was convinced that Roosevelt's vast, unnecessary schemes would greatly augment the power of the federal government and, with its attendant bureaucratization, would end only by obliterating the cherished old order. [3] "You cannot extend the mastery of government over the daily life of a people," Hoover warned, "without somewhere making it master of people's souls and thoughts." [4] And, thus, at the very outset, one of the enduring themes of the Hoover-Roosevelt antithesis was clearly and firmly enunciated by Hoover himself.

In this influential speech, Hoover also provided the basic outline and some of the more important clues for the subsequent elaboration of his defense by conservative admirers. Among those sharing this responsibility were William Starr Myers and Walter H. Newton in *The Hoover Administration* (1936), Ray L. Wilbur and Arthur M. Hyde in *The Hoover Policies* (1937), and John T. Flynn in *The Roosevelt Myth* (1948), Hoover himself again, more fully, in the three volumes of his *Memoirs* (1951, 1952), and Edgar E. Robinson in *The Roosevelt Leadership, 1933–1945* (1955).

Collectively, the historical claims made in this literature for

Hoover and the efficacy of his policies for dealing with the economic crisis are large, important ones. In looking at the past for precedents of forceful executive leadership in the nation's struggle against periodic economic depressions, Myers and Newton found none at all. Hoover, in fact, was the precedent-setter in this crucial matter. For them,

> President Hoover was the first President in our history to offer Federal leadership in mobilizing the economic resources of the people, and in calling upon individual initiative to accept definite responsibility for meeting the problem of depression. . . . The depressions that arose in the Van Buren, Buchanan, Grant, Cleveland, Theodore Roosevelt, or Wilson Administrations were practically ignored by the government in any official action. An examination of Presidential messages will show that but little of importance was done officially by previous Presidents to relieve either depression, distress or unemployment, or to cushion the financial and business situations that resulted from such conditions.[5]

Unlike his predecessors, Hoover responded immediately and forcefully. He held a series of meetings with business, industrial, labor, and political leaders and won their support and cooperation for his program. The depression, caused by the economic dislocations set in train by the First World War and the impact upon America of the subsequent European collapse in 1929, was contained through the combined effect of holding to the current wage scale and spreading the work, through maintenance of the existing construction rate, supplemented by expanded public works at all governmental levels. In addition, tight credit was eased when the Federal Reserve System's lowered the discount rate, and began its large-scale open-market purchasing of securities. Finally, the needs of the unemployed were cared for by private charity and local and state welfare, assisted by federal encouragement.[6]

Subsequently, during the next two years, in response to further upsetting shocks from abroad, which menaced the nation's basic business and banking structure, Hoover strengthened his program with additional policies: a moratorium on intergovernmental debts (June 1931), creation of the Reconstruction Finance Corporation (January 1932), passage of the Glass-Steagall Bank Credit Act (February 1932), and the Home Loan Bank and the Emergency Relief and Construction Acts (July 1932). Together these measures constituted the principal ideas and legislative enactments that made up Hoover's antidepression program.[7]

Conservative commentators and historians have advanced three major claims with regard to this program, all of them highly complimentary to Hoover's wisdom, leadership, and historical reputation. The national response set in motion by President Hoover to overcome the economic crisis marked a dramatic, unprecedented exercise of executive iniative, in sharp contrast to the passive acquiescence of previous depression presidents. Furthermore, his program succeeded economically, if not politically, on at least five separate occasions when the incipient American recovery was set back either by disruptive forces from outside our borders or by unfavorable domestic political developments, such as the election of a Democratic controlled House of Representatives in 1930. But in each instance, Hoover successfully parried the blow, so that after July 1932, when the economy reached its low point, recovery resumed once again.[8] As Myers and Newton put it, "The forces of depression were definitely checked and the road to full recovery was freed from obstacles during the Hoover Administration." [9] But then, unfortunately, the greatest shock and setback of all occurred: the election of Roosevelt, which provoked a new decline, this time in earnest. Hoover's patient labors to right the economy were now permanently undermined, largely because the delicate barometer of recovery, business confidence, was upset by Roosevelt's disquieting talk of fiscal and monetary experimentation.[10] Not yet undone, however, was Hoover's abiding achievement: he had devised an economic recovery program without compromising the integrity and viability of the American system.

It was the claim that Hoover had successfully blocked the subversion of the American system that John T. Flynn emphasized as a point of departure for his sweeping attack upon President Roosevelt and his New Deal. Unlike Hoover, Roosevelt had willingly accepted planning-collectivist proposals that resulted in the transformation of the old, traditional American system into the new welfare state. And this development, as Flynn saw it, was an important part of the preparation for an eventual American totalitarian dictatorship. Flynn's praise for Hoover's foresight and restraint, in this regard, was one way of fashioning a bludgeon to batter Roosevelt and all his works.[11]

Evocation of a past far superior in all its particulars to the new order created by the pervasive alterations of the New Deal became the central theme of Edgar E. Robinson's assessment of Roosevelt's leadership. The acknowledged hero in Robinson's view was Herbert Hoover; and it was *Hoover's* qualities of leadership in an older, better America that provided the reference point for an extremely adverse judgment of Roosevelt.[12] For Roosevelt unhinged the nation from its past by a complex of changes that amounted to nothing less than a revolution. "Roosevelt's leadership," as Robinson summed up the major ingredients of this revolution,

> resulted in fundamental changes in the government itself: in tremendous concentration of power in the Executive; in building up a vast system of bureaucratic control of private business; and by adding direct economic support of the citizen to the careful adjustment of conflicting economic interests in a free enterprise system.[13]

According to the conservative scale of values, therefore, the drastic innovations of Roosevelt seemed a meager, mean substitute for the venerable American system that stood intact during the Hoover years. The New Deal was simply an accurate yardstick measuring the nation's decline down the road toward Europe's totalitarianisms.[14]

While conservatives were perfecting their defense of Hoover, liberals were fashioning a far different reconstruction of the Hoover years and the meaning of his policies. This interpretation, the work of many hands, was closely intertwined with and influenced by the liberal response to President Roosevelt's handling of the Great Depression. Since liberals welcomed Roosevelt's broad conception of the powers of his office, his openness to new ideas and willingness to experiment, and the consequent burgeoning of federal responsibility, they reversed the conservatives' mode of perception and evaluation. For liberals, Roosevelt was the model of what ought to be, and it was *his* leadership in transforming the old order into something new and more viable that became the reference point in judging Hoover's custodianship.[15] The result was a highly critical interpretation of Hoover, his ideas and achievements, and, of course, his historical standing and reputation.

In the liberal version, Herbert Hoover became a pitiful, tragic figure. Devoid of public *charisma* and political skills, Hoover was an inept player in the vital game of politics, unable to dramatize his policies or to control the Congress. Incapable of seeing, let alone acknowledging, the economic defects of the existing structure, he failed to devise an energetic and realistic recovery program. Instead, he grievously misled the public with a continual stream of optimistic statements affirming the essential soundness of the system and the workability of his program; moreover, he proclaimed its success, in the very face of overwhelming evidence to the contrary. But, most fundamentally, Hoover's failure was an intellectual one: he was the prisoner of an outmoded political philosophy, defending a faith whose time had long passed but which still held the power to mesmerize Hoover in pious ineffectuality.[16]

Such a critical appraisal of Hoover and his policies clearly reveals the major assumptions and values underlying liberal political thought and how their pattern of beliefs, in turn, influenced historical perception. For the Great Crash and the Great Depression exposed what were regarded by liberals as inherent defects in the existing economic order; namely, a maldistribution of national income, a weak banking structure, a top-heavy business structure, an unbalanced international trade, and erroneous economic policies.[17] The resolution of the economic collapse, therefore, demanded extended reform of the economic structure. And economic reconstruction—on this scale, at least—was conceivable as a solution only through the agency of forceful political leadership, one that recognized the scope of the task and was willing to enlarge the federal responsibility and power to meet it. In short, what the liberals considered necessary was President Roosevelt and the New Deal. Hoover, who denied and resisted both the economic analysis and the political cure, was put down simply as a stubborn, misguided ideologue preoccupied with burning incense to a dead past.[18]

The liberal scales of judgment, of course, have by no means been used solely on Herbert Hoover; they have been applied broadly throughout the twentieth century as a basis for historical appraisals. Yet Hoover has been a peculiarly apt illustration of the liberal analysis, primarily because he was so evident and forthright in opposing this whole frame of thought and its expectations. He understood the liberal program thoroughly and rejected it emphatically, and he received in consequence the full burden of liberal disapproval. But beyond this, the issues at stake were not merely an interpretation of the past but a proper program, a correct way for the country to travel for the immediate, foreseeable future. And since it was not possible to hold to Hoover's American system and still follow the liberal prognoses, one or the other had to be abandoned. Clearly the liberal's choice was to drop Hoover and with him the constraining limitations of the old order.

Superficially, at least, liberal and conservative historians share much in common in regard to this subject. Both groups have conceived of Hoover and Roosevelt as polar opposites, with antithetical philosophies concerning the proper role and functions of the national government and with opposed policies for handling the Great Depression. The two schools of thought differ markedly, however, in which president should be historically celebrated and which castigated. And yet the liberal judgment, with its commanding professional standing and wide public circulation, has not been accepted universally by all who share liberal assumptions and values. Three notable exceptions, for example, have been Walter Lippmann in his "The Permanent New Deal" (1935), Broadus Mitchell in *Depression Decade* (1947), and Carl N. Degler in "The Ordeal of Herbert Hoover" (1963).

The significant point of departure in this third revisionist interpretation of Hoover was each author's rejection, in varying degrees, of the common conservative-liberal procedure of contrasting the two presidents as opposites and then supporting such an assumption by emphasizing the essential discontinuity between the policies of the two administrations. Instead, these authors made a case for the continuity of policy during the Great Depression, assigning and crediting Hoover with the role of innovator. The implications of the revisionist interpretation, if accepted, were far-reaching indeed. It shifted Hoover from the conservative camp into the progressive-liberal tradition, and it required a reassessment not only of Hoover's historical reputation but of Roosevelt's as well. In a very real sense, the proper subject of these years became Hoover-Roosevelt and the Great Depression.

Within this new conceptual framework, Lippmann made the largest, most flattering, and least qualified claims for Hoover. "The policy initiated by President Hoover in the autumn of 1929," he argued, "was something utterly unprecedented in American history. The national government undertook to make the whole economic order operate prosperously." [19] Furthermore, in implementing this radical new idea, Hoover devised a series of policies that anticipated "most" of Roosevelt's *recovery* program. Specifically, according to Lippmann's account, "in all essential matters of policy—monetary management, the budget, the agricultural disparity, and industrial 'stabilization'—there has been no break in principle, and . . . the Roosevelt measures are a continuous evolution of the Hoover measures." [20] In sum, the one significant new idea of this period and the essential means devised to carry it out were the product of Hoover's initiative and leadership.

Lippmann's analysis was formulated midway during the New Deal. Broadus Mitchell, on the other hand, wrote after the domestic New Deal had run its full legislative course, which provided him with the greater advantage that perspective afforded. Moreover, Mitchell's judgments were the product of a full-scale economic analysis of the Great Depression decade. Consequently, his more careful assessment moderated in some particulars Lippmann's statements and expanded them in others. Although Mitchell repeatedly urged the point that many New Deal policies were anticipated by Hoover, he also defined the areas wherein the two administrations diverged; and he frankly recognized the limits which Hoover's philosophy imposed upon him. Specifically, Hoover anticipated the New Deal in the creation of the Reconstruction Finance Corporation, the agricultural policies adopted by the Farm Board, and the reluctant acceptance of federal relief for the states. He differed most markedly from his successor in his more circumscribed conception of public works, deficit spending, and direct federal relief for the unemployed, and in his opposition to social security and public electric power.[21]

The two presidents, Mitchell added, were nonetheless committed to the common overall objective of preserving capitalism. But the *means* each was willing to accept and use for attaining this central purpose differed significantly. In Mitchell's judgment,

> Hoover, by and large, was content with socializing the "public" losses of corporations because these would reach to the private losses of individuals. The New Deal properly went further and was willing to socialize the private losses of unemployed individuals on the ground that, unless aided, these would destroy the public, including corporate welfare. The Hoover analysis stopped cruelly short. . . . The New Deal, by contrast, endeared itself for its sympathy with individual misfortune, when equally deserved thanks might have gone to it (but did not) for its industrious attempt to preserve capitalism.[22]

Then, with a fine, impartial hand, Mitchell proceeded to criticize both Hoover's percolation theory of recovery and Roosevelt's nationalistic approach and his resort to the economics of scarcity. For ultimately neither succeeded in the immediate, overriding task of ending the depression.[23]

Carl Degler's essay—a cogent, judicious statement of the liberal revisionist interpretation—can serve here as a convenient summary of this viewpoint. "Hoover's principles," he stated, "were distinctly and publicly progressive." [24] Adopting the liberal equation of progressive as being equivalent to the expansion of federal responsibility and power, Degler added that "perhaps the most striking example of Hoover's willingness to recognize the new role of government in dealing with the complexities of an industrial economy was his breaking precedent to grapple directly with the Depression." [25] The ensuing program, which carried Hoover close to the New Deal, was restrained finally by Hoover's ideology, primarily his commitment to the principles of individualism and a balanced budget. It was, in other words, Hoover's fidelity to this principle that led him to oppose such additional measures as federal relief for the unemployed, creation of a government corporation to run Muscle Shoals, and a government system of old age and unemployment insurance.[26] Hoover, therefore, was best understood as a "transition figure in the development of the government as an active force in the economy in times of depression." [27]

The liberal revisionist account was intended as an historical corrective to the exaggerated claims of both Hoover and Roosevelt partisans, with their neat contrast of the two administrations: the one defending the old tradition, the other ushering in a new order. Beyond this function, revisionism, particularly Mitchell's work, inadvertently served another purpose: it provided a logical bridge to a subsequent left revisionist interpretation distinct from its own.

In *The Contours of American History* (1961), William Appleman Williams used the continuity approach in regard to the depression policies of the two administrations, but it was set in a different, larger context—that of corporate capitalism. Hoover, in his attempt to halt the depression, "pulled out every antidepression tool the Progressives ever owned." [28] And it was these policies that "provided the rudiments of Roosevelt's program." [29] But Hoover's refusal to go further than he did in enlarging the government's role was not motivated by a pious reverence for the past; it signified instead the deliberate restraint of a man who thoroughly understood the dangers that could arise if the state were given the dominant position in the American political economy. It was Roosevelt, lacking Hoover's sophisticated understanding of the corporate economy and its potential pitfalls, who plunged recklessly ahead, making the latent danger an actuality. It was thus during the New Deal years that a syndicalist nation was created, that is, a system dominated by a coalition of leaders representing capital and government. All that Hoover had feared and sacrificed to prevent had come to pass.[30] Ironically, therefore, Williams' account of Hoover—informed as it was by a different time and political stance, graced with a new terminology, and utilizing continuity—ended up echoing much of the conservative's defense of Hoover and his policies.

One is not accustomed to thinking of President Hoover as an ambiguous figure, but when one considers the entire historiographic spectrum that has developed on Hoover and his depression policies, it is evident that ambiguity, even outright contradiction, are rampant. Taken collectively, all that is claimed for Hoover, or charged against him, cannot be reconciled easily, if it can be reconciled at all. He has been cast, by admirers and detractors alike, as the defender *par excellence* of the values and the institutions of an older America. At the same time—one is tempted to say in the same breath—he has been credited by practically everyone as a great innovator: the first president to accept national responsibility for overcoming an economic depression and restoring prosperity. To this end, Hoover is said to have devised a set of policies which significantly enlarged the function and role of government in the nation's economic life. Indeed, according to some, he went so far in this new direction as to anticipate the essentials of Roosevelt's New Deal. It appears, consequently, that Hoover upheld the traditional concept of limited government, a basic value in the American system, while with his left hand he inaugurated a fatal departure from that tradition. Thus, if one is tempted to follow a process of indiscriminate eclecticism, one can consider Hoover as both the defender of the old order and the precursor of the new. If this form of synthesis is unacceptable, which indeed it is, then there is an alternative procedure that is conceivable: to examine more closely the claims made for Hoover both in relation to the years preceding and the years following his administration, thereby using a double vantage point for judging Hoover's historic contribution as a depression president.

In the course of the twentieth century, prior to President Hoover's confrontation with the Great Depression, the American economy was subjected to three major disruptions: the banking panic of 1907, the recession of 1914, and the depression of 1920–21.[31] These episodes, involving the administrations of Presidents Theodore Roosevelt, Woodrow Wilson, and Warren Harding, respectively, constitute a sufficient testing ground for determining the degree of credibility that should be accorded the claims made for Hoover as an innovator; that is, for gauging the extent to which his policies measure a departure from the *past.* Was nothing, in actual fact, done by Hoover's predecessors during these times of severe economic crisis? Or to state the issue positively, what response, if any, was made by the three presidents on these occasions: and did their behavior and policies anticipate Hoover's own own responses?

On 22 October 1907 the Knickerbocker Trust Company, whose

officers were involved in an unsuccessful copper corner, suspended in New York City, marking the beginning of the panic.[32] The bank's collapse provoked a sharp break on the New York Stock Exchange, further runs on other trust companies, and a critical shortage of currency. Moreover, the crisis was not confined solely to Wall Street; in the South and West, already faced with a serious shortage of cash and credit to finance the seasonal movement of crops, the money panic resulted in some states declaring bank holidays and a further decline in commodity prices and the closing of some commodity exchanges. The repercussions of the panic even reached across the Atlantic to the European money markets, forcing the Bank of England and the Imperial Bank of Germany to raise their discount rates to unprecedented levels as a means of protecting themselves against the outflow of gold to the United States.[33]

President Theodore Roosevelt was fully alive to the possibility that the public would hold him responsible for the panic and its consequences. As he remarked privately, "when the average man loses his money he is simply like a wounded snake and strikes right and left at anything, innocent or the reverse, that presents itself as conspicuous in his mind." [34] Roosevelt's initial move was therefore aimed at the public psychology of fear, in a form we would subsequently recognize as the classic response of a depression president: he issued a public statement of reassurance that, despite appearances, all was well. "No one who considers calmly," he declared soothingly, "can question that the underlying conditions which make up our financial and industrial well-being are essentially sound and honest." [35] Surely, the purpose, even the choice of words resounds familiarly in our ears.

More concretely, Roosevelt used a set of policies devised essentially to strengthen the country's financial institutions by direct federal assistance in order to place them in a position where they could meet all demands and thereby stem the panic at its source— the teller's window. To this end, Secretary of the Treasury George B. Cortelyou arranged for a $25 million deposit of government funds in New York City's national banks, supplementing the private ef- forts of J. P. Morgan and others, including the New York Clearing House, to amass currency at the banks sufficient enough to cover the demands of frightened depositors.[36]

These measures were only temporarily successful; within a week the New York bankers were fearfully anticipating the collapse of an important brokerage house and another trust company, and with them the closing of the Stock Exchange. To avert this chain of

events, Roosevelt was persuaded by Morgan's associates, Judge El-
bert Gary and Henry C. Frick, to permit United States Steel to
absorb the Tennessee Coal and Iron Company as a means of but-
tressing the assets and financial standing of the shaky brokerage
house. Roosevelt's decision, severely criticized later, succeeded in
saving Moore & Schley and keeping the Trust Company of America
open; but the money shortage was not yet resolved.[37]

The administration next considered the problem of facilitating
an expansion of the money supply through the national banks.
Cortelyou at first authorized the banks to use bonds other than the
authorized government ones as a substitute basis for issuing notes.
This maneuver was ineffectual because all bonds were currently at
high prices and in short supply. Roosevelt and Cortelyou then
turned to a more direct approach: the government announced an
issue of 2 percent Panama bonds and 3 percent Treasury certificates
and made them available to national banks for a down payment of
10 percent and 25 percent, respectively. In other words, the government manufactured the bonds needed to expand the currency and
sold them to the banks on easy credit terms. This action resolved
the money stringency and ended the panic.[38]

The next crisis, that of 1914 during the Wilson administration,
was directly tied to the outbreak of European hostilities between
28 July and 4 August.[39] The effect of the First World War upon the
American economy was immediate and widespread, involving a
major crisis on the New York Stock Exchange, great pressure on the
banking structure, and severe agricultural and industrial disruption.
The nation's foreign trade practically ceased, primarily because
America depended heavily upon foreign shipping for delivering its
goods to all parts of the world. In response, the Wilson administration energetically set about to relieve the pressure on the financial
structure and to remove the obstacles to its foreign trade by direct
intervention in the economy.[40]

The first task was to cushion the stock market. Europeans held
a total of $2.5 billion in American stocks and bonds and began
heavy selling on 30 July. With the closing of the London Stock
Exchange the next day, an avalanche of additional selling orders
was expected. The New York bankers averted the threat by closing
the New York Stock Exchange that same day after consulting with
Secretary of the Treasury William G. McAdoo, who approved the
decision.[41] Subsequently, in October, the market faced a new crisis:
the prospect that bankers holding some $1 billion in notes, with
securities as collateral, would demand payment, resulting in whole-

sale dumping of securities. The Treasury intervened by notifying "national bank examiners to approve all loans secured by listed stocks at their value as of July 30, 1914, thus in effect putting a floor under security prices." [42] On 29 November the New York Stock Exchange reopened for bond trading; and on 12 December it resumed full operations.

At the outset of the war, American bankers and merchants were indebted to London by some $450 million in short-term obligations. When British bankers began calling these loans, the American banks came under heavy pressure from their frightened depositors. With a first-class panic facing them, the bankers turned to the federal government for assistance. McAdoo, like Cortelyou before him, went immediately to New York City after providing Wall Street with $100 million in emergency currency. Discovering there that the bankers were unable to obtain the necessary, additional relief via the Aldrich-Vreeland Act because of its overly restrictive provisions, McAdoo promised to try to get Congress to amend that act within the next twenty-four hours. True to his word, the next morning McAdoo was waiting for the chairman of the Banking Committee, Senator Robert L. Owen, with appropriate amendments. Congress passed the bill that day and President Wilson signed it the next.[43] Meanwhile, Wilson reassured the public in the classic mode:

> There is great inconvenience, for the time being, in the money market and in our Exchanges, and, temporarily, in the handling of our crops, but America is absolutely prepared to meet the financial situation and to straighten everything out without any material difficulty. The only thing that can possibly prevent it is unreasonable apprehension and excitement. . . . There is cause for getting busy and doing the thing the right way, but there is no element of unsoundness and there is no cause for alarm.[44]

In this case, at least, a combination of words and actions quieted public fear, stopped the runs on the banks, and restored confidence.

The administration also exerted itself in an attempt to untangle the barriers obstructing the nation's foreign trade. Wilson conferred with congressional leaders in an effort to devise means of persuading foreign ship owners to register under the American flag, and he discussed plans for building an American fleet. McAdoo conceived of a plan for creating a government-owned corporation to buy foreign ships, including those of Germany stranded in port, but this scheme was blocked in Congress. However, Congress was willing to create a War Risk Insurance Bureau to provide low-cost marine insurance as an inducement to get ships out unto the sea again. These difficulties, however, were settled instead by the British, in September 1914, when they succeeded in clearing the sea lanes of surface German raiders. Shipping then became readily available at reasonable rates, and large orders for goods soon revived American foreign trade.[45]

Among the more sombre Wilsonian legacies bequeathed to his Republican successor was the depression that began in 1920.[46] Warren Harding, in his presidential campaign, had emphasized the need for restoring prosperity and reducing the cost of government, two objectives that were not regarded in the wisdom of that day as incompatible. Once in office, Harding turned at once to the political problem of translating these objectives into legislative actualities. His prosperity program aimed at providing assistance to three major interest groups: business, agriculture, and labor.[47] And in a remarkably short space of time, he succeeded in accomplishing his purpose.

Harding and his Secretary of the Treasury, Andrew Mellon, had a ready, conservative prescription for business recovery. Its main tenets included reestablishing a lean economy in governmental expenditures, instituting a tax reduction, and paring the national debt. The rationale for this program was that by relieving the investing classes of the heavy tax burden, they would be in a position to resume their important function of providing the risk capital vital for economic growth. Similarly, the payment of the national debt would place money in hands that would use it for additional capital investment.[48]

The business program was carried out with impressive dispatch. The Budget and Accounting Act of 1921 established the Budget Bureau, which substantially cut governmental expenditures. In the Revenue Act of 1921, the excess-profits tax and the surtax on individual incomes were lowered, although not to Mellon's complete satisfaction. Furthermore, Herbert Hoover was busily transforming the Department of Commerce into an active agent for promoting business confidence and foreign trade in furtherance of Harding's goal of restoring the nation's prosperity.[49]

The agricultural counterpart of this recovery program included the Fordney Emergency Tariff, passed in May 1921, with an antidumping provision and high protective rates on a number of farm commodities. Then after Harding met with farm leaders and spokesmen to determine their priorities, there followed in quick succession the Packers and Stockyards Act, the Future Trading Act, two amendments to the Farm Loan Act which made it easier for farmers to get larger loans, and the Emergency Agricultural Credits Act. The latter, an administration-conceived measure, expanded the loaning powers of the War Finance Corporation to include farmers' cooperatives and livestock growers and permitted the corporation to buy agricultural paper secured by farm commodities as a means of assisting rural banks. This program, enacted in the special session, was completed by 24 August 1921.[50]

During the winter of 1920–1921 there were an estimated 4,754,000 workers unemployed; by the late summer of 1921 the figure had climbed to 5,753,000.[51] "The laborer," Robert Murray has remarked, "was the Harding era's forgotten man." At Hoover's initiative, an unemployment conference was held in September 1921, where Harding "warned . . . that the conference should not seek unemployment subsidies from the federal government as a solution."[52] Instead, the conference members were offered a program conceived by Hoover, one which he later reapplied during his own presidency. His program called for stepping up construction work, spreading jobs, increasing public works, and furnishing local relief for the unemployed. All this was to be carried out by Hoover's preferred method of voluntary cooperative action among the people themselves, spurred on by a high-powered public-relations campaign. The results of his program were no more successful in 1921 than they were to be during the Great Depression.[53]

The conclusion that emerges from this summary account of the economic crises in the Roosevelt, Wilson, and Harding administrations is that the long-standing contention that no president, prior to Hoover, accepted federal responsibility for assuring the economic well-being of the nation needs to be considerably modified, if not abandoned altogether.[54] None of these presidents was an exponent of laissez-faire ideology; all of them attempted to correct the economic dislocations of their time and restore prosperity. And in each instance, their commitment involved a considerable measure of direct federal intervention. There were, then, ample executive precedents during peacetime for Hoover to use and to build upon when he came face to face with an even graver crisis. And he used them.

Specifically, Hoover imitated the past in his protracted efforts to protect and strengthen the financial structure of the nation. The

Federal Reserve System followed an easy-money policy by lowering the discount rate and by large open-market purchases of securities. When obstacles appeared that hindered this policy, they were removed by amending the rules to broaden the types of paper eligible for rediscount and by substituting government securities for commercial paper as backing for Federal Reserve notes. Also, additional support for financial institutions was provided by the creation of the Reconstruction Finance Corporation, by an act increasing the capital of the Federal Land Banks, and through the establishment of the Home Loan Banks. These measures were designed to improve the liquid position of financial institutions, thereby diminishing the danger of runs and improving the banks' capability and willingness to make loans.[55]

Hoover coordinated this financial policy with a complementary one to encourage business and industry. However, in this area, Hoover's means were significantly limited to persuading businessmen of the wisdom and utility of carrying out the recovery measures voluntarily. The federal government's role in the program of expanding the levels of construction and capital investment, maintaining wage scales, and refraining from layoffs by spreading the work, was limited to persuasive encouragement and a massive propaganda effort to convince business and the public alike that these efforts were succeeding. In effect, this meant that the success of Hoover's program rested finally upon the willingness of businessmen to assume the risks of conducting business as usual in spite of the depression. None of these vital policies was made mandatory by law because recourse to such direct compulsion was repugnant to Hoover's political philosophy.[56]

Similarly, Hoover's labor program was constructed to use identical methods and to conform to the same values and restraints. Labor's two overriding objectives at this time were work and relief. For the successful implementation of one, the workers were dependent upon the goodwill and success of businessmen cooperating voluntarily in a national undertaking and in the other upon the resources and cooperation of private and local-state agencies. The federal government's proper role here, Hoover believed, was one of promoting and coordinating voluntary action; the social and political price for going beyond this to direct federal action was too high to pay.[57]

For agriculture, Hoover devised the Federal Farm Board with authority to assist farm organizations in creating a system of national cooperative associations and to set up stabilization corporations.

The onset of the depression, however, shifted the Board's main effort from the cooperatives, where Hoover intended them to be, to the stabilization corporations, which had been originally conceived for temporary emergencies. After the corporations failed to hold wheat and cotton prices up by buying surplus stocks, the Board retreated from the field, advising the farmers to control their own production even if that involved the destruction of excess crops. Like President Harding before him, Hoover was unwilling to support agricultural prices by federal subsidy.[58]

Thus, Hoover's policies for dealing with the Great Depression drew fully from the peacetime precedents of the past. He also added refinements and some outright innovations to the government's armory against depression. And some of the new devices, notably the practice of increased federal spending through an expanded public-works program, involved direct federal commitment. But even here the scope and effectiveness of the venture was circumscribed by Hoover's insistence that all projects be self-liquidating. When Congress tried to go beyond this conception to much more ambitious schemes, Hoover denounced the attempt as pork-barrel legislation and firmly exercised his veto power. For he remained a true believer in a balanced budget, regarding it as crucial to the nation's financial soundness and as vital for restoring business confidence.[59] And even though Hoover failed here, it was not because he faltered in his belief; the deficits were the unintended outcome of declining federal revenues. Hoover continued to insist that the primary responsibility for increased spending, sufficient to revive economic activity, must rest upon the private and not the public sector.

Hoover was therefore a significant figure in the evolution of governmental policies for dealing with depressions. But by the time he left the White House he was standing solidly upon a principled opposition to any further expansion of direct federal intervention. He never thought it worth the candle to gain prosperity at the expense of undermining the American system. So that when one contemplates his modest program in light of Roosevelt's New Deal, there remain a great many things which he refused to do, as Mitchell, Degler, Williams, and others have pointed out.[60] For the limits of Hoover's program can be understood only when one sees the intimate relation of his restraint to his political philosophy, his image of America past, and his vision of her future.

Hoover and Congress: Politics, Personality, and Perspective in the Presidency

JORDAN A. SCHWARZ

Jordan Schwarz was born in 1937, in Chicago, Illinois. He did his undergraduate work at City College of New York and received his M.A. and Ph.D. degrees from Columbia University in the years 1960 and 1967, respectively. He taught at Cedar Crest College in Pennsylvania in 1964–65 and has since been on the history faculty at Northern Illinois University. He has published numerous articles and his recent publication, The Interregnum of Despair: Hoover, Congress and the Depression *(Urbana, Illinois: University of Illinois Press, 1970), is viewed as a vital work on the Hoover period.*

Schwarz describes Hoover's concept of how the American system ought to operate—a system emphasizing voluntary organizations and state and local governments. He underscores Hoover's fear of the federal government and especially, of the factionalism in Congress that threatened his American system. Schwarz contends that Hoover defined his presidential mission as one of organizing voluntary forces within a community to encourage a spirit of cooperation. And the president saw federal legislation as "the last resort in any problem."

The adjournment of the Seventy-First Congress on 4 March 1931 brought a welcome political tranquility to Washington. America had passed its second winter of economic depression and the number of unemployed workers was still growing. The legislators, fresh from renewed contacts with their constituents in the election of 1930—a disastrous experience for many of them—had become increasingly skeptical about the Hoover administration's recovery and relief policies. Numerous relief bills were initiated during the lame-duck session, most of which never emerged from Congress. Bitter words had been exchanged between the administration and congressmen in both parties. President Hoover had vetoed a dozen bills and threatened to veto all relief measures that endangered the nation's recovery. As one newspaper saw it, "war" had erupted between the president and a "continuously contentious Congress." And so it was that Hoover sympathizers rejoiced over the departure Congress. As another newspaper hyperbolically exclaimed, "Congress has provided farm relief, unemployment relief, drought relief, veterans' relief and its adjornment will provide general relief." [1]

But the end of the Seventy-First Congress did not signal peace between Capital Hill and the White House. After serious differences with the Republican Seventy-First Congress, Hoover had no reason to expect accord with the acutely divided Seventy-Second. The 1930 election had destroyed big Republican majorities; their seventeen vote margin in the Senate had been reduced to one; a GOP majority of one hundred in the House of Representatives would be a Democratic majority of five after the special elections of 1931. Moreover, weak party discipline and cohesion made an active Congress a threat to a beleagured president.

Every plea for a special session in 1931 met with presidential admonitions against disturbing the processes of recovery already at work. Congressional advocates of federal relief had been promoting a special session that would legislate relief and Hoover replied with his own propaganda against it. The mere possibility of an extra session of Congress, he told the Gridiron Club, had created "apprehension and fear" in the country and had evoked protests from the press and labor, agricultural and business groups. On 22 May he gave newsmen a terse declaration that "we cannot legislate ourselves out of a world economic depression" and claimed the support of a large majority in Congress in opposing an extra session.[2]

But that was not the last word on the matter. Many times during 1931 the administration confronted depression crises that led to legislative remedies and renewed suggestions from its friends for a special session. In June he called for a moratorium on European debt payments, an action requiring congressional approval. By phone and telegram Hoover secured an unofficial authorization from hundreds of individual lawmakers and thereby circumvented demands that a special session legislate the moratorium. Then the impending collapse of American financial institutions inspired recommendations for reviving the War Finance Corporation. Eugene Meyer urged Hoover to call Congress in September, but Hoover preferred to use bankers' capital for a public finance corporation. However the bankers would not create their National Credit Corporation until Hoover assured them he would ask Congress to enact the Reconstruction Finance Corporation. That, it was understood, would not happen until the regular session convened in December. In addition, Hoover favored Federal Reserve changes that would liberalize lending practices. Senator Arthur Vandenberg of Michigan earnestly discussed such legislation with Hoover beginning in July and, after suggesting a special session in September to deal with the money-supply problem, found that Hoover ended those discussions until January.[3] Like Eugene Meyer, Vandenberg learned the hard way that nothing would move Herbert Hoover to call Congress before the Constitution required it to meet on 7 December 1931.

Why was Hoover hostile to Congress?

The answer to that question is as complex as the man. It involves his philosophy of American government and society, his concept of American history, and his perception of American society in the Great Depression. Also, Hoover's experience with Congress during his service under three presidents, and his knowledge of their relations with Congress, influenced his attitude toward the lawmakers. Finally any portrait of Hoover would not be complete without a consideration of his political personality. Part of Hoover's problems with Congress stemmed from the fact that he was an unyielding ideologist. His concept of Congress's place in the American system began with his model of how the American system ought to operate. Our democracy, he believed, was a centrist concept precariously balanced between regimented systems to the left and the right of the American system. Only in America had the integrity of the individual been preserved from government coercion. Only in America did there prevail a spirit of cooperation that eschewed the excesses of anarchy and regimentation in favor of voluntary cooperation. Hoover maintained that the principal driving force in the American system was its voluntary organizations and state and local governments. They preserved participatory democracy and fostered our spirit of voluntary cooperation while protecting us from the inefficiency of big government and the selfishness of sectional and group interests.[4]

Hoover believed that the great evil of twentieth-century America was broker-state politics. The term did not have currency then, but it is appropriate for labeling his bête noire. Broker-state politics most often showed its ugly factionalism in Congress, where special pressure groups mischievously negotiated favors with each other for their own benefit at the expense of the American system. If Congress was given free rein, Hoover feared it would pass laws creating a gigantic governmental bureaucracy that would erect a regimented fascism or a collectivist communism. As American society grew more complex and interests multiplied and grew stronger, how could America protect the initiative of its voluntary organizations and their spirit of cooperation?

In a sense, that is how Hoover defined his mission: he organized the voluntary forces of our community and encouraged its spirit of cooperation to develop solutions independent of the broker state. The last resort in any problem should be federal legislation. As secretary of commerce or as president, he approached most problems by bringing representatives of all interested groups together in a conference or on a commission. They investigated problems and proposed solutions which could require legislation that ratified their cooperative decisions. Only after this free exercise in voluntary cooperation, and guided by the recommendations of voluntary organizations, did Congress have a mandate to legislate on national problems. The executive branch never permitted Congress to take the initiative. If congressmen initiated legislation that Hoover considered inimical to voluntary cooperation, he would build a fire against it with alternative legislation. If neither passed, so much the better. If the undesirable bill passed, there was still the veto. The president, Hoover believed, better understood the general interest than the special-interest-minded legislators.

In the words of one close observer of President Hoover: "He has never really recognized the House and Senate as desirable factors in our government." [5] Hoover disliked most electoral politicians. Too many of them, he suspected, looked out only for themselves, the sectional or group interests they represented in Washington. Most of them he classified as fools or knaves; anything constructive would meet with their obstruction. Congress had some statesmen, but they were few compared to the demagogues and collectivists.

In late 1927 many politicians had wondered if Hoover possessed the qualities needed for a successful presidency. Undersecretary of the Treasury Ogden Mills was certain that Hoover had the best "intellectual vigor, knowledge, experience, judgment and training" of any presidential candidate Mills could remember.[6] Indeed, even Hoover's antagonists dared not doubt his superior intelligence, administrative experience, or executive abilities. What made everyone pause was his temperament for politics. For if, as Oliver Wendell Holmes said of Hoover's successor, Franklin Roosevelt was a second-class intellect with a first-class temperament,[7] Hoover possessed a first-class intellect with a second-class temperament, or worse.

In a political milieu which valued gentlemanly conviviality, Hoover was ill at ease. He did not have to be, like Harding, one of the boys and join senators in a friendly poker game over bourbon and branchwater, tell the latest blue jokes, or spin yarns for them. Those old politicos in Congress respected an able man who remained apart from their clubbiness and kept his word—especially when he was president. All congressmen expected from the man in the White House was candor, courtesy, and a willingness to meet them as peers with an engaging, good-humored countenance. They were dismayed to find him a dour personality. As early as 4 January 1919, Colonel Edward M. House told his diary that Hoover "takes, as usual, a gloomy outlook. . . ."[8] In the Great Depression his morose bearing had a tragic aspect. Aside from his own intelligence, little about him radiated cheer. His humor, when evident, was sardonic and ironic. "Herbert Hoover is a man of extreme reserve," Senate Republican leader James E. Watson wrote. Watson, a gregarious rogue, bemoaned Hoover's singleminded seriousness and lack of humour. Complaints about Hoover's demeanor were endless. Colleagues constantly noticed that Hoover was "too easily disturbed," responded to a crisis "with all the blackest possible surmises for it," and was "inclined to have a persecution complex."

Working with Hoover could be a morbid experience. On one occasion, Secretary of State Henry L. Stimson fled from the White House to get away from "the ever present feeling of gloom that pervades everything connected with the Administration." He told his diary: "I really never knew such unenlivened occasions as our Cabinet meetings. When I sat down today and tried to think it over, I don't [sic] remember that there has ever been a joke cracked in a single meeting of the last year and a half, nothing but a steady, serious grind, and a group of men sitting around the table who apparently have no humanity for anything except business."[9]

Much has been written concerning Hoover's seriousness and lack of humor. Many of his supporters however, have gone out of their way to note a subtle sense of humor beneath his shy exterior. As his press secretary wrote, "That Herbert Hoover has a gift of humor—a vein of whimsicality known to all his associates—would come as news to most people." Yet, twice a year throughout his presidency, Hoover spoke at the Gridiron Club's dinners attended by Washington correspondents, events which Hoover described as intended for "'rubbing the salt of wit, the vinegar of hyperbole, and the iodine of satire into the raw wounds of politics.' " [10] Hoover's format for speaking at these affairs called for a few minutes of displaying his wit and then a stern dissertation on what he was doing, why he was doing it, and what others should be doing. Of course, levity by itself might have drawn public accusations that Hoover laughed while Americans starved. Yet, given the Hoover public personality, the Gridiron performances were unbearably consistent. Even at events intended for relaxing frivolity and gaiety, Hoover could not resist giving a lecture on everyone's civic duty.

For all his savvy of economics the president appalled everyone with his political ineptitude. His voluntaristic philosophy and temperament omitted any place for the give-and-take negotiations of politics. He worked hard to build convincing cases for his proposals and depended upon the cold logic of massive data. While his presentations were always impressive for their factual content, his austerity removed any touch of camaraderie from a collaboration of personalities. "He didn't like the human element," recalled a farm-group leader who held two positions under Hoover; "He couldn't slap people on the back." [11] Nevertheless, Hoover did not have to be a back-slapper; as an apostle of cooperation, all he had to show was a willingness to go along in order to get along.

But Hoover, since his days in the Food Administration, had a reputation as a "solo player," who acted on his own without consulting other bureaus or congressmen. " 'He has been a dictator,' " Senator William E. Borah of Idaho complained. " 'But you cannot run the Presidency the way you run a Food Administration during a war.' " [12] He seemed to feel that his leadership did not require negotiation with Congress. He expected Congress to be unquestioningly responsive to his leadership; after all, it should appreciate that he had all the necessary facts.[13]

In a way, Hoover considered himself America's indispensable man. He had nobody to originate suitable schemes for him or to execute them. An aide recalled that he "had to do it all by himself. . . . " He lacked the capacity to delegate authority with confidence. Stimson felt that Hoover hindered and interfered with his subordinates. Also, the president suspected that Republicans conspired to deny him renomination and White House assistants kept lists of people considered disloyal to him. Such behavior betrayed his own insecurity in politics.[14]

Republican senators were contemptuous of Hoover's political fumbling. To Watson, the Hoover tenure proved the dictum that "to be a successful president, a man, among his other qualifications, should be a successful politician." Many senators had experiences with Hoover that convinced them that there was more to the presidency than executive ability. Hiram Johnson, always a quick detractor of Hoover's, believed he was "in total ignorance of the real working of the system. . . ." [15]

Hoover returned their contempt. On one occasion when they had to calculate their legislative support, he and Secretary of State Henry L. Stimson "talked over the Senators to be seen and . . . he had bad impressions about everyone of them, and bad news about some of them. . . ." [16] It was not that Hoover lacked slavish followers in Congress. In fact, several senators gave him total fealty, some of them doing it out of political necessity, others because they respected his leadership and agreed with his policies. But the Hoover loyalists were few. Most congressmen were like the Republican who sadly recalled, "He didn't know where the votes came from. . . ." [17]

Hoover believed that Congress had no constructive role to play in an economic crisis. Legislators tended to be meddling and obstructive because they catered to special and parochial interests at a time when efficient economic organization was imperative. His perspective of Congress had its roots in his Food Administration experience of World War I and in the Commerce Department during the twenties.

Hoover's appointment in 1917 as head of the Food Administration brought him into contact with Congress for the first time. Later he recalled that he "learned that even in such an august institution there was the same minority of malicious and dumb that there was in the rest of the world, and their opportunity was greater." To diminish their political opportunities, Hoover demanded separation of the Food Administration from the Agriculture department, thereby keeping a consumer agency from the influence of producers. With the avuncular support of President Wilson, Hoover won most of his demands and became known as the Food Administration dictator. Shrewdly manipulating the press, Hoover earned a reputation as one of the powerful managers of the nation's wartime economy.

Several times the Food Administrator clashed with Congress. The lawmakers delayed formal organization of the agency while agricultural groups squabbled over the Lever-Simmons bill. Congress likewise delayed the appointments of state administrators while Republicans and Democrats made partisan issues of executive offices. Some senators charged Hoover with arbitrarily favoring certain interests at the expense of others. Congressmen accused Hoover of interference with the free market and seeking too much power to control prices and ration food. Even wives of congressmen blamed the food dictator for their "Hooverized" meals—"bad coffee, bad chocolate, and four kinds of war bread and cake." [18]

Hoover was politically persona non grata to Republican senators when they learned in 1921 that Harding was considering him for the Cabinet. "Hoover gives most of us gooseflesh," one Republican exclaimed and several senators pleaded with Harry Daugherty to use his influence to keep Hoover out of the new administration. They doubted his Republicanism. Hoover had declared his party affiliation only after calling for the election of a Democratic Congress in 1918. (He believed the Congress must be responsive to the president.) That action and its justification marked him as an enemy of their party and their legislative prerogatives. They branded him an internationalist who would enhance executive power at their expense. Many Democrats were more receptive to having Hoover join their party than were Republicans. [19]

Antagonism between the executive and Congress was frequent during the Harding and Coolidge administrations, and usually Hoover was at the center of the battle. These were instructive experiences for the secretary of commerce in his training for the presidency. Harding's first Congress had large GOP majorities (182 seats in the House, 22 in the Senate). Yet Harding found himself constantly bickering with his former colleagues. When its lame-duck session adjourned in 1923, despite the fact that it gave Harding most of what he requested, the press berated the Congress for an unresponsive performance. It was blamed for delaying tariff changes, inaction during national strikes, excessive generosity with subsidies to shipping companies, and, the most profligate stroke of all, passing a veterans' bonus over the president's veto. Not only would the bonus endanger the nation's fiscal integrity, Harding argued in his veto message, it would also "establish the precedent of distributing public funds whenever . . . it seemed politically appealing to do so." Undoubtedly Hoover, whom Harding relied heavily upon as "the smartest 'gink' I know," helped shape the president's thinking on the bonus. [20]

The Commerce portfolio afforded Hoover an opportunity to gain experience in national economic voluntary organization during peacetime. At Hoover's behest, Harding convened an unemployment conference of national leaders in the economy in 1921 and set the tone for its resolutions by telling the conferees that only voluntary and local action, not federal intervention, would create jobs. Needless to say, the conference's resolutions were written by Hoover and followed that theme. Federal bureaus concomitantly speeded their public-works projects in 1922 so that by 22 May Harding could proclaim, "We have passed the winter of the greatest unemployment in the history of our country." He attributed this accomplishment to the cooperation of federal, state, local, and voluntary agencies. Congress had been excluded from any role in the recovery process. When the economy-minded Congresses of the twenties were later called upon to appropriate funds for public works to offset unemployment, they responded negatively. Hoover promoted public works but seemed reluctant to become unecessarily embattled with the lawmakers on this issue. Besides, the importance of public-works planning for economic stability seemed diminished by the apparent success of Hoover's voluntary organization activities in 1921–1922.[21]

Again and again Hoover demonstrated the speed and efficacy of voluntary action under his organizational leadership while Congress debated, delayed, and took counsel with its lobbyists. When he occasionally sought legislation and it met defeat, he blamed the setbacks upon industrial lobbyists or propagandizing bureaucrats. For example, although he generally preferred voluntary action to revive the "sick" bituminous coal industry, the industry proved to be too chaotic and disorganized for unified action. After five years of frustration he reluctantly endorsed proposed legislation to empower the secretary of commerce to organize the industry, only to be defeated by the owners' lobbyists.[22] Hoover boasted that through corporative voluntarism he had brought about the end of the twelve-hour day in the steel industry "without the aid of a single law. . . ."[23] He averted federal intervention in the nation's railway industry by getting the carriers and the unions to introduce their own legislative proposals.[24]

Although Hoover constantly complained about Congress, he usually enjoyed a fair amount of success with it. Between 1921 and 1928 he nearly doubled the Commerce Department's appropriations and increased its personnel by more than 50 percent. Congress gave his department an aeronautics branch in 1926 and a radio division in 1927, both of which he desired in order to rationalize those new industries. Also, Hoover proved himself an expert bureaucratic imperialist by accessioning agencies from the departments of the Treasury, Labor, Interior, and Agriculture. But special-interest groups in various departments used their congressional contacts to thwart Hoover's scheme for a vast governmental reorganization.[25]

No interest group gave Hoover as much trouble as the farm bloc. As a strong advocate of market control by agricultural cooperatives, Hoover opposed every farm bill which would have had Washington aid farmers in the sale and distribution of commodities. He blocked the Norris bill of 1921 and assisted in the passage of a substitute measure. But Congress's passion for the McNary-Haugen bill gave him trouble. Several times he endeavored to sidetrack McNary-Haugenism to no avail. The farm bloc saw it as a panacea to the depression, but Hoover considered it wrong-headed and potentially dangerous to the whole economy. The farm cooperatives lined up against Hoover and only Coolidge's vetoes prevented the McNary-Haugen scheme from becoming law.[26]

Despite substantial Republican majorities throughout the twenties, except during 1923–1925, the Harding and Coolidge administrations were constantly embroiled in fights with Congress.[27] By the time Hoover reached the White House he and many prominent congressmen were old antagonists. Nonetheless, the new president was confident of his ability to deal with them. What he did not count on was a protracted depression.

At the outset of his presidency, Hoover convened a special session to consider a farm relief bill and tariff revision. The Agricultural Marketing Bill, when he signed it on 16 June 1929, closely followed his own farm proposals. The tariff debate, on the other hand, confirmed Hoover's pessimistic view of pressure-group politics. Farm-bloc senators tried to force an unwanted export debenture scheme upon the administration while Hoover vainly demanded a "flexible provision" that would have enabled the executive to adjust rates as justified by scientific observations. But the Democrats opposed the flexible provision as an intrusion upon Congress's taxing powers. The result was a fifteen-month standoff before Hoover finally received and signed the Hawley-Smoot tariff into law. His only request to Congress had been the flexible provision, which led critics to accuse him of failing to provide adequate legislative leadership and permitting Congress to logroll a monster. Still, the tariff was not a defeat for Hoover. The only major defeats he suffered in the Seventy-First Congress which could not be corrected with a veto were the Senate rejection of a nominee for the Supreme Court and an overridden veto of a veterans' bonus.[28]

But the depression, he believed, demanded a curb upon legislation. Confronted with the divided Seventy-Second Congress, Hoover
developed legislative strategy for his own reelection in 1932. He
wanted Republicans to stand aside and permit Democrats to organize the Senate in order to give the opposition full responsibility
for legislation. He was in a credit war: if the Democrats passed his
program, he got credit for leadership; if they balked, they were
blamed for obstructing recovery. He would present Congress with a
recovery program, but he would limit its role by insisting upon a
balanced budget as a requisite for recovery. He would veto any
spending bill that threatened to create a budgetary deficit and pin
the onus of profligacy upon the lawmakers. If Congress failed to
pass his proposed legislation or balance the budget, it would be
responsible for the continuing depression.

But he never achieved his first goal. The Senate Republican
leadership, which enjoyed outsmarting Hoover on other occasions,
would not surrender its majority privileges. Only Hoover would
benefit from a struggle with an "irresponsible" Congress, and Republicans did not care to sacrifice themselves to build his "heroic"
image. He confided to a White House visitor that he could with a
clear conscience and much political profit make a record of vetoes
of Democratic bills which would greatly strengthen him even if
they are passed over his veto. At the same time he would piously
plead for an adjournment of politics for the duration of the crisis.
Republicans, however, scorned his amateurish legislative strategy;
it once more proved to them how little he understood politics.[29]

Despite his political ineptitude, Hoover enjoyed remarkable political success during the first few months of the Seventy-Second Congress. His emergency proposals were approved with dispatch. Passage
of the moratorium resolution and the Glass-Steagall bill took two
weeks each, the Reconstruction Finance Corporation a little longer.
The Senate rejected the LaFollette-Costigan bill in February and
headed off a certain presidential veto. During early 1932 Washington basked in an unusual period of cooperation between the
legislative and executive branches. But, to a suggestion that he
enjoyed a honeymoon with Congress, Hoover retorted, "There has
been no honeymoon. . . . You know that the Democrats have
taken my program because they had none of their own and because
the attitude of the country compelled them to take the one I put
forward. They would murder our plans in a moment if they dared.
The truth is that they do not dare." [30]

Hoover was right. The Democrats were frightened by the prospect of a fight with the president. With the election so near and Hoover's popularity so low, Democratic leaders were perfectly content to second his leadership in a statesmanlike fashion. America had a bipartisan economic policy in 1932. Democrats wanted nobody to hurl the charge of legislative obstruction or political mischief at them. They preferred caution to foolish jousting with the president.[31]

Nonetheless, Hoover trapped them on one issue: balancing the budget. Democratic control of the House gave them responsibility for the tax bill and the administration let it be known that a federal deficit would destroy business confidence and ruin recovery. As on the other Hoover proposals, a bipartisan consensus prevailed on the budget issue. Democratic leaders would not listen to backbenchers who suggested that deficits were common and inescapable in crises like war and depression. (Two previous Hoover budgets could not avoid deficits.) But when the Democratic leaders attempted to raise revenue by passing a $2\frac{1}{4}$ percent manufacturers' sales tax, the rank-and-file House Democrats rebelled and joined maverick Republicans in upsetting the scheme. By 1 April the sales tax lay in ruins alongside the fiction of a balanced budget.[32]

Still Hoover never relented in his quest for a balanced budget. It had become the most potent weapon in his political arsenal. With it he could courageously veto any public-works relief bill not to his liking and expect to benefit politically by standing for an economic principle against congress's political expedience. Of course, according to a White House source, balancing the budget was "more a slogan than an actual belief." Economist Herbert Stein has written, "administration warnings about the dangers of deficits became more and more terrifying . . . partly for the purposes of the 1932 election." The White House carefully kept a file of Democratic vows to balance the budget for Hoover's use in the coming campaign.[33] He may have been maladroit at politics, but Hoover was as devious as anybody else when he stood for relection in 1932.

As Congress documented the collapse of Hoover's relief program in 1932, federal relief became imperative. The same Democratic Senators who had squelched the LaFollette-Costigan bill in February were ready to vote for the Garner-Wagner pork-barrel bill in June. Hoover had opposed legislating public works earlier, in part because he believed he had licked the depression of 1921 without them and he anticipated that voluntary cooperation would succeed again. Although he finally conceded that the time for legislative action had arrived, he insisted upon a public-works bill that would not break the Treasury. With a stern message he righteously vetoed the Garner-Wagner bill; then Congress accepted the Hoover guidelines for the Emergency Relief and Construction Act of 1932.[34] In the end he had what he wanted: he had demonstrated courage in vetoing a politically inspired spending bill and could claim credit for Congress's "constructive" measures.

Rarely had Congress been held in such low esteem as it was during the Hoover years. Such a sweeping generalization may seem like hyperbole, even in our time, but certainly that was one contemporary point of view. By divorcing Congress from any substantive role in recovery, Hoover had spotlighted all the worst characteristics of representative government. He considered pleas for legislative remedial action as ideological or political hostility, rather than acknowledging their merit. Yet he had to justify his intransigence to legislating and could only do so by demeaning Congress. To be sure, Hoover was himself the target of considerable vilification on Capitol Hill, in the press, and in the nation. But most of the anti-Hoover jibes were personal, rather than directed at the institution of the presidency. On the other hand, Hoover's antilegislation campaign brought representative government under reproach. Craving firm leadership in the crisis, many Americans blamed Hoover as a person and Congress as an institution for the lack of national direction. By late 1932 Americans had discarded Hoover and his approach to recovery; many people wondered if they should likewise discard an ineffectual Congress.

Alternatives to congressional government were seriously discussed in those months immediately preceding the inauguration of Franklin Roosevelt. The Seventy-Second Congress's lame-duck session, 5 December 1932 to 4 March 1933, was a farce filled with over one hundred retired or retiring legislators, who bided their time or amused themselves with the antics of Huey Long. It confirmed the worst suspicions concerning representative government. Journalists and congressmen themselves ridiculed the institution and its personalities. Intellectuals like Charles Beard and Henry Hazlitt assailed Congress as an anachronism that ought to be replaced by an efficient body suited for a technological society. A few senators speculated that America needed a Mussolini—at least for the duration of the crisis. Magazines like the *Saturday Evening Post* and *Colliers* ridiculed Congress; journals like the *Nation* and the *New Republic* earnestly defended the institution as worthy if it had a legislative leader in the White House. A few people like Felix

Frankfurter and Representative Thomas Amlie of Wisconsin suspected that there existed a concerted campaign to discredit Congress. Perhaps more people should have heeded to words of Newton
Baker, who wrote: "The fact is, Congress is not any more uncertain
than the country and its muddling impotence is not greatly different from the cross purposes, hesitancies and lack of conviction
which one hears in the very best circles of private life." [35] In other
words, Congress was only as good as its constituency.

In a sense it is unfair to Hoover to contrast his relations with
Congress against Franklin Roosevelt's. (Besides, some critics can
point to the mixed results of the first hundred days as evidence that
Hoover was the more knowledgeable and principled of the two.)
At any rate, the contrast is useful. Roosevelt, like most products of
the World War One bureaucracy, subscribed to voluntary cooperation. But he disagreed in degree with Hoover on the federal role,
Roosevelt advocating a congressional initiative that subordinated
the community's initiative. Secondly, not only did Roosevelt's governmental philosophy include a constructive role for Congress,
temperamentally he needed legislation and the legislators. The road
to recovery was not clearly marked and had to be built by an
executive-legislative collaboration that justified all action in the
name and best interests of the people they served. Roosevelt enjoyed broker-state politics. He reveled in the give-and-take with
congressmen and sought them out regardless of party affiliation.
They were seen as assets—not antagonists. The new Senate Republican leader, Charles McNary, visited Roosevelt in January and
March 1933 and came away each time warmed by FDR's ingratiating
personality. "He is very affable and I think much on the square," an
ecstatic McNary wrote of the new chief executive; ". . . I am sure
it will be a pleasure to work with him . . . I like him very much." [36]
The new relationship between the president and Congress provided
the nation with a productive beginning. That harmony did not
restore prosperity, but it did restore a nation's faith in representative government, which is no small achievement.

Herbert Hoover and American Corporatism, 1929–1933

ELLIS W. HAWLEY

University of Iowa

Ellis Hawley received the B.A. and M.A. degrees in the state of his birth, at the University of Wichita and the University of Kansas, respectively. In 1959 he received his Ph.D. degree from the University of Wisconsin. He has taught at North Texas State University and Ohio State University and currently is Professor of History at the University of Iowa. His interest in Herbert Hoover and the Hoover presidency stems from his profound research for his publication, The New Deal and the Problem of Monopoly *(Princeton: Princeton University Press, 1966). He has written a number of important articles including "Secretary Hoover and the Bituminous Coal Problem,"* Business History Review *(Fall, 1968) and the lead article in* Herbert Hoover and the Crisis of American Capitalism *(Cambridge: Harvard University Press, 1973). Currently he is working on a study of Hoover and associational activities, 1917–1933.*

Hawley's theory that Hoover's concept of American corporatism was prophetic arises from his considering Hoover within the framework recently developed by neoinstitutional historians and students of modernization. He argues that this presidency can be regarded as the end of an era—that by 1933 the model of informal corporatism and "cooperative competition" which Hoover and his associates developed in the twenties had been discredited. Yet, Hawley contends, the dividing line between the Hoover and Roosevelt presidencies has been exaggerated. The difference between the two consisted of different types of managements, and Hawley sees Hoover's attempt as "one of a long series of efforts to provide America with a 'middle way' between atomistic individualism, a state-directed economy, and 'new forms of the Middle Ages.' "

In recent years, a number of new perceptions have been altering older interpretations of twentieth-century American history, particularly those interpretations that have focused chiefly on liberal politics and have viewed the modern American state as a triumph of an indigenous liberal democracy. For neoinstitutionalists, neoconservatives, and neoradicals alike, the dominant theme in recent American development has been the quest for order, stability, and system, not the pursuit of liberal ideals.[1] For recent students of comparative history, the focus has shifted from the uniqueness of the American experience to its similarities with other modernizing societies.[2] And for other scholars, it has become apparent that the American version of the regulatory state was shaped not only by pragmatic tinkering within a framework of liberal-democratic ideals but also by persistent and sometimes powerful strands of what is best described as guildist or corporatist thought.[3]

This is not to say that Americans were ever much influenced by the fascist perversion of corporatist ideals or that they have ever been ready to scrap completely the ideals of the independent trader, the bourgeois republic, or the free marketplace. Nevertheless at times they have been strongly attracted to the central vision in corporatist ideology, to the notion, in other words, of a decentralized, yet harmonious, organic, interdependent social order, organized around and regulated by specialized functional groupings, which are held together and stabilized by responsible leadership, established principles of social equity and efficiency, and institutionalization of a "natural" mutuality of interests. Here, as in Europe, the late nineteenth and early twentieth-century concerns with "destructive competition" and "social anarchy" produced a burgeoning maze of private "regulators," new visions of social harmony through scientific coordination and moral regeneration, and a pervasive nostalgia for lost Edens and earlier "communities." Here, too, the experience of World War I intensified these developments, and here as in Europe, the vision of "industrial self-government" was offered as a way to provide direction and reform without sacrificing property rights or building oppressive bureaucracies.[4] In America, to be sure, there was less inclination to translate this vision into formal philosophical disquisitions. But for a time, especially in the 1920s, it was hailed as the "American way," an organic yet modern outgrowth, so it was said, of America's older traditions of voluntarism, local autonomy, and frontier neighborliness. And despite subsequent attacks on "private power," the vision has remained an influential component in the "partnership," "pluralist," and "neofederalist" formulas of recent years.[5]

Viewed in this context, then, the American regulatory system has been shaped not only by interacting pressure groups and liberal-democratic ideals but also by repeated efforts to convert private regulators" into components of a larger "community of interests," reconcile such arrangements with persisting commitments to economic and political individualism, and devise governmental machinery that could secure "constructive" private actions without creating new instruments of tyranny. In the history of such activity, so it now appears, the effort made by Herbert Hoover and his associates looms especially large.[6] And it is to the task of delineating the later phases of this effort and placing them in the larger context of corporatist thought and influence in America that the present paper is devoted. Hopefully, by focusing on the "cooperative system" that Hoover tried to build and defend, on the disillusionment with it under depression conditions, and on the alternatives that were waiting in the wings when Hoover left office, such a study can further our understanding both of the forces shaping economic policies during the Hoover administration and of the relationship between these policies and longer-range developments.

By the time Hoover entered the White House he had already become the nation's leading spokesman for what he felt to be a new and superior form of "self-government." In America's burgeoning network of self-governing associations, he had come to believe, lay the nucleus of an ideal regulatory structure, one that could bring order, efficiency, and equity without producing industrial dictatorships, closed cartels, or stultifying bureaucracies. As guildlike collectivities led by enlightened and public-spirited men, these cooperative institutions could develop codes of ethical behavior, desirable patterns of social obligation, and the harmonious productivity of which an integrated and purposeful commonwealth was capable. Yet given their dependence on moral suasion, informal pressures, and "educational" activities, they could not encroach unduly upon individual initiative, grass-roots responsibility, and self-adjusting market mechanisms. The "essential" benefits flowing from these older arrangements could be retained, and for Hoover the road to "progress" lay in developing a synthesis that would do so.[7] The task ahead, as he saw it, was to expand and coordinate this emerging "system of co-operation," guide it into "constructive" channels, and protect it from those who would either dismantle the system or turn it into an instrument of tyranny and stagnation. These had been his goals as secretary of commerce. And while critics would soon disagree, he believed that his earlier activities had done much to preserve traditional liberties yet to remedy social ills, raise living standards, and achieve "stable employment and profit." [8]

As president, moreover, Hoover quickly indicated that his goals had not changed. Just as in the 1920s, he hoped to achieve greater order, efficiency, and equity, primarily by organizing areas that were still "sick" or "chaotic," providing economic leaders with better information and advice, and bringing cooperative groups into closer and more regularized relationships. Yet at the same time, he hoped to preserve and expand the benefits flowing from individual initiative, local responsibility, and health rivalry. The right kind of organization, he believed, could achieve both ends; and while this might require some modernization of the antitrust laws, it also required that the main features of these laws be retained and enforced. They were needed both to improve the economic performance of the "cooperative system" and to prevent it from developing abuses that enemies of the system could seize upon to pervert or destroy it.[9]

From the beginning, then, the Hoover policies cut two ways, a situation that seemed to flow partly from the dialectic in the president's own thought, partly from conflicting pressures and the larger ambivalence characteristic of most New Era leaders. At times, particularly in noting the evils of economic disorder and "destructive" competition, the guiding vision seemed to be a structure of semiformal guilds or estates, each represented in a larger economic community and each having positive social obligations. Yet repeatedly, as this vision collided with the desire to preserve traditional liberties and incentives, Hoover and his lieutenants drew back, insisting that it was vital to the "American system" that market forces, individual opportunity, and existing political arrangements be retained. And repeatedly, they seemed to be saying that the evils of "big government" stemmed both from the lack of private controls and the failure to hold private power blocs within narrowly defined limits.[10]

To bring greater purpose and planning to the "cooperative system," for example, Hoover was ready to enlarge the network of expert studies, informational "clearing houses," and cooperating committees that he had helped to promote earlier. By encouraging private leaders to set up such a network, he believed, and by tying

private groups into it through functional representation, the activities of the nation could be "integrated" and guided without
being "regimented" or "bureaucratized." [11] Consequently, he moved
quickly to expand existing activities and to add new machinery of
the same sort in such fields as social reform, education, and child
welfare.[12] When it came to moving beyond this, however, and creating some sort of functional representation in an established economic council, a project that some of his associates had long
urged,[13] Hoover seemed of two minds. Initially, he appeared enthusiastic about a proposal advanced by his old friend Julius
Barnes, one that, if adopted, would have set up a "continuing" economic directorate composed of functional group leaders, heads of
the major regulatory agencies, and Cabinet members having interest-
group clienteles. This, so Hoover told Robert Lamont, could serve
both as an over-all economic coordinator and an informed sponsor of
new "conferences or commissions for development of special subjects."
Yet within a matter of weeks, he had backed away. After consulting
with Senators James Watson and George Moses and being told that
any such move would necessarily be interpreted as "turning Government over to big business," he dropped the idea, decided that
the "American system" could function better without such a council, and developed a marked reluctance to consider it again.[14]

A similar blend of corporatist with antitrust ideals seemed to
characterize Hoover's attitude toward private "stabilization" programs. On several occasions now, particularly in urging studies of
how the antitrust laws could be "reoriented," conferring with pro-
ponents of "reorientation," and giving pep talks to selected trade
associations, he seemed inclined to remove some of the legal checks
on private power to support guildist regulations.[15] Yet at the same
time, he was emerging as something of an antitruster. In April
1929, after Attorney General William Mitchell had refused to grant
antitrust immunity to a plan for curbing oil production, Hoover
defended the ruling and drew sharp distinctions between the proposed plan and real "conservation." [16] In August he told the new
antitrust chief, John Lord O'Brian, that the law must be enforced.[17]
And partly because of his own commitment to "healthy" competition, partly because it seemed that rising criticism of the anticom-
petitive arrangements previously encouraged by William Donovan
might discredit all cooperative programs,[18] he backed the efforts of
O'Brian to dismantle the semiformal cartels taking shape in a
number of industries. In late 1929 the Justice Department abandoned the policy of approving cooperative schemes in advance, and

in early 1930 it began moving against a series of trade association programs that Donovan had once encouraged.[19]

Under O'Brian's prodding, too, the Federal Trade Commission began changing its policies and revising the industrial codes that it had helped to formulate through its trade practice conference procedure. In the guise of eliminating "uneconomic, unmoral, or unsound practice," so it was charged now, the commission had been "fomenting conspiracies in restraint of trade." And in early 1930, after O'Brian had filed vigorous complaints and FTC Chairman William Humphrey had switched sides on the issue, a major revision of the codes got under way. Eventually, despite strong protests from the affected industries, more than sixty codes were stripped of rules considered conducive to "illegal conduct" or questionably close to the "twilight zone." [20] Hoover, moreover, seemed to approve. Although he had once hailed the trade practice conference approach as an immensely constructive procedure leading toward a new "law merchant," [21] he offered no encouragement now to those who claimed to be defending it. Spokesmen for affected industries were told that the president had neither the power nor the desire to interfere with the actions of an "independent" agency. And when former commissioner Abram Myers complained that Humphrey was tearing down the very thing that Hoover had tried to build, the president again drew sharp distinctions between the ethical practices he had hoped to encourage and the "price-fixing" that the FTC was refusing to sanction.[22]

The major area in which both Hoover and the business "stabilizers" could see far too much "destructive" and "wasteful" competition was that of the natural-resource industries, especially lumber, petroleum, and bituminous coal. In these fields, he did seem inclined to remove some of the legal checks on private power,[23] and probably, had he been able to shape matters as he desired, he would have liked to see the industries stabilized by cooperative groupings similar to those he hoped to foster in agriculture. The industries involved, however, were badly divided. In each of them, strong minorities were ready to attack almost any stabilization scheme as being "oppressive" and "monopolistic." And Hoover, caught in the crossfire and dubious about either the wisdom or legality of federal coercion, developed a marked reluctance to do much of anything until internal conflicts could be adjusted. Urged to call a coal conference, for example, he refused to do so, arguing that it had no chance to succeed and could only aid those advocating radical or political rather than "constructive" solutions.[24] Urged to organize a timber "conservation" program, he was hesitant about doing this.[25] And once the Colorado Springs Conference of June 1929 had demonstrated how badly the oil industry was divided and how unlikely it was to accept his proposal for regulation through an interstate compact, he was much more pessimistic about what could be accomplished in that field.[26]

In agriculture, on the other hand, Hoover did make a strong effort to build the type of organization that his ideology called for. Here victory at the polls had insured that his "farm plan" would be tried.[27] And here, as one historian has noted, the Agriculture Marketing Act provided an "almost perfect illustration" of Hoover's regulatory philosophy translated into practice.[28] Under it, stability, modernization, and equity were to be achieved for agriculture, not by statist controls, collective farms, or massive corporations, but rather by organizing and nourishing cooperative associations that could regulate behavior while preserving the individuality and rural virtues of their members. Viewed from one angle, the solution seemed to implement corporatist ideals. This was apparent, for example, in the carefully devised functional representation, the notion that disorder in agriculture threatened the whole social organism, and the efforts of the new Farm Board to establish one official "regulator" in each commodity.[29] Yet as Hoover saw it, there would still be room for individuals, innovators, and sturdy yeomen. "Compulsory" contracts were to be avoided. And while government might "stabilize" markets during "emergencies," it was not to set aside the "normal laws of supply and demand," convert voluntary institutions into instruments of stagnation and tyranny, or listen to those who would impose "rigid" schemes of production control. If it did so, it would destroy the very soul of a healthy system, and the "new day for agriculture" would never come.[30]

Finally, in devising a countercyclical program following the panic of 1929, Hoover tried again to translate his synthesis of corporatist and individualist ideals into practice. Acting much as he had during the recession of 1921,[31] he called the nation's economic leaders together, secured pledges of wage maintenance and expanded construction, and entrusted the implementation of these to cooperating trade bodies coordinated by the Business Survey Conference, a companion agency in the construction field, and a variety of governmental "advisers."[32] Again, there were clear elements here of a corporatist design, particularly in the "regulators" being used, the functional representation in coordinating bodies, the concern with maintaining "just" or "socially efficient" wages and prices, and the overriding notion that liquidation could and should be avoided by "responsible" decision-makers interested in preserving the social fabric and the organic unity of society. Yet again, as Hoover saw it, his approach would also preserve the flexibility and vitality of a market system. There would be no legal coercion. The program would not prevent long-range adjustments to consumer demand. And by using ad hoc coordinaters and limiting the government's role to "advice" and "assistance," the dangers of creating either a stultifying statist bureaucracy or a "superorganization" of industry would be averted.[33]

During Hoover's initial months in office, then, he tried with varying results to apply the policy guidelines that he had worked out in the 1920s and, unwisely perhaps, credited with helping to achieve the "remarkable" stability, creativity, and growth of that period.[34] His problems came when continued application of the guidelines failed to produce what it was supposed to. By mid-1930, it was becoming increasingly clear that Hoover had not found the way to maintain permanent prosperity or to provide ever-increasing benefits for all. As distress and disorder mounted, his formula for balancing the regulatory roles of the individual, the functional group, and the national state seemed increasingly inadequate. And the months that followed would bring simultaneous and ever stronger attacks from those who would increase the power and responsibilities of the state, those who would implement the corporatist vision by creating formal guilds and a "superorganization" of industry, and those who blamed the nation's difficulties on too much private or public interference with individual freedom and self-regulating market mechanisms.

From one side now, a side populated by classical economists, orthodox bankers, and antitrust traditionalists, came charges that the corporatist and statist aspects of the Hoover approach were causing the difficulties. Public and private "regulators," in other words, were holding back readjustments and blocking the competitive processes that could purge the "rottenness" from the system and restore it to economic health. And depending upon which "regulators" were seen as the primary villains, different programs were offered for dealing with them. From business quarters, for example, came a growing assault on the uneconomic" wage scales that Hoover and his allies were trying to maintain. From defenders of fiscal orthodoxy came an attack on the "wasteful" and "artificial" spending that he was encouraging. From antitrusters came charges that

Hoover-encouraged "monopolies" had destroyed purchasing power and were preventing its reestablishment. And from a variety of hard-pressed businessmen came indictments of their "monopolistic" and "prosperity-destroying" rivals, suppliers, or customers. While each group had different "restraints" or "rigidities" in mind, their general prescription was that Hoover should now permit "natural" readjustments to take place or, if necessary, help them take place by blasting away the obstacles that were preventing them from doing so.[35]

From the other side, however, came growing demands for either strengthening the "regulators" or replacing them with others that could do a better job. Economic well-being, so it was argued, had foundered on the rocks of "destructive competition" and "uncoordinated development." Its restoration required stronger or different controls than Hoover was using. And again, depending upon which regulatory weaknesses were seen as the chief villains, different programs were offered as a way to correct matters. From one set of critics came a variety of proposals for strengthening Hoover's "educational" apparatus and expanding the governmental supplements to purchasing power.[36] From another set came an increasingly powerful attack on his efforts to retain the antitrust laws and maintain "healthy" competition.[37] And from a third came proposals for replacing existing "regulators" with new ones, particularly with public and private agencies that would be less interested in "scarcity profits" and more in full employment, social justice, and the restoration of mass purchasing power.[38] Again, while different regulatory weaknesses were seen, the general idea was that Hoover should reorient his policies so as to strengthen controls over economic behavior and provide a higher degree of over-all economic coordination.

Increasingly, it seemed, Hoover's dreams of "cooperative competition" and "flexible" coordination were dissolving into a bitter struggle for contracting benefits. As in the "sick" industries earlier, a welter of conflicting groups and interests were trying to redistribute the burdens of the depression, and in pushing measures to do so, each was arguing that its preservation and prosperity were "basic" to the nation's future well-being.[39] The crying need, so growing numbers of Americans felt, was for new forms of coordination or shifts in power that could restore harmony and "progress." And among those who would strengthen or alter existing "regulators" rather than trying to revive some type of automatic economy, two broad visions of what should be done were emerging, each drawing, to some extent, on memories of the war government, the dreams associated with scientific management, and the "lessons" provided by Hoover's "failure." One would blend a statist-backed "democratization" of industrial government and social benefits with a powerful planning and disciplinary apparatus responsive both to democratic aspirations and scientific expertise. The other called for a fuller realization of the incipient corporatism that Hoover had encouraged. Voluntary associations, in other words, would become compulsory guilds; clearing houses and "educators" would give way to central coordinators, superassociations, or "integrative" arrangements backed by coercive power; and "antisocial" or "anarchic" minorities would no longer be allowed to undermine the order, security, and "scientific" direction needed for socioeconomic health.

Indicative of what one set of "coordinators" had in mind was the flurry of "national plans" that began appearing in 1931. In the spring and summer of that year, such liberal "programmers" as Stuart Chase, Charles A. Beard, and George Soule published detailed proposals, schemes that, in general, would revive the wartime apparatus, create functional syndicates representing all interests, and use them to control investment and build purchasing power.[40] Articles also appeared examining the "experiments" abroad and how they might be adapted to American needs.[41] Discussions of the broader applications of "scientific management" dominated the 1931 meeting of the Taylor Society.[42] And out of a progressive conference in March 1931 came a "stabilization" committee chaired by Robert LaFollette, Jr., further proposals for a national economic council, and, beginning in October 1931, a long series of Senate hearings focusing on a variety of planning schemes.[43] For a whole group of "neoliberals" now, some updated form of the New Nationalism, "war socialism," or Veblenian technocracy seemed desirable; and while they disagreed about how much autonomy the individual and the business group must give up, they all envisioned more power for labor and consumer groups and for a central planning and regulatory apparatus manned by disinterested experts and representatives of the "public."

What the other set of "coordinators" had in mind was also becoming increasingly clear. Throughout 1931 the attack on the antitrust laws intensified, both from groups seeking special legislative treatment and from organizations like the National Civic Federation, the American Bar Association, and the American Mining Congress, all of whom favored a system of administrative exemptions.[44] Revision became the subject of a number of business and academic conferences,[45] and in Congress bills appeared to save the trade practice codes that the FTC had been scuttling.[46] At the same time, sentiment for legal sanctions against "chiselers" was growing. Some "stabilizers" now wanted not only the right to form cartels but a law that would force all elements of their industries to join and comply.[47] And finally, disillusionment with Hoover's "coordinators" was bringing forth numerous proposals for a "superorganization" of industry, one that would be strong enough to weld these units of "self-government" into a harmonious whole, bring "responsible" group leaders into a broad "concert of interests," and thus keep statist expansion to a minimum. In essence, this was to be the function of the Peace Industries Board proposed by Bernard Baruch, the Council of Industries suggested by R. H. Whitehead, the Board of Trade advocated by Mark Requa, the Institute of Industrial Coordination urged by Benjamin Javits, the Economic Congress envisioned by Matthew Woll and James Gerard, and the less known but similar institutions projected by other corporate systematizers.[48]

As such proposals multiplied in late 1931, two particular schemes caught national attention, both, significantly perhaps, emanating from segments of the business community that Hoover had long relied on for leadership and coordination. One came from General Electric's Gerard Swope and Owen D. Young, men long regarded as prototypes of the "industrial statesman." Speaking before the National Electrical Manufacturers' Association on 16 September, Swope set forth an elaborate scheme of economic and welfare planning, one that he had worked on since May and had already discussed with a number of associates. The system, as he envisioned it, would operate through compulsory trade associations, made up of all major firms and empowered by law to regulate production, prices, and trade practices. Labor would benefit from a system of old-age, life, and unemployment insurance administered by labor-management committees in each industry, and coordination in the "public interest" would come through a supervisory agency and public representatives on the association boards.[49] The result, as some critics saw it, would be either an administrative nightmare, a closed and stagnant economy, or a "semisyndicalist" alliance of "big government" and "big business." But for Swope, Young, and their supporters, adoption of the scheme would free industry from outmoded "fetishes," revive markets and investments, and allow government and business to "cooperate" for the "benefit of the people." [50]

The other scheme was that developed under the auspices of the

United States Chamber of Commerce, chiefly by Henry Harriman, the chairman of its Committee on Continuity of Business and Employment. Set up in May 1931, this committee had studied both the proposals being made in the United States and the types of agencies being established abroad.[51] In September it turned to writing its report, and in October it released to the public a scheme calling for legalized trade-association planning, balanced by private unemployment insurance and coordinated through a "national economic council" made up of "public" men but ones chosen by the leaders of functional interest groups.[52] In essence, the plan combined the main features of Swope's proposal with a more elaborate version of what Julius Barnes had urged on Hoover in 1929. And the fact now that Chamber members approved the scheme by a majority of nearly eight to one [53] demonstrated the lengths to which a growing segment of the business community was willing to go. The "neo-liberals" on the left had their counterparts in "neocorporatists" on the right; and while these advocates of compulsory guilds and centralized "business planning" were having difficulty in capturing organizations other than the Chamber of Commerce,[54] they could no longer be dismissed as an insignificant minority.

As conditions worsened, then, growing numbers of critics could agree that Hoover's approach was a failure yet could not agree on the "lessons" to be drawn or the alternative that should take its place. Badly divided over what the new role of the individual, the private group, or the state should be, they tended for a time to cancel each other out and make innovation by anyone difficult. Yet even if change had been less difficult, it seems unlikely that Hoover would have regarded it as desirable. Ideologically committed to the guidelines he had worked out earlier and always reluctant to admit failures or "mistakes," [55] he quickly came up with his own explanation of the continued economic difficulties, blaming them not on the failure of his policies but on developments abroad over which Americans had no control.[56] And having accepted this diagnosis, he coupled continued efforts to develop and apply the "cooperative system" with an increasingly defensive campaign, one that poured more and more of his energies into answering his critics, explaining why he was promoting neither big government nor monopoly nor economic anarchy, and holding the line against the statist "short cuts" and "new forms of the Middle Ages" [57] that could put an end to the American dream.

One theme, increasingly insistent now, was the dehumanization that Americans would suffer and the libertarian institutions they must sacrifice if they turned to a system regimented, subsidized, and regulated by the state. In the summer and fall of 1930, as cooperative committees were set up to organize drought and unemployment relief, the president laid great stress upon how these agencies would preserve the roots of "self-government." [58] In 1931 the Muscle Shoals veto, the efforts to hold down federal appropriations, the launching of the President's Organization for Unemployment Relief, and the explanations of why the Farm Board should discontinue its "stabilization" activities and resist schemes to regiment agricultural production all provided opportunities for expounding on the evils of big government.[59] And in a series of formal addresses, the theme appeared again and again. Yielding to temptations of this sort, Hoover told a Lincoln Day audience in 1931, would eventually make every man a "servant of the State;" and speaking at Indianapolis four months later, he depicted the flurry of "national plans" as being an infection from Russia, argued anew that his original program would work once the shocks from abroad had been overcome, and proposed his own "Twenty Year Plan," one that would achieve its goals by giving the "American system" a chance.[60]

At the same time, despite charges that "cooperation" was being rendered impossible,[61] the Hoover administration was also resisting the notion that its informal corporatism should be converted into a formalized and compulsory system. Again, if Amerians tried to do so, the cure would be worse than the disease. It would generate pressures for elaborate regulatory bureaucracies or other anticapitalist institutions; and even if these could be resisted, it would gradually undermine progressive and creative forms of association, converting them into instruments of extortion or into closed and stagnant arrangements where men must either remain in their places or advance only at the expense of others. This, so the argument ran, had been the experience abroad.[62] And while Hoover would concede that the Sherman Act could stand some revision, especially as it applied to natural-resource industries,[63] he stubbornly refused to suspend antitrust prosecutions or to issue blanket denunciations of those who were cutting prices or selling below cost.[64] When approached by business "planners," moreover, his Commerce Department kept urging them to forget about "grandiose schemes" and concentrate on devising better "educational campaigns," improved forms of voluntary cooperation, and sounder planning by individual firms.[65]

Not surprisingly, then, the "grandiose schemes" set forth in late

1931 seemed to impress Hoover more with the evils they could bring than with any benefits that might accrue. On 11 September, after reading an advance copy of the Swope Plan, he found "only about five percent" of it to be of "some use." The rest was a scheme for "gigantic trusts such as have never been dreamed of in the history of the world." And to combat the proposal, he quickly secured an opinion that it was unconstitutional, forwarded this and other materials to Senator Felix Herbert, and persuaded the latter to issue a statement denouncing the plan and pointing out how it would destroy constitutional government, saddle the nation with inefficient and monopolistic cartels, and eventually force the creation of a vast bureaucracy.[66] Subsequently, the president also made it clear that he would have nothing to do with the Chamber of Commerce scheme. Although Julius Barnes kept supplying him with documents and pointing out how important it was to move against "destructive competition," [67] Hoover's State of the Union message merely reiterated his earlier request for a congressional investigation. Schemes for repealing the antitrust laws, he declared again, would "open wide the door to price fixing, monopoly, and destruction of healthy competition." [68]

It would be a mistake, however, to see the Hoover administration as merely holding the line against welfare statists and corporate systematizers. Although pleas of powerlessness in the face of foreign developments and domestic obstacles were now creeping into its rationale, it had not given up on its own efforts to manage economic and social behavior. The search continued for its own alternative to laissez-faire, for a regulatory structure that would remain within Hoover's guidelines and could serve both as an economic governor and a bulwark against the threats of big government or industrial dictatorship. And the result in 1930 and 1931 was a further burgeoning of Hoover's "cooperative system." There were new efforts, for example, to develop a type of "planning" compatible with "progressive" and "creative" institutions. There were new cooperative programs for some of the natural-resource industries. And much better known, there was a further proliferation of committees and governmental aids designed to secure "constructive" private and local action in providing relief, expanding credit, and solving social problems.

The first of these efforts, the campaign to develop an "American program" of planning, got underway in mid-1931, partly as an adjunct to the work of the Emergency Committee for Employment, partly in an effort to head off the agitation for coercive controls.[69]

The central idea, as developed by such Commerce Department officials as Frederick Feiker, Julius Klein, and Louis Domeratzky, was to revitalize the traditional work of trade associations and mold this into a "nationwide pattern" capable of bringing balanced and stable growth. While rejecting "centralized planning," they believed, it was possible to do much more in the way of promoting market research and cost education, setting up budgetary and investment controls, adjusting production "through statistical knowledge," and regularizing employment, trade practices, and interindustry relationships.[70] In September 1931 Feiker persuaded the American Trade Association executives to back the Commerce Department program rather than schemes for compulsory cartels, and in the months that followed he and his associates urged the approach on other groups.[71] The Cotton Textile Institute and the cement producers also received official encouragement in their efforts to curb "destructive" competitive behavior.[72] A model trade-association charter was worked out. And renewed efforts were made to publicize and expand the Department's advisory and promotional services, thus helping an "individualistic" people to "plan from the bottom up" rather than the top down.[73]

Working with established associations, the Hoover administration was also able now to set up some special "conservation" programs. In late 1930, for example, following a series of negotiations with lumber leaders, the president appointed a privately financed Timber Conservation Board, which was made up of both Cabinet members and industrial representatives and was allowed to forecast demand, suggest quotas, and recommend other remedies for economic "chaos."[74] Similar arrangements, too, were made with oil leaders. In 1930 and 1931 the Federal Oil Conservation Board, headed by Secretary of the Interior Ray Lyman Wilbur, began cooperating with the American Petroleum Institute to provide forecasts of demand, suggest quotas, and set up voluntary import controls.[75] And in June 1931, apparently under strong pressure from both the industry and interested Cabinet members, the Federal Trade Commission abandoned its efforts to revise the petroleum code and reinstated trade practice rules encouraging price maintenance.[76] In addition, plans for a coal program were repeatedly considered, and, had operators been less opposed to making labor a partner in stabilization, might have been adopted. Calls for a national coal conference continued to founder on the rock of union-management conflict, and by late 1931 the National Coal Association had turned to a plan for regional marketing cooperatives, one that O'Brian proposed to contest, but which William Donovan and other association lawyers hoped to slip inside the antitrust laws as being a "reasonable" measure of "economic self-defense." [77]

Finally, the years 1930 and 1931 brought the creation of such agencies as the National Drought Relief Committee, the Emergency Committee for Employment, the Home Building and Child Health Conferences, the President's Organization for Unemployment Relief, and the National Credit Association. All of these, as Hoover saw them, were to provide a middle way, an alternative to laissez-faire that could secure "constructive" action and relief without resorting to big government or politicized cartels.[78] His cooperative machinery, however inadequate his critics felt it to be, kept growing. And in such areas as resource management, construction planning, and credit relief, he seemed willing to back it with new federal supplements. He supported legislation for a permanent Federal Power Commission. He welcomed the creation of a Federal Employment Stabilization Board. And in December 1931, after his National Credit Association had failed to relieve a growing credit paralysis, he finally called for a new framework of governmental credit and controls within which cooperative measures might be successful.[79] His policies hardly merited the label "do-nothingism." But in holding the line against statist regulation, federal welfare, and formalized corporatism, he was being thrown into an increasingly negative stance.

In early 1932, moreover, Hoover continued to hold the line. In spite of some urging from Cabinet members, he refused to endorse the coal-stabilization or trade-practice measures being considered in Congress.[80] In the face of new spending and relief proposals, he continued to expound on the evils of big government, demoralized federal credit, and "non-productive" public works.[81] And when confronted with new formulas for business planning, he continued to see them as opening the way to "monopoly" or "socialism." In February, after meeting with a new business group put together by Charles Abbott and Gordon Corbaley, he considered but quickly rejected their scheme for a two-year "truce in destructive competition" so as to allow an "experiment" in production planning.[82] Subsequently, the administration shunted aside similar proposals advanced by such trade-association leaders as Gilbert Montague, George Sloan, and Z. L. Potter.[83] And in June, when a group of industrialists and American Legion officials urged revival of the Council of National Defense as an "emergency cabinet," the president's reaction was strongly negative. Such a body, he argued, was unneeded. It would merely add a "fifth wheel to an already much taxed coach," and if the public should become alarmed about the economic or political implications of reviving it, any effort to do so would result in far more harm than good.[84]

The difficulty, as Hoover continued to see it, was not with the regulatory structure he was trying to preserve and develop. It lay rather in the "credit paralysis" induced by shocks from abroad and irresponsible behavior at home. And to cope with this, he was not only adopting the classical prescription of budget balancing but also deploying a new array of cooperative committees and federal "supplements." New Laws in the first half of 1932 established the Reconstruction Finance Corporation and provided special credits for farm groups and holders of real-estate mortgages. A new Citizens' Reconstruction Organization conducted a campaign against hoarding.[85] And a new network of Business and Industrial Committees, set up in each Federal Reserve district and coordinated through a national conference, attempted once more to persuade businessmen that they should use the new credit facilities, expand their operations, and hire as many workers as possible.[86] In Hoover's mind, moreover, the brief upswing in the summer of 1932 became proof that his analysis was correct. For him the subsequent downturn was a politically inspired crisis, due chiefly to political uncertainties following the election and to the fears created by a new wave of irresponsible behavior on the part of Democratic politicians.[87]

Given a chance, Hoover felt, his policies could still bring economic and social well-being. And during and following the campaign of 1932, he continued to expound on the evils of "state-directed" systems and closed or politicized cartels. New governmental initiatives, as he saw it, should be limited chiefly to mobilizing additional cooperation, helping farmers to retire marginal lands, and reestablishing confidence in the financial system.[88] And to the cartelizers, his only concessions were to express further sympathy for the coal, lumber, and textile industries, suggest that test cases like the one being tried in the coal industry might provide an answer, and point out that he had urged Congress to find suitable controls for these areas where competition was truly "destructive." [89] In September 1932, when Henry Harriman threatened political retaliation unless he endorsed the Chamber of Commerce plan, Hoover heatedly declared that he would stand firm against any such attempt to "smuggle fascism into America through a back door." [90]

In October, as a new wave of business meetings and speeches attacked the antitrust laws, he refused to alter his stand; and in late 1932 and early 1933, even though some Commerce Department officials were now in close touch with those who hoped to sell some version of the Harriman plan to the incoming administration, the president himself would have nothing to do with the effort or its instigators.[91]

For a majority of Americans, though, Hoover's approach had now become either a study in weakness, an excuse for doing nothing, or a mask for economic exploitation. Demands for a "new order" had become insistent; and while Americans could still not agree upon what the proper balance between competitive rivalry, group action, and statist direction should be, they would soon have a president who was willing to give "something" to nearly everyone, institutionalize the divisions, and allow competing administrators and groups to determine where the balance should be struck. A new burst of energy and experimentation was in the making, one that would demolish the lines that Hoover had been holding but would be slow to settle on a new regulatory model. In essence, what it would provide was not a coherent alternative but a set of "economic charters" under which an alternative might take shape, frameworks, in other words, that different sets of administrators could use to build quite different versions of an "industrial democracy." And within these frameworks, sharp clashes would persist, not only between the interest groups, but also between the conflicting ideals of a corporatist order, a planning and social-service state, and a revitalized market system. Initially, policy would veer toward an approximation of what Harriman and Swope were advocating, but the resulting collision with entrepreneurial, antitrust, and welfare-statist ideals would bring a sharp reaction, forcing this version of corporatism to give ground on all sides, and postponing the emergence of a new consensus on a regulatory model until the advent of "neo-pluralism" in the 1940s.[92]

In some respects, then, the Hoover presidency can be regarded as the end of an era. Its governing model in economic policy, the model of informal corporatism and "cooperative competition" that Hoover and his associates had worked out in the 1920s, became during his presidency an increasingly discredited model. Under depression conditions, it seemed to block the search for order, abundance, and equity rather than promoting it, and the discrediting of the model marked the beginning of a long search for a new and presumably more satisfactory way of reconciling a modern technocorporate system with America's liberal-democratic and rural heritage. Yet the significance of this dividing line can easily be exaggerated. The shift was not from laissez-faire to a managed economy, but rather from one attempt at management, that through informal private-public cooperation, to other more formal and coercive yet also limited attempts, efforts that still made numerous concessions to individualistic and village ideals.[93] The tensions inherent in Hoover's system persisted in the vacillating policies of the New Deal and in the subsequent synthesis that "neopluralism" was supposed to provide. And the later excursions into guildist government and welfare statism built upon and were in some degree limited by the cooperative institutions that Hoover had encouraged and the federal "supplements" that he was willing to establish.[94]

Viewed in longer perspective, the Hoover years appear as a distinctive yet integral stage in the continuing process whereby twentieth-century policy-makers have tried to reconcile conflicting visions of a new order with the dreams that they inherited from nineteenth-century liberalism and agrarianism. In America, to be sure, these visions of order have frequently been disguised as "new liberalisms." But just as in Europe, they have tended to come in two varieties, one stressing statist direction and services, the other, often ignored, envisioning a regulatory system built around modern guilds and corporations. For Hoover, the latter vision was far more attractive than the former. And while his attempt to blend and balance it with "healthy competition," local communitarianism, and statist "supplements" became a casualty of economic contraction and internal tensions, it cannot be ignored by those who would understand the larger patterns of twentieth-century American development. On the contrary, it should be seen as a major attempt to work out a modern corporatist order compatible with American ideals and traditions, as a forebear of different but similar attempts in the post-World War II period, and as one of a long series of efforts to provide America with a "middle way" between atomist individualism, a state-directed economy, and "new forms of the Middle Ages."

III

The Interregnum

The View from the State House: FDR

ALFRED B. ROLLINS

University of Vermont

Alfred Rollins was born in Presque Isle, Maine in 1921 and received his B.A. and M.A. degrees from Wesleyan University in 1942 and 1946 respectively. Harvard University awarded him his Ph.D. degree in 1953. He taught in the State University of New York for nearly two decades (at New Paltz and Binghamton) prior to becoming Dean of Arts and Science at the University of Vermont in 1967. Recently, he was appointed Vice President for Academic Affairs at that institution. His books about the Hoover-Roosevelt era are superb, the most significant being Roosevelt and Howe *(New York: Alfred A. Knopf, Inc., 1962).*

Rollin's essay analyzes Hoover's public-image plight and attributes it to Franklin Roosevelt's stock stereotype of Republican leadership: "the old melodrama of a Republican gang of power and perquisite serving special interests." Rollins sees competition between the two men developing as early as 1920, and by 1929 Roosevelt was "locked in on the Hoover matter" and worked to discredit Hoover. The essay compares Hoover and Roosevelt in several instances. Hoover obviously grows in reputation as scholars research further into the Roosevelt era.

Herbert Hoover will always suffer from the judgments of hindsight. His enemies grasped not only the rewards of their victories, but even the obituaries of the vanquished. As John Quincy Adams, James K. Polk and James Buchanan disappeared into the historiography of Jacksonian and Radical Republican scholars, so Hoover and Coolidge have literally vanished into the New Deal historiography which has contrived our image of their world. Hoover, in particular, became merely the polar opposite of those characteristics popularly arrogated to Roosevelt. He became the man that Roosevelt was not, a mere foil for his artful and persuasive adversary. Actually it was Hoover to whom Roosevelt reacted. But it was a Hoover whom

Roosevelt himself created and sometimes flexibly recreated from time to time.

Hoover's image had to dramatize the folk-hero Roosevelt—St. George, the White Knight, and Davey Crockett all rolled into one. Everything before 1932 must be reduced to mere transition. The United States must appear to have moved insensibly, like some relentless pattern of tragedy, toward the stock market crash and the "Great Failure" of Herbert Hoover. Then came the interregnum—a three-year drama in which the hapless Hoover purged his sins under the whip of public conscience while yearning for the recovery that would justify his faith in the old system. Driven increasingly to do *something,* he seemed to find the things he did made empty by the inhibitions of his own dour faith in laissez-faire, made fruitless by the hard weight of public distrust.[1]

In its simplest forms, this vision had grown from Roosevelt's own personal and partisan perceptions of his predecessor and antagonist. My generation of historians accepted Roosevelt's Hoover almost uncritically. Even those, such as Carl Degler, who sought to give Hoover higher marks, did so in a Roosevelt frame of reference. One must credit Hoover for some of the New Deal, Degler insisted. One must recognize that the changes came earlier than 1933. But one still saw the Hoover administration as mere transition to greater things.[2] And when E. E. Robinson sought to redress the balance, he managed only to reverse the image, judging Roosevelt by the values of Hoover.[3]

When one looks closely at Roosevelt's "Hoover," one sees at once two significant problems. First, the reaction to the Hoover administration from the Governor's Mansion in Albany was seriously affected by the fact that the "Great Engineer" and the Hyde Park Roosevelt had been barely friendly enemies ever since 1919. Second, Hoover had become an almost endlessly flexible target for Roosevelt, a moving foil for rapidly changing and inconsistent charges by FDR, depending upon the changing compulsions of politics. One cannot ask, "What did Roosevelt think of Hoover?" One must specify, when, where, and in what context. What continuity there was in Roosevelt's view was supplied by his stock stereotype of Republican leadership—the old melodrama of a Republican gang of power and perquisite, serving special interests and sacrificing the people to "privilege" before the shabby ikons of nationalism, imperialism, and laissez-faire. In addition to that, Roosevelt sometimes found Hoover to be an insensitive, calculating engineer, bent upon solving problems with statistics and committed to heartless interference with all kinds of personal and private matters. Yet at other times he found the Great Engineer to be inefficient, incapable of handling complex problems, illogical, meddlesome, with no real sense of direction, and often insensitive to the need for planning and direction of the national economy.

According to Roosevelt, reading the Hoover administration was like responding to alternating current. Sometimes Hoover interfered; sometimes he failed to lead. Often he tried to plan everything in sight; yet he failed to develop the information necessary for planning. He expanded Federal power; but he failed to address the nation's problems. And Roosevelt's friends often reinforced these views. During World War I, Josephus Daniels found Herbert Hoover to be cold and distant. And Colonel Edward M. House once described Hoover as "simply reveling in gloom." [4]

Hoover's reactions to Roosevelt, on the other hand, were fairly simple. He apparently didn't think much about FDR until Roosevelt ran for the governorship. A frequently cited letter of congratulations from Hoover to FDR on his 1920 vice presidential nomination is really nothing more than the courteous kind of note which a young member of the administration might sent to any colleague who had achieved this signal honor. When he did notice the man, in 1928, Hoover was quite literally appalled. Hoover never saw in Roosevelt anything more than a rapidly shifting politician, apparently without principle, who could do anything to be elected and even worse to stay in office.

If Roosevelt's view of Hoover was partly personal, Hoover's view of him was almost entirely so. Hoover didn't like the man, didn't trust him, and barely found the tolerance to be in Roosevelt's presence at those absolutely essential and unavoidable moments. It was partly this rigid, personal, almost abhorrent view of Roosevelt that made Hoover such an easy butt for FDR's facile and inspired politiking. If Hoover had been willing to understand his insouciant enemy, he might have dealt with the menace more effectively.[5]

Roosevelt *did* understand *his* enemy. He knew the immense vulnerability of a humorless, sensitive, rigid personality, and he made the most of that knowledge. And Roosevelt also learned that one effective quip was worth twenty pages of turgid Hoover rhetoric. Roosevelt darted lightly about, stinging now here and now there, prodding Hoover to react and then blaming him for the reaction, while the president complained that Roosevelt would not play the campaign by the president's rules and stay put so that he might be swamped by the weight of the humorless presidential argument.

But the explanations must go further. For one thing, Roosevelt shared most of Hoover's economic views. Once the Californian had preempted the stage for enunciating these views, Roosevelt was left in a defensive position which he found neither profitable nor comfortable. And a good part of the Roosevelt image of Hoover which has become part of our genetic baggage can be explained fairly simply by the fact that one was a Democratic governor, cast in the role of challenger and committed for the moment to enunciate the interests of a state and of a region, while the other was a Republican president chosen by fate to defend and to approach problems on a broad national scale. Yet the personal roots of their conflict ran deep and it would be worthwhile to search them out at least briefly.

The fact is, Hoover had been a challenge to Roosevelt personally and a threat to his career ever since 1920. Hoover not only preempted many of the economic grounds upon which FDR might have chosen to stand, but he also symbolized exactly the kind of vigorous, dynamic leadership for which Roosevelt himself would always stand. We have tended to forget, in the wake of his later troubles, that Hoover the war administrator and Hoover the secretary of commerce had seemed to his colleagues and the nation a man much more in the image of Theodore Roosevelt than most other figures on the national scene. It was only in the 1930s that we all began to think of the Great Engineer as a sober, tired, and charmless man in the shadows of Coolidge and of Mellon. Both Hoover and Roosevelt looked back to the heady atmosphere of the Progressive era for their models, and it was only in the depression that Hoover seemed to be reverting to the sober intellectualism of Woodrow Wilson, while FDR seemed to reassert the inspired and agile dramatics of his cousin, Theodore.

Both of these men were limited intellectually, but their limits were significantly different. FDR was shallow and superficial, as almost everyone would agree. But Hoover was narrow. Roosevelt seldom understood a complicated problem with any degree of mastery, but he grasped the main lines and related them superbly to human concerns and to other peoples' understanding. Hoover almost always went deep with a problem, but the depth was like a mineshaft, straightly walled by Hoover's presumptions. Though his views were always well documented, they frequently lacked all understanding of the complex human and social ramifications of the problem. At the moment of their impact on history, Hoover's narrowness betrayed him and Roosevelt's insouciance worked superbly because Hoover had been compelled to make the first moves.

Hoover and Roosevelt had first become acquainted in the second Wilson administration. They were rivals from the start, but appropriately friendly and polite. And they were thrown into conflict with each other by their mutual involvement in the logistical phases of the postwar settlement in Europe. Roosevelt, as assistant secretary of the Navy, had the responsibility of dismantling the Navy's European establishment, and he made the most of it in both headlines and political contacts. Hoover, as director of European Relief, drew a better lot; his job was to save Europe from hunger and he emerged a hero. At the end of the first round, Hoover was an international figure, glamorous, positive; Roosevelt was still a junior bureaucrat whose earlier political flamboyancies had long since been forgotten, and whose name one saw in the newspapers only occasionally. Roosevelt recognized their relative status; one suspects that Hoover hardly noticed.

FDR certainly admired his more successful colleague. He included Herbert Hoover in a list of the "right men" in the War Administration—he was talking about vigor and efficiency and positive goals. He apparently urged Hoover to be available for the Democratic nomination in 1920. He certainly worked to nominate Hoover for the presidency. But there may well have been a little gamesmanship in all of this. It was a close friend of Hoover, to whom Roosevelt wrote the now frequently quoted letter: "He [Hoover] is certainly a wonder and I wish we could make him President of the United States. There could not be a better one." This was probably no more than a harmless gesture, but young FDR was honest in viewing Hoover as a good potential Democratic candidate, in a year of Coxs and McAdoos and worse. And he was obviously upset to discover that the Food Administrator was a Republican. He had presumed to appear much closer to Hoover that he had any chance of being.[6]

Roosevelt's own vice presidential nomination in 1920 gave him his first national platform. But his vigorous campaign tied him to a weak candidate, James Cox of Ohio, and to confused and discredited issues, particularly Woodrow Wilson's handling of the League of Nations question. Both Roosevelt and Hoover were eager supporters of the League. But FDR went down to defeat in association with his president; Hoover remained remote in Europe, doing good and staying clear of the political disaster at home. As a pro-League Republican, he was free of the taint of Wilson's confused tactics, but could associate easily with whatever positive reactions the League of Nations could evoke.[7]

Hoover found himself at once on the crest of a new wave. As secretary of commerce in the Harding and Coolidge administrations, he stood for liberal internationalism, along with Charles Evans Hughes, while benefitting politically from the popularity of Coolidge conservatism. As a Republican Wilsonian, he flourished at court, while Democratic Wilsonians were cast out of influence in both Capitol and party.[8]

In his new role, Hoover aroused both Roosevelt's jealousies and his fears. If he had noticed at all, the secretary of commerce might have been amused at the resentments of this defeated vice presidential candidate, whom fate had additionally disabled with polio. But what was marginal, at best, for Hoover was central for Roosevelt. The scattered contacts of the two during the 1920s left FDR moderately bitter. One involved the initial attempt of Roosevelt to play a public role during his recovery from polio. In searching for a vehicle to regain national attention, FDR had hit upon the American Construction Council, a trade organization which sought to develop just the kind of industrial self-government which Secretary Hoover had been preaching for the nation as a whole. Roosevelt fell eagerly in with the idea of self-stabilization. And he was soon building support by manipulating, much as Hoover was doing, the fears of governmental intervention and of extreme, unregulated competition: government regulation, he said, would be "unwieldy . . . expensive. . . . It means higher taxes. The public doesn't want it." [9] As did Hoover, he took a light view of the antitrust laws and planned for broad programming to smooth out the economic cycles, for the development of a "code of ethics," the allocation of construction dates, materials, and labor, and the development of a "guild" spirit to control the industry.[10] He failed, and eventually concluded that such anarchy could not be organized, that only the disaster of depression and bankruptcies would reduce the number of firms to a small enough group so that order might be reestablished in the construction industry. But, as failure came in upon him, he came to blame increasingly the lack of support from Secretary Hoover and the failure of the Department of Commerce to provide the information, statistics, and communication upon which self-regulation might be made to work.[11]

By 1924 the Construction Council had been abandoned. By 1927 Roosevelt and Louis Howe were taking advantage of the Mississippi

Valley floods to mount a major attack on Secretary Hoover. The motivation was clearly political. Roosevelt was looking for issues over which to attack the national administration. Louis Howe advised him to hit Hoover's ineffective flood-relief program. Issue a "ringing demand in the name of humanity," said Howe. "In other words, raise Hell generally." [12] They proposed a broad program of inland waterways and flood control under federal management and suggested a citizens' committee to study the problem and compel federal action. When Hoover proposed a similar committee, however, Roosevelt protested that this was just a delaying tactic which would submerge any real action in "too broad a consideration" of the problem.[13] Roosevelt went on to outline a plan similar to what later became the Tennessee Valley Authority.[14]

A year later Roosevelt was attacking Hoover vigorously, in his support of Alfred E. Smith for the presidency. Again the issue was water power. He assailed the Republican-controlled State Power Commission for proposing fifty-year leases of public sites to private interests, scorned the claim that Hoover would put an end to unemployment with projects such as the Boulder Dam. When Hoover charged that his own public-power views smacked of socialism, Roosevelt noted that the secretary of commerce had entered the "panic" stage of the campaign.[15]

It was a personal campaign. Roosevelt, running for governor of New York, made the most of the opportunity to compare the "great human engineer," Al Smith, with the cool, restrained secretary of commerce. Hoover, he said, was not "temperamentally fitted or able to handle a great many problems at the same time." He was a weak man who had accepted Harding corruption and Coolidge inaction. On the other hand, he had, said Roosevelt, shown "a disquieting desire to investigate everything, and to appoint commissions and to send out statistical inquiries on every conceivable subject under Heaven. He has also shown in his own Department a most alarming desire to issue regulations and to tell businessmen generally how to conduct their affairs. . . ." [16]

By now the antagonistic roles for which they had been programmed in the postwar world had been fairly rigidly established. By the time he reached the 1928 campaign and won the governorship, Roosevelt had been locked in on the Hoover matter. It was not that he was committed to some one specific view on a particular issue. His precise views could and did change. This sort of thing never bothered Roosevelt very much. What he did find it impossible even to consider changing were his personal, instinctive reactions to the man. If by 1932 Hoover came to see Roosevelt as abhorrent and distasteful, Roosevelt had long since come to view Hoover as a cold, arrogant, and insensitive man, who had better be viewed with fear and treated with contempt. He did, on occasion, refuse to attack Hoover personally, but this appears to have been merely a sensible recognition of the fact that others could attack more profitably without being discredited for personal motives. About the most positive thing he would find himself saying would be his comment to Raymond Moley in 1932, ". . . old Hoover's foreign policy has been pretty good. . . ." The presidential election had now been passed; he could afford a moment of patronizing comment for poor "old Hoover." [17]

If the inevitable combat between Roosevelt and Hoover had ever a chance of being equal, that chance was destroyed by the fact that Hoover had to meet the depression first in the White House, while Roosevelt could stand aside and watch. FDR learned and put the lessons to work. He was free to criticize Hoover for not acting; then chastize him for his actions; then mount his own solutions with the benefit of two to four years hindsight. In such a game, Roosevelt was compelled to discredit Hoover even when he knew the president was correct. Even when he learned from Hoover—and he did —he must somehow differentiate his own plan. This was all the more compelling because he must win the White House and build his program with the same Democratic congressional majority from which Hoover had wrested his own handful of achievements.

Fortunately for Roosevelt, Hoover elected to go it alone without congressional help as much as possible. As Albert Romasco and others have pointed out, he sought, in fact, to "exclude Congress from participation in the recovery." [18] When young Bob LaFollette, New York's Robert F. Wagner, and Colorado's Edward P. Costigan took the lead in labor reform legislation, Hoover rushed to use the veto.[19] The president's activities on agriculture and on the Muscle Shoals question also gave Roosevelt popular issues. Roosevelt was left free to woo the dissident congressional majority, while the negative feelings and unfriendly headlines focused upon Hoover. He stopped in Washington frequently for personal conferences with Democratic leaders and made "ringing statements" on a number of subjects in which they were interested. As he wrote to Senator Royal S. Copeland of New York, he feared that his party might "be misled along conservative or reactionary paths by those who fatuously compete with our Republican friends for the support of of certain interests." He needled Hoover on the tariffs, relief, the airmail scandals, the war-debt moratorium.[20]

But, if he warned against conservatism, Roosevelt also, in 1929 and 1930, talked up states' rights. He gleefully assailed Hoover's attempts as president to enforce prohibition laws and claim that right for the states, while happily opposing the whole idea of prohibition itself.[21] He virtually ignored unemployment in New York during the early days of the depression, but he was delighted to pillory the president for his naive predictions that the depression would end shortly. He seemed to have no sense of urgency himself, calling as he did for a long-range study of unemployment conducted as "dispassionately and constructively as a scientist faces a test tube of deadly germs. . . ." He satisfied himself with asking employers to be proper Boy Scouts and do a good deed a day. But he was happy to demand of the federal government extensive unemployment and social-security insurance programs and at the same time to assail Hoover for abandoning the "law of supply and demand" and inventing a "new theory that, although a man cannot pull himself up by his bootstraps, a nation can." [22] In his 1930 campaign for reelection, Roosevelt relentlessly associated his hapless opponent with Hoover's boast: "The poor man is vanishing from among us. . . ." Roosevelt claimed, ". . . if Washington had the courage to apply the brakes . . . the fall from the heights would not have been appallingly great." He did not try to explain why the governor of the state which contained the financial nerve center of the nation had done nothing to apply the brakes, and he did not have to explain that his own budget expansion was not a planned antidepression measure but an accidental outcome of his reform program.[23]

By the summer of 1931 Hoover was trying to turn the tables by challenging the governors to take action against the depression, so that "self-government" might be saved and federal intervention avoided. Roosevelt had little to show for his claims that the states should become the "experimental laboratories" of the nation.[24] And meanwhile the public-power victories he had won painfully in New York were frustrated by President Hoover's insistence that no action could be taken along the St. Lawrence until the Senate had approved a federal treaty with Canada.[25]

If Roosevelt had pursued Hoover with lively inconsistency for ten years, he moved in upon him almost viciously in the 1932 presidential campaign. Light, incisive humor alternated with the most direct charges of incompetence and dishonesty, until Hoover was left seething with rage and unable to mount an effective defense. If Hoover tried to support the federal treaty-making authority in the St. Lawrence power negotiations, Roosevelt would embarrass him with a public telegram inviting the president's help to get the "great public work" underway at once.[26] If Hoover became mired in inconsistencies of foreign and domestic economic policy, Roosevelt would pursue him with the famous lines about Alice in Wonderland and Humpty Dumpty:

"Will not the printing and selling of more stocks and bonds, the building of new plants and the increase of efficiency produce more goods than we can buy?

"No," shouted Humpty Dumpty. "The more we produce, the more we buy."

"What if we produce a surplus?"

"Oh, we can sell it to foreign consumers."

"How can the foreigners pay for it?"

"Why, we will lend them the money."

"I see," said little Alice, "they will buy our surplus with our money. Of course, these foreigners will pay us back by selling us their goods?"

"Oh, not at all," said Humpty Dumpty. "We set up a high wall called a tariff."

"And," said Alice at last, "how will the foreigners pay off these loans?"

"That is easy," said Humpty Dumpty, "did you ever hear of a moratorium?"

But then, if Hoover had predicted optimistically about the depression, Roosevelt would charge, "the administration did not tell the truth. . . ."[27] And amidst all this, Roosevelt was claiming Hoover's own ground, the pursuit of "individualism." Individualism must be, said FDR, "what it was intended to be—equality of opportunity for all, the right of exploitation for none." Government could, he said, "act as a check and counterbalance to . . . oligarchy" and could do that "without becoming a prying bureaucracy. . . ."[28] In San Francisco he demanded planning; a few days later in a radio speech he attacked Hoover for "reckless" spending and for his resort to federal controls. The president complained sharply that FDR was merely a "chameleon [in] plaid." [29] Roosevelt ran a campaign of lively and inconsistent maneuver, developing "compromises" with his conflicting advisors. Hoover moved almost alone, with clean logic from narrow presumptions that made him miss both the essence of the nation's problems and the hearts of its people.

It is a delight that scholars are beginning to break through the New Deal mold and to face the twenties with some fresh points of view. Among the best possibilities at the present time are those which attempt to get historians back to that age as it actually was and to view Hoover in the terms of 1926–1927–1928 rather than in terms of 1930, 1931, 1932, 1933. This is not to say that one should shrink from deciding whether the results of Hoover's policies were successful. It is rather that one should seek explanations of his action in context, not from afterthought. One distinct possibility will be to view Hoover against our national understanding of the presidency as it was in 1928. Another is to approach Hoover as a legislative leader and to examine the cross-party management and leadership which was the essential challenge of his administration. Perhaps another would be the study of the internal consistencies and tensions of Hoover's theory and practice. Undoubtedly there are many more possibilities. But it is clear that we are only beginning research and understanding of the twenties in American history. Now that we no longer feel compelled to destroy or defend Herbert Hoover, we may even begin to approach him as part of a complex society, rather than as the simplistic symbol for an whole era of history.

The Interregnum Struggle Between Hoover and Roosevelt

*Frank Freidel was born in Brooklyn and was educated at the
University of Southern California (B.A., 1937) and at the University
of Wisconsin, where he received the M.A. and Ph.D. degrees, in
1937 and 1942 respectively. Among institutions where he has taught
are Shurtleff College, the University of Maryland, Pennsylvania
State College, Vassar College, the University of Illinois, Oxford
University, and at Harvard University, where he has been
since 1955. He is a prolific and eminent author, his major work
being his multivolume study of the life of Franklin D. Roosevelt,
the latest volume,* Launching the New Deal, *published in 1973.*

*Friedel sees the relationship between Roosevelt and Hoover
deteriorating further during the interregnum. Hoover feared the
coming New Deal and by February 1933 admitted that he was
attempting to convince the president-elect to abandon it. Freidel
attributes much of the personal animus which developed between
the two as stemming from their futile discussions regarding the
gold standard and the banking crisis. He concludes that both
should be criticized for their activities during the interregnum—
Hoover for pushing the gold standard and Roosevelt for not acting
in the bank situation.*

For Herbert Hoover, the long bleak months between his landslide
defeat in November 1932 and his relinquishing of office in March
1933 were one final ordeal culminating his tribulations as president.
As the national economy plummeted toward the nadir of the depression crisis, Hoover felt that its deterioration was an inevitable
consequence of Franklin D. Roosevelt's victory and his dangerous
New Deal program. Hoover began to act as though he felt it was
his duty to save the nation, indeed the world, from the folly of the

American voters. In the weeks and months that followed his defeat until midnight of the day before he left office, Hoover doggedly, repeatedly, tried to persuade Roosevelt to modify his program, to abandon its many errors and accept the Hoover formulae for recovery. By February 1933 Hoover was actually admitting that what he wanted was for Roosevelt to abandon the projected New Deal.

Thus put, in bare outline and in retrospect of over forty years, Hoover's endeavor at best appears quixotic. Even at the time, anyone who was aware of Roosevelt's stubbornness would realize how hopeless Hoover's persistent efforts were. That made little difference. Hoover was a president with an intense feeling of moral stewardship. At first he set upon his course rather hopeful that he could win some modifications from Roosevelt; later he continued the fight not only out of righteousness but also with some notion of setting forth a record which might win him vindication from posterity.[1]

On the narrative level, the struggle between the outgoing and incoming presidents is a fascinating tragedy. Since the end of the thirties there have been Raymond Moley's able reminiscences, which, although written after Moley had changed his mind about Roosevelt, are sympathetic toward the president-elect. Hoover, in his memoirs, did not present his own case nearly as effectively. For one thing, he apparently did not consult his papers, with the result that along with his passionate exposition of his views, he made a number of minor, rather annoying errors. In the past several years, certain aspects of the relationship between the two men have been described, most notably in Herbert Feis's quasi-memoir, quasi-history, *1933*. Within various manuscript collections, and especially in the papers of President Hoover, opened several years ago, there is sufficient material to enable historians now to make a three-dimensional reconstruction of the painful struggle between the outgoing and incoming chief executives. It is also now possible to tell the story more fully from Hoover's standpoint. In the telling, he comes out somewhat better than in his memoirs, which apparently he wrote when he was particularly bitter toward Roosevelt and convinced that the New Deal was little short of communist in its implications. To this extreme Hoover had come from his pleasant early friendship with Roosevelt when they were both young administrators under President Wilson during the First World War.[2]

It was the acute hostility and mistrust between these two upright sensitive men that made cooperation between them almost impossible after the 1932 election, although the frightful economic plight of the nation called for immediate redress. There is no need to remind historians of America in the twentieth century how very bad conditions had become—with a quarter or more of the working force unemployed and many of the rest receiving only part-time work at low wages; with a large number of the farmers having already lost their farms and some of the remainder malnourished. Relief was so inadequate that it was scarcely above the starvation level, even though the price of corn was so low that some farmers in Iowa found it cheaper to burn the previous year's corn to heat their houses than it would have been to buy coal.

How under these horrible circumstances could the American best known for his humanitarian feeding of the European victims of World War I and that other decent leader, soon to establish himself as the great champion of the dispossessed, fail to join in at least some minimal emergency action? The answer is, of course, that these two devotees of Woodrow Wilson, who as late as 1929 or 1930 were little different ideologically, had developed in response to the depression quite distinctly different views concerning the limits of government action. Hoover had remained true to the older Wilsonian limitations, which distinctly emphasized voluntarism. Roosevelt continued to talk in those terms, but in private conversations with his advisors and to some degree in hazy campaign statements he had begun to espouse much more vigorous government action. Both men still believed in the precepts of the New Freedom, but Roosevelt was ready to move on toward the New Nationalism, and indeed toward experiments that both Wilson and T. R. would have abhorred as heresies. Hoover, as the ideological heir to Wilson, did so detest them that before the campaign of 1933 was over, he was denouncing them most emphatically. One comment of Hoover's so angered Roosevelt, listening on the radio, that he claimed Hoover was impugning his patriotism.

The personal side was even more painful, the falling out of old friends. It must have been very hard for Herbert Hoover in years after he left the White House, and indeed even after Roosevelt's death, to face up to the fact that he had once enjoyed Roosevelt's warm admiration. He preserved in his files a letter that Roosevelt had written to Hugh Gibson, in which Roosevelt had expressed his warm admiration for Hoover and his hope that Hoover would become the candidate for president in 1920, on the Democratic ticket. When, it was Roosevelt who was picked in 1920 as the Democratic vice presidential candidate, Hoover sent him a charming message of congratulations. This too Hoover kept in his files, but when Rexford G. Tugwell, some years after Roosevelt's death, came upon a copy of it at the Roosevelt Library and asked Hoover's permission to publish it, Hoover refused.[3]

It is pleasant to relate that by 1958 Hoover had mellowed sufficiently to write a few more kindly pages on his personal relations with Roosevelt. (He then decided not to publish them.) In these recollections, Hoover says that they met socially when they were serving under Wilson and became good friends. He recounts their numerous pleasant meetings in 1919 and 1920 and quotes Roosevelt's laudatory letter to Gibson. The cordiality, Hoover points out, continued during the years when Hoover was secretary of commerce and had correspondence with Roosevelt who was chairman of the American Construction Council. Then comes an interesting revelation, that Hoover was grievously hurt by a letter which came into his hands after the campaign of 1928 and which "seemed to indicate less than fair play in political debate from a personal friend." The letter, which was spread broadside, and was probably the work of Roosevelt's "amanuensis," Louis M. Howe, is surprising only for its mildness, considering what campaign missives usually are. In it, Roosevelt suggested that Al Smith would probably be more Wilsonian in his actions than the administration of the Republican candidate, surrounded by "materialistic and self-seeking advisors." That was all. There was not a word of direct criticism of Hoover. In fact, throughout the campaign Roosevelt scrupulously avoided any public attack on Hoover, refusing to write an article against "an old personal friend." He did, however, remark in private that he thought Hoover cold.

Sensitive would have been a better word, since apparently Hoover never forgot and never forgave that campaign letter. It is too bad, since obviously Roosevelt was not intending to malign his friend.[4]

The reason for Roosevelt's anger toward Hoover was something that Hoover could never have remotely guessed. There was a reception at the White House at the time of the annual governors' conference in the late spring of 1932, not long before the Democratic Convention. Other Democratic contenders for the nomination were whispering that Roosevelt did not have the physical stamina to be president. Roosevelt was particularly determined, therefore, to give the impression that he was merely lame, and not a paraplegic dependent upon a wheel chair. When he arrived at the East Room of the White House, the president and Mrs. Hoover were not there, and for a full half hour he and the other governors were kept waiting. Roosevelt regarded this as a trial of his strength, refused offers to take a chair, and despite acute discomfort from his steel braces stood with the perspiration rolling down his face, suspicious that President Hoover was purposely putting him through this ordeal. Neither he nor Mrs. Roosevelt ever forgot. And yet nothing could have been more contrary to Hoover's sense of fair play than to have engaged in such a low political stunt. Hoover's unprinted reminiscences of Roosevelt bear this out:[5] "I greatly admire the courage with which he fought his way back to active life and with which he overcame the handicap which had come to him. I considered that it was a great mistake that his friends insisted upon trying to hide his infirmity, as manifestly it had not affected his physical or mental abilities." [6]

It would be difficult, of course, at the end of any hard fought presidential campaign for the two candidates to regard each other except with a considerable measure of distrust and distaste. Normally, it does not make much difference, but at a time of crisis it was unfortunate. It can be argued too that the hostility of these two men toward each other did make a difference, but one contrasts it with the cooperativeness that was to develop between Roosevelt and Hoover's secretary of state, Henry L. Stimson.

In the aftermath of his election, Roosevelt would not have expected to have much involvement with Hoover. True enough, in a relaxed talk with Adolf A. Berle the Saturday before the election, he speculated that if he were to win by a very heavy margin that there would be pressure for Hoover to place Roosevelt in succession to the presidency as secretary of state, persuade the vice president to resign, and himself resign so that Roosevelt would immediately become president.[7]

Nothing could have been further from President Hoover's thoughts. Rather, he felt that the election of Roosevelt was precipitating a panic which began to be evident when the Maine election in September indicated that Roosevelt would win and Hoover's policies be reversed. Hoover, in his own thinking, as he has suggested in his memoirs, was nonetheless conciliatory, hoping that he could work with Roosevelt to persuade Congress to enact certain recovery bills that both of them favored, particularly the balancing of the budget, the administrative reorganization, and changes in banking and bankruptcy laws. Hoover has written, "Indeed, if these matters were out of the way, such political liabilities as were in them would be on my back, and the new administration would have a propitious beginning." Hoover also hoped there could be agreement on certain foreign problems, since there had been no question concerning them raised during the campaign. On policies toward Japan and the World Disarmament Conference, Roosevelt was to continue much as his predecessor.[8]

On the acutely difficult and delicate problems of war-debts payments and the forthcoming World Economic Conference, the two men soon found themselves at loggerheads. Behind these was a prime domestic issue which had received some slight airing during the campaign, the question whether or not the United States government should as a mild palliative to the acute deflation go off the gold standard. One cannot understand the complicated negotiations between the two men in the months that followed if one does not keep in mind Hoover's profound faith in the gold standard and his determined efforts at all costs to keep Roosevelt from abandoning it. Even in the aftermath of World War II and the Bretton Woods monetary agreements, Hoover still talked in private of the gold standard with the almost religious fervor with which William Jennings Bryan had once expounded the gospel of silver. During the campaign, rumors had reached him from the Democratic camp that Roosevelt was toying with the notion of going off gold, and indeed, such was the case. Near the end of the campaign, Roosevelt persuaded Carter Glass to deliver a fervent speech to scotch these rumors, something which thereafter Hoover could hold against Roosevelt as a prevarication. Defense of the gold standard, therefore, was very much in Hoover's mind as he initiated discussions with Roosevelt. Also there was his hope that the United States could negotiate an agreement for the British to return to the gold standard and make trade concessions in return for an American reduction or abandonment of war-debt payments. The debts in Hoover's mind were an American asset which could be used to obtain economic cooperation from Western Europe—including the maintenance of a gold standard. Hoover felt that if the major nations of the world were on gold that the resulting security and international financial arrangements could help restore business confidence. The thesis continued that business had been regaining confidence and was pulling out of the depression until the prospect of Roosevelt and his experiments shattered it. Therefore, through all of the months of the interregnum what Hoover basically sought from Roosevelt, in one way and then in another, was a pledge to keep the United States on gold; as a second, more distant object, he would have liked Roosevelt to work toward the restoration of the gold standard in London.

It was a forlorn dream on both counts. Roosevelt was purposely obscure about his plans concerning gold if for no other reason than to prevent speculators from making a killing, but he seems to have been stubbornly determined to retain the option of going off gold if he wished. That point is well known. Less familiar is how the British would probably have reacted if Roosevelt had cooperated with Hoover. One can guess from a Foreign Office internal memorandum written when the British ambassador, Sir Ronald Lindsey, cabled on 14 November 1932 the inaccurate information that Roosevelt might want to exchange debt concessions for a trade agreement. The analyst wrote unkindly that it was "nothing more than a rehash of Mr. Hoover's hair-brained scheme," totally contrary to the Ottawa arrangements of a few months earlier. The Foreign Office and the rest of the British administration had no interest in making any real concessions on war debts, but rather were determined to reduce them as rapidly as possible to the point of elimination. In his relations with both Roosevelt and the British, and incidentally with the French, Hoover was to be most unhappy all that winter.[9]

There was one other obstacle that Hoover would encounter in his dealings with Roosevelt. Hoover insisted upon asserting that the depression was worldwide in origin and that recovery could come only through worldwide cooperation. Throughout his campaign, Roosevelt had been equally emphatic in blaming the depression upon Republican policies in the 1920s and emphasizing the view of his two chief advisers, Moley and Tugwell, that solutions must be of a national sort. Although during the first hundred days of his administration, Roosevelt tried to pursue both nationalistic policies and ones of world economic cooperation, earlier during the interregnum he firmly refused to commit himself to Hoover.

The drama began on the Sunday after the election when President Hoover, en route by train from California to the White House, sent a long telegram from Yuma, Arizona to inform Roosevelt that the British had unexpectedly asked for an immediate review of war debts and a postponement of their installment due under existing arrangements on 15 December. Hoover invited Roosevelt to a personal conference to take up not only debts but also the interrelated questions of the World Economic Conference and the Disarmament Conference. "The building up of world economic stability," Hoover emphasized, "is, of course, of the greatest importance in the building up of our recovery."[10]

Roosevelt instantly recognized the telegram as transcending the question of war debts and dealing with the fundamental differences between Hoover's program for remedying the depression on a worldwide scale and Roosevelt's emphasis upon nationalism. Further, Roosevelt, as Moley remembers, was absolutely certain that he did not want to accept responsibility before he assumed power. He was pleasant enough in his reply to Hoover, but there was no likelihood that a meeting between the two men could reconcile these two basically different positions. They did not appear so contrasting on the surface, but underneath there was, throughout the interregnum as various matters arose involving negotiation, this fundamental block—Roosevelt's refusal to accept responsibility and to limit in advance the freedom of action he would need when he became president.[11]

There was another problem, and that was the suspicion with which the two antagonists faced each other. Hoover prepared for the meeting so wary of Roosevelt that he even took the unprecedented step of having a transcript made of his telephone conversation with Roosevelt. Further, he told Stimson that he did not want to see Roosevelt alone, that there must be witnesses present so that Roosevelt could not later go back on his words.

An unconscious handicap to Hoover was his staunch belief in his own correctness, which must have antagonized Roosevelt in its repeated manifestations. Stimson noted in his diary that Hoover "had wrapped himself in the belief that the state of the country really depended upon his reelection." [12]

Roosevelt was equally wary as he prepared to confer with the president, especially because he was convinced that the Democratic leaders in Congress, upon whom he must depend for his New Deal program, would be vehemently opposed to any new reduction in war debts at that time. He was far more concerned with them than he was with President Hoover. Under these circumstances, Roosevelt's meeting with Hoover was foredoomed. Hoover had brought Secretary of the Treasury Mills into the meeting, and Roosevelt had Moley with him. From notes that Hoover on the one hand and Moley on the other jotted almost immediately after the interchange, it is possible to reconstruct it with some accuracy. There is no especial need to go into the factual details of the conversation, except to note that Hoover wanted to reconstitute the Debt Commission, which had negotiated the Dawes and Young war-debt and reparations agreements of the 1920s. He would ask Congress to nominate three members from each house and add to them three presidential appointees. The presidential appointees were to be ones of whom Roosevelt approved. By the close of the meeting, Hoover thought he had Roosevelt's assent to the proposal, whereas

Roosevelt felt that he had been telling Hoover that he was perfectly agreeable to Hoover going ahead on his own with the proposal. Also Roosevelt was agreeing to the method of issuing a communique on the meeting. Roosevelt, as was characteristic, was so affable during the discussion that Hoover understandably thought he was obtaining Roosevelt's approval. There is also the plausible possibility that Roosevelt did not decide definitely until he had left the meeting that he would not agree to reconstituting the debt commission.

In subsequent years, Hoover was certain that Roosevelt had engaged in serious treachery. It is interesting that his immediate reaction after Roosevelt had left the White House was not so black: "The impression he left on my mind was a man amiable, pleasant, anxious to be of service, very badly informed and of comparatively little vision. My impression at the moment is that he will not carry through on this agreement."

There is one sidelight to the discussion which has become apparent only through Hoover's notes. The two men did have several minutes of private discourse, during which Roosevelt asked Hoover if he would help persuade Congress to enact a farm bill which would establish the domestic-allotment scheme. Hoover declined, saying that he thought the domestic allotment was unsound. This minor episode shows as clearly as anything that Roosevelt was perfectly willing to act with Hoover if in so doing he could obtain part of his future program. On the other hand, Hoover was willing to act with Roosevelt only if he approved of Roosevelt's goal.[13]

Unhappily the meeting at the White House and the two contradictory statements to the press that followed were damaging rather than remedial. Both Hoover and Roosevelt suspected treachery on the part of the other. During the next few weeks the relations between them deteriorated further, and the inevitable result was for Roosevelt to draw closer to the Democratic leaders in Congress and the popular position that the war debts must not be reduced. (It was a view which did not represent Roosevelt's private opinion.) On the other hand, Hoover enjoyed the strong support of Republican newspaper columnists and editorial writers. The clash did little but confirm each of the antagonists in feeling his position was right. By the end of December there was a hopeless impasse between them on the debt question.

In his own eyes, President Hoover was a man of good will who had been doing no more than to try to help a misguided tyro. In a private, off-the-record conversation with the United Press White House correspondent, Henry F. Misselwitz, Hoover confided:

There is little I can do now. It isn't going to be as simple as he seems to think. He is going to find it tough going. . . . Those war debts are a liability to any administration, and the poor devil is going to discover they can't be solved by talking about them. . . .

[Every] new man that comes to this job thinks he can fix things up right off. We all come into it with the idea the other fellow was mostly wrong and with our own ideas of what should be done. But it doesn't work out always the way we think it will. . . .

I offered to share that great liability with him, to let him use me in any way he wished in these two months. I'm rid of a lot of grief now that he turned it down—but I'm filled with anxiety about what it means. If we had shown solidarity and a united party front, it would have meant much in these debt negotiations. It might have stopped the world from its present rapid downsliding. . . . I am most anxious about it, and doubtful what may come next. We'll just wait and see.[14]

Although Hoover could speak thus charitably to a White House reporter concerning Roosevelt, his stance in relation to the incoming president had become almost one of stalemate. How different it might have been is indicated by Secretary of State Stimson's success in reaching working arrangements with Roosevelt. Stimson put his foreign policies above party considerations, and found that the most difficult part of his task was to persuade Hoover to let him see the president-elect. Stimson's attitude toward Roosevelt in its way was almost as patronizing as that of his chief, but Stimson managed better to keep it to himself. He had written in his diary just before Hoover's first conference with Roosevelt:

My chief fear is the attitude in which Hoover is approaching the meeting: he has allowed himself to get so full of distrust of his rival that I think it will go far to prevent a profitable meeting. It is true that we here feel that his fear about Roosevelt and his untrustworthiness seems to be pretty well founded from information which has come from every side, from people who have known him intimately; but I have found in life that the best way to make a man trustworthy is to trust him, and Mr. Hoover has not learned to do this as to Mr. Roosevelt.[15]

Hoover, after his unfortunate encounters with Roosevelt, warned Stimson that he was "a very dangerous and contrary man and that he would never see him alone." Stimson then went so far as to tell the president that when he was governor-general of the Philippines, he had won the support of the Filipinos, ordinarily thought a treacherous race, by trusting them. Further, said Stimson, if Roosevelt were "as bad as Hoover thought he was, it would be worse to give him the grievance of refusing to see him than any treachery he might perform." This argument caused Hoover to give way and to allow his secretary of state to visit the president-elect.[16]

The meeting between Stimson and Roosevelt was a most cordial one and led to frequent subsequent telephone conversations. Stimson without difficulty got Roosevelt to endorse the Stimson Doctrine, which refused recognition of Japanese conquests on the Asiatic mainland, together with his approval of other State Department policies. For his part, Stimson began serving Roosevelt rather informally in Roosevelt's contacts with other countries, whether Stimson approved of Roosevelt policies or not. Through January and February of 1933, Stimson found himself in fact operating as secretary of state under both the outgoing and incoming presidents. Stimson's cooperation contributed to an interesting result, that the State Department continued under Roosevelt to be staffed by most of Stimson's key lieutenants, and Stimson himself, in the background, was frequently consulted and of considerable influence. Felix Frankfurter was being flattering that winter to Stimson when he predicted that the secretary of state would have more influence with the incoming administration than he had with the outgoing one, but the prediction was not too far off the mark.

Yet even after the establishment of liaison between Stimson and Roosevelt, when Hoover had a second meeting with Roosevelt in January 1933, he fared no better than before. The only outcome of this meeting was that Roosevelt gained firm control, in point of fact if not of law, of the forthcoming negotiations involving both war debts and the agenda for the World Economic Conference. And at this point the unpleasant negotiations between Hoover and Roosevelt might have come to an end had it not been for the frightening gold and banking crisis which grew out of hand in February 1933.[17]

In mid-February there were twin shocks in the nation; the first was the attempt of a mentally unbalanced assassin to kill Roosevelt in Miami—a quite near miss which fatally wounded Mayor Anton Cermak of Chicago. President Hoover immediately wired Roosevelt expressing his relief. The other was the growing drain on Treasury gold reserves and the mushrooming runs on banks. Banks throughout the United States, weakened by the long attrition of the depression, could not withstand the heavy withdrawals and hoarding that gained momentum in the latter half of the month. Basically the crisis occurred because millions of small depositors and businesses had exhausted their resources, which in turn exhausted bank resources. The problem was compounded, on the one hand, because depositors mistrusted banks and desperately needed their remaining savings, and on the other because the expectation that the incoming administration would take the nation off the gold standard and devalue the dollar had caused a heavy drain on the federal gold reserve.

As the pressure upon the banks became acute, President Hoover came to believe that Roosevelt was responsible for it and that Roosevelt alone could bring it to an end. Consequently, he sent a lengthy handwritten message to Roosevelt through a secret service operative, only three days after the attempt on Roosevelt's life and two weeks before Inauguration Day.

Roosevelt read the letter unperturbed and, although he discussed it far into the night with his advisors, took no action. Perhaps President Hoover's tone had something to do with Roosevelt's attitude, for in the letter Hoover once more outlined at length his theories, counter to Roosevelt's, on the nature and course of the depression and by implication blamed Roosevelt for the current state of alarm. Since the crisis was due to lack of confidence in the Democratic leadership, the way to end it, Hoover asserted, would be for Roosevelt to clarify the public mind on certain essentials: "It would steady the country greatly if there could be prompt assurance that there will be no tampering or inflation of the currency; that the budget will be unquestionably balanced, even if further taxation is necessary; that the Government credit will be maintained by refusal to exhaust it in the issue of securities." [18]

Hoover was well aware how drastic a change in course he was demanding of Roosevelt. Several days later, trying to bring pressure upon Democratic leaders of the Senate, he sent a letter to a Republican senator, presumably to show the Democrats, in which he wrote with remarkable self-revelation: "I realize that if these declarations be made by the President-elect, he will have ratified the whole major program of the Republican Administration; that is, it means the abandonment of 90% of the so-called new deal. But unless this is done, they run a grave danger of precipitating a complete financial debacle. If it is precipitated, the responsibility lies squarely with them for they have had ample warning—unless, of course, such a debacle is part of the 'new deal.' " [19]

It would have taken someone with more forbearance than Roosevelt to reply favorably to a letter written in as antagonistic a tone as Hoover's. He took Hoover's letter so seriously that he meticulously wrote on the envelope the place and time of receipt, then for days failed to answer the letter. Roosevelt had every intention of balancing the budget and keeping the domestic debt ceiling low, but he was not willing to abandon his option to take the United States off the gold standard and devaluate its currency to a level competitive with that of other nations.

In any event, if Roosevelt had given his pledge, he might have stemmed the gold drain, but it is questionable whether the run on banks would have stopped. As it was, his view of the worsening crisis was that there was nothing within the United States that Hoover could do with his aid that Hoover could not do without it; Hoover was still president, and he, Roosevelt, was as yet a private citizen. What would transpire after 4 March, Inauguration Day, was something different, and Roosevelt quietly made his plans. Meanwhile he did nothing as the crisis intensified, bringing banking holidays and severe restrictions from coast to coast.

Economists are perhaps in a better position than historians to evaluate the failure of Hoover and Roosevelt to cooperate with each other. My own suggestions are only those of a political historian.

Beyond question the United States had suffered from remaining on the gold standard while its main competitors for world markets, especially the British, had devalued their currencies. During the depression years, 1929–1932, although world trade had declined only a quarter, American exports had gone down 50 percent. Of course, many factors other than the relatively high valuation of the dollar were involved, including the tariff. While President Hoover was interested in using war debts to obtain some tariff concessions from the British, he was especially hopeful he could persuade the British to put the pound sterling back on gold, which would have lost them the edge they had in obtaining foreign trade. This was the scheme Foreign Office officials regarded as a utopian dream.

Many of Roosevelt's advisors were strongly urging him to abandon the gold standard and let the dollar fall to a level which would make it attractive to nations seeking American goods. It is significant to add that during the interregnum Roosevelt had not entirely abandoned gold orthodoxy; he was tentatively ready to push the British toward a return to gold. His interest was only in obtaining a more competitive relationship for the dollar in the world trade and in using devaluation at home as a means of getting up agricultural prices—in short, he wanted what was being urged upon him by certain international bankers and by some agricultural economists, especially Professor George Warren of Cornell University and his coterie. Once Roosevelt attained these goals he planned to seek international stability through gold. So the plans seemed to read. It is certain, however, that Roosevelt and his advisors were not ready to maintain the gold standard at the cost of a continued outflow of gold and acute deflation.

Two years later, Roosevelt's and Hoover's secretaries of the treasury gave conflicting views in the *New York Times* concerning the gold drain and its effect upon the banking crisis. Henry Morgenthau, Jr., wrote: "Europeans knew that we could not maintain our currency at the old gold level without a ruinous deflation of our prices, trade, and industrial activity. Facing that crisis, the previous administration stubbornly refused to take action, evidently under the impression that that was a proud achievement, when it was obviously economic suicide."

On the next day, Mills retorted: "It was not the maintenance of the gold standard that caused the banking panic of 1933 in the outflow of gold . . . it was definite and growing fear that the new administration meant to do what they ultimately did—that is to abandon the gold standard, and their refusal to cooperate in any way with the outgoing administration." [20]

Put in other words, President Hoover, at the time of the crisis in February 1933, simply would not take the drastic step of embargoing gold or abandoning the gold standard, nor would Roosevelt bind himself in advance to maintain the gold standard. Furthermore, Hoover tried throughout to bend Roosevelt to his wishes, rather than to accommodate himself to the incoming president. He even went so far as to get in touch with the great Democratic conservative, Senator Carter Glass of Virginia, who was considering Roosevelt's offer to become Secretary of the Treasury, and urge Glass to obtain some commitment on Roosevelt's part to gold orthodoxy. Financial editors of the nation's great newspapers had demanded no commitment of Roosevelt, then in the last week before inauguration they began to do so—probably through President Hoover's indirect intervention.[21]

In all of President Hoover's pressuring, there was the assumption that a pledge not to tamper with the gold standard would stop the runs on banks. This is a dubious point, since many individuals with small deposits, and for that matter a good many business corporations, were near the bottom of their financial resources. Lack of confidence in banks and desperate need for money were prime factors in the withdrawals. The temptation to make profits out of a rise in the price of gold was only one cause of the runs.

Concerning the quarrel between Hoover and Roosevelt over the banking problem, Hoover in later years made one telling point— that was the refusal of Roosevelt to support legislation to stop publication of Reconstruction Finance Corporation loans to banks. Speaker John Nance Garner had forced the publication, for he was suspicious of politics being involved in the granting of loans to banks. Publishing lists of these banks no doubt was unsettling, but Roosevelt apparently had reached the point, much like Hoover, at which he would make no concession to his antagonist. The best that can be said for Roosevelt is that the damage had already been done and preventing further publication would have made no particular difference.

Nor can much be said for Roosevelt's own conservative view of the crisis, that the bankers had been engaging in malpractice and now should suffer their punishment. Roosevelt would not endorse massive R. F. C. backing of the banks, which could have saved a great deal of the trouble. Nor did he seem to realize, as the champion of the common people, that they were desperately in need of banks which were open and safe.

On the other hand, throughout the frightening final days before Roosevelt took office, the president-elect was correct in his basic legal view; that is, he, Roosevelt, was a private citizen, and any legal action that President Hoover could take would be one not requiring Roosevelt's agreement. Nothing happened, and at the end of the interregnum the basic position of the two men was as it had been at the beginning.

President Hoover would take no action without the endorsement of the president-elect, but he would also make no concessions toward Roosevelt's point of view, insisting, rather, that whatever was done be something he, Hoover, believed in. Therefore, he did nothing. President-elect Roosevelt, while he became deeply involved in the conduct of foreign relations and in suggesting to the Democratic leaders in Congress what legislation they should or should not support, refused to limit his freedom of action in advance through capitulating to Hoover's requests. Through thick and thin he continued to take the position that he would not accept responsibility until the oath of office made him president.

In retrospect, it is hard to accept Hoover's apocalyptic view that

Roosevelt and the New Dealers were happy to see the economy plummet to new depths so that they could start to build from the bottom. Yet while it is understandable that Roosevelt would not commit himself on gold, it is shocking that he was unwilling to use his great power over Congress to obtain quick emergency passage of some measure to stem the bank runs. True enough, it can be argued that bankers and experts on banking could not agree among themselves as to what needed to be done and that President Hoover certainly would have vetoed any measure which did not fit his own precise specifications. That is scant excuse. Through quick action, the president-elect might have helped cushion the collapse, and even if he had failed through a Hoover veto, he would have had the satisfaction of the attempt. The onus would then have been on President Hoover. But the very fact that a historian, like the contestants, can get involved in trying to assess blame upon either Roosevelt or Hoover is an indication of the nature of the tragedy. This writer would not access blame impartially upon both men, since as the contents of this paper indicate, he is more sympathetic toward Roosevelt and his advisors. Yet there are shadings of grey as well as black and white in the sketch, and the overall impression is one of tragedy. While the grim contest between incoming and outgoing presidents fills the foreground, in the background, as bleak as a Doré etching of Dante in hell, are the American people struggling painfully, trapped in a lake of ice.

IV

Foreign Policy

Hoover's Foreign Policy and the New Left

SELIG ADLER

State University of New York at Buffalo

Selig Adler was born in Baltimore, Maryland. He received his B.A.
degree from the University of Buffalo in 1931 and his M.A. and
Ph.D. degrees from the University of Illinois in 1932 and 1934
respectively. Professor Adler has devoted his teaching career to the
University of Buffalo (presently State University of New York at
Buffalo) where he serves as Samuel P. Capen Professor of History.
He has been a Visiting Professor at Cornell University and the
University of Rochester. His major publications have been the
Isolationist Impulse: Its Twentieth Century Reaction (New York:
Abelard-Schuman, 1957) and The Uncertain Giant, 1921–1941:
American Foreign Policy Between The Wars (New York:
Macmillan, 1965).

The revision of Hoover foreign policy, marked in recent years by
writings of William Appleman Williams and his students, is
emphasized by the Adler essay. He assesses the revisionists'
rehabiliation of Hoover in terms of neo-isolationism, an idea that
is both important and relevant. Furthermore, Adler's analysis is
extremely provocative in declaring that there is a conscious effort
on the part of leftist historians to rehabilitate Hoover in order to
downgrade Roosevelt's accomplishments.

Prior to the advent of the New Left, only minor differences divided
those historians who assessed Herbert Hoover's approach to foreign
affairs. This consensus is not surprising, since strong bonds of
personal memories united those writers who vividly recalled the
depression, the Axis ordeal, and the profound disillusionment
stemming from the postwar rift with Russia and the communization
of China. To these defenders of the American faith, the lessons of
history seemed clear. The Republican Restoration of 1920 had led
to a fragile prosperity, whose collapse triggered a train of foreign
calamities. In contrast, the New Dealers were regarded as forward-

looking men who saved the country from economic chaos and later spared western civilization from the hands of the fascist outlaws. Amidst such a climate of opinion, isolationism became a pejorative term; a catchall word denoting unpreparedness, appeasement, and a denial of global responsibility.[1]

Herbert Hoover proved a favorite target for these writers of the liberal internationalist school. His presidency was portrayed as an era of darkness before the dawning of the New Deal. This animus was exacerbated by the fact that Hoover spoke out and wrote vociferously on contemporary issues during his thirty-two years as expresident. Almost all of his admonitions ran contrary to prevailing trends of opinion and his dire prophecies were usually wrong. The United States, despite his warning, did not become a fascist society because of the war. Moreover, long after the concept had been outmoded, Hoover still boasted of America's ocean moats.[2] At mid-century, the expresident and his disciple, Senator Robert A. Taft, demanded a severely limited American perimeter of defense. They were promptly charged with sounding the bugle for a retreat from global peacekeeping. Further, by equating the Yalta agreements with an appeasement of communism and by holding the Democrats responsible for the loss of the Chinese mainland, Hoover and Taft associated themselves with the right-wing backlash so despised and feared by the liberal intelligentsia.[3] The time was not yet ripe for a new isolationism, for the way had not yet been paved by the prolonged frustration of the Vietnamese War.

While Hoover generally fared badly at the hands of the consensus historians, some of his diplomatic policies did receive accolades. His administration was credited with making public the Clark Memorandum and with returning to de factoism in its recognition policies.[4] Alexander De Conde's seminal monograph convinced our guild that Hoover laid the foundations for the Good Neighbor policy. It was also the Quaker president who withdrew the marines from Nicaragua, planned the evacuation from Haiti, and scrupulously refrained from intervention during a spate of depression-spawned Latin America revolutions.[5] But here, too, luck was not on Hoover's side, since the business collapse undermined the United States market for Latin American staples and cut off the flow of borrowed funds to our southern neighbors. Moreover, the depression led to the ill-fated Smoot-Hawley tariff, which impeded trade with Latin America.[6]

However, the liberal historians did accept at face value Hoover's denunciation of the old-fashioned gunboat imperialism.[7] Yet even in this area misfortune marred the president's record, for he vetoed, on conscientious grounds, a bill providing for the eventual independence of the Philippine Islands. Some writers have recognized the soundness of Hoover's arguments, but inasmuch as Franklin D. Roosevelt cheerfully signed a similar measure, the net result detracted from Hoover's reputation.[8]

The Hoover moratorium on war debts and reparations is usually dismissed by the conventional historians as an intelligent but ineffective approach to a particularly troublesome problem.[9] In addition, the more perceptive orthodox interpreters acknowledge that despite Hoover's postpresidential effusions, during his White House years he was more internationally minded than any of his predecessors save Theodore Roosevelt and Wilson.[10] Yet at this point come the caveats which, in the eyes of the liberal writers, negated Hoover's internationalism. No single American, so the argument runs, did more to promote the American economic empire, cut down on the foreign carrying trade by subsidizing the United States merchant marine, and reduce overseas imports by developing substitute domestic products. These selfish measures made it virtually impossible for America's foreign debtors to collect the dollar reserves needed to pay the war debts which their hard-nosed creditor in Washington insisted on collecting.[11] Further, it was President Hoover who signed the detested Smoot-Hawley tariff bill with six gold pens. Countless college students have learned that 1028 economists warned the president of the consequences of his act; consequences which produced sheer chaos in the field of international exchange.[12]

Nothing that Hoover did, however, did more to invoke the scorn of the diplomatic specialists than his handling of the 1931 Manchurian crisis. To understand this prejudice, it is necessary to recall the prevailing intellectual climate prior to the seismic shift of opinion set in motion by the Vietnamese catastrophe. Until then the great majority of post-Pearl Harbor observers of international relations reasoned that the Axis nightmare could have been avoided had the Japanese been halted in their attempt to disrupt the Versailles and Washington Conference settlements. The events that followed the Manchurian coup had proven that peace was indivisible. Therefore, the liberal school argued, each act of aggression, no matter how remote from American shores, had to be promptly halted.

Inasmuch as the chain reaction of aggression was touched off while Hoover was president, the blame fell upon him for clinging to the notion that the mobilization of condemnatory world opinion could halt the drift toward international anarchy. His critics often forgot that until 1937 Roosevelt's brand of isolationism did not differ from that of his predecessor. The liberals, however, preferred to recall FDR's later actions, which allowed Americans to emerge "strong and respected, refreshed in their faith . . . in the ultimate triumph of justice in human affairs." [13] Hence historians concluded that the foreign problems that beset Roosevelt came because Hoover refused to take the calculated risks which might have stopped the Tokyo war hawks.

This simplistic interpretation is vulnerable on several counts. First of all, writers tended to overemphasize the differences at the time of the Manchurian crisis between President Hoover and Secretary of State Henry L. Stimson; they stress the latter's willingness to risk war in order to preserve peace. Stimson, we are told, viewed nonrecognition as merely a prelude to stronger action, while Hoover relied entirely upon moral suasion. But if one reads Hoover's *Memoirs* today regarding his 1931 actions, his reasoning is convincing. The president thought that there was something to be said for Japan's rights in Manchuria, that the United States could not patrol the world, and that therefore it was highly dangerous "to stick pins in tigers." [14] Sensible as this sounds in 1973, as long as the concept of global policemanship remained popular, it seemed to historians that Hoover's decision to condemn Japan without agreeing to use either economic or military coercion served only to focus Tokyo's enmity upon Washington. To oppose aggression with weapons that are irritating but ineffective, Julius W. Pratt wrote at the height of the Cold War, "is worse than not to oppose it at all." [15] On the other hand, Richard Hofstadter early grasped Hoover's dilemma by observing that had the president threatened Japan with force, his domestic critics would have promptly accused him of blowing up a foreign crisis in order to distract attention from his domestic failures.[16] But less sagacious observers complained that Hoover's Quaker orientation led him first to weaken the striking power of the navy by underbuilding and then failing to use what navy he had. The net result was that the ease of Japan's success in Manchuria became "a signpost beckoning Mussolini and Hitler" on the road to aggression.[17]

In this fashion, with the exception of rock-ribbed conservative writers, right-wing revisionists, and members of Hoover's personal retinue, the guild took historical judgment upon the diplomacy of 1929–1933. It is significant, however, that a brace of left-of-center historians were among the first professional historians to view Hoover in a more objective light.

In his celebrated vignette of 1948, Richard Hofstadter praised Hoover for his cogent realization that the harsh Versailles settlement would force Germany to choose between communism and reaction. While the Columbia professor classified the Quaker president as the last authentic spokesman of "laissez-faire liberalism," Hofstadter, like William A. Williams after him, seemed more sympathetic to Hoover than to the second Roosevelt.[18] This is not mere coincidence, since Hoover and Roosevelt have traditionally formed historical antipodes. Hence those writers on the left who were skeptical of New Deal reforms have been prone to narrow down the differences between the two men. Thus Hofstadter concluded that FDR was simply more subtle than his predecessor, but no less determined to replace the European imperialisms "by a liberal and benevolent American penetration" of the colonial world under the guise of "international welfare work." [19]

Richard N. Current, a progressive in the LaFollette tradition, tried in the 1950s to reverse the consensus' approval of Stimson's spirited diplomacy in favor of Hoover's innate caution.[20] Current admired Hoover's recognition of the limitations of American power; a restriction that he felt served the country far better than the "combat psychology" of Stimson.[21] Hoover, Current argued, understood that only a revision of the post-Versailles status quo would save Berlin and Tokyo from quixotic foreign adventures. However, Current wrote at a time when the Hoover variety of limited internationalism was distinctly out of fashion. Hence he did not convince many of his colleagues of Hoover's diplomatic foresight, albeit he did succeed in calling attention to the president's part in formulating what is now generally termed the Hoover-Stimson Doctrine.[22]

Meanwhile, there emerged from William A. Williams's seminars at the University of Wisconsin a new generation of iconoclastic diplomatic historians destined to challenge many long-held dogmas. As far as Williams himself is concerned, his appreciation of Hoover's sterling qualities came only gradually. His 1952 survey of American-Soviet relations contains little but disdain for the Quaker president. Hoover, Williams wrote, matched his faith in capitalism by an unflinching belief that Bolshevism would collapse of its own errors. Hoover's sneaking sympathy for Japan in 1931, Williams explained, stemmed in part from his fear of Asiatic communism. Hence the president rebuffed indirect overtures from Moscow during the Manchurian crisis despite the fact that some of these offers might have strengthened his hand. As to Hoover's post-White House career, Williams pointed out that the former president was naive enough to believe that he could give Bolshevism the *coup de grâce* by organizing a special group to help Finland during the Winter War of 1939–40.[23]

The first glimmer of empathy for Hoover came two years later in Williams's oft-quoted article, "The Legend of Isolationism in the 1920s." The author here conceded that while secretary of commerce, Hoover pushed the United States's "informal empire" into distant parts of the globe in order to promote domestic prosperity, foment counterrevolution, and preserve global respect for free enterprise. But Williams had good things to say about Hoover's dislike of Wilsonian "moral imperialism," his opposition to Theodore Roosevelt's blatant expansionism, and his distrust of certain vulnerable parts of the League Covenant. Further, Hoover was credited with expanding the "opportunistic nationalism" of the pre-1914 progressives into a bond of union among capitalist powers joined together by a "mutuality of interests." [24]

Williams's next major work, *The Tragedy of American Diplomacy*, proved of cardinal importance in revising the findings of the orthodox interpreters. It was in this book that Williams's surprising attraction to Herbert Hoover began to take concrete form. He portrayed Hoover as a hardheaded realist, far ahead of his generation in comprehending that only a drastic reform of liberal capitalism would halt the global trend toward socialism. Recognizing the weak spots in the American economic system long before its 1929 collapse, Secretary Hoover tried to shore up the economy at home. Further, Hoover foresaw that a new general war would yield a rash of Marxist revolutions and he sought to prevent this conflict by forging bonds of mutual interest between the Atlantic powers.[25] Hence Hoover sought to restrict foreign loans to productive enterprises, but Wall Street did not heed his admonitions, preferring to play a short-run game.[26] Williams also emphasized that Hoover was a friend of trade unionism, that his suggestions to relieve the farm plight were constructive and that he saw presciently "the kind of syndicate capitalism that the New Deal would fasten on the country." [27] While admitting that Hoover was a die-hard enemy of communism, Williams explained that he never risked war with the Soviets, always believing that Moscow would be lured from its economic errors by the gainful aspects of free enterprise.[28] Obviously Williams was attracted to Hoover's essential pacifism, for he underlined that while the president did not approve of Japanese expansionism, he refused to court the "general disaster" of war. Nonetheless, Williams's favorable treatment of Hoover is paradoxical, for the principal thrust of his book is against the very kind of informal American economic empire that the secretary of commerce did so much to promote.[29]

The Contours of American History, Williams's next book, poses a similar perplexity. Hoover, we read, recognized the fragile nature of the post-Armistice prosperity. He also realized the true potential of world revolutionary movements and tried to reduce that potential by refurbishing capitalism. But he also understood that other nations regarded the United States as an imperial power in the Leninist sense of the word and that this recognition could lead to a new war. He tried to head off this catastrophe by making American economic expansion helpful to the development "of backward or crippled countries." [30] But in this effort Hoover failed because the leaders of the "corporation community" of Coolidge's America refused to accept his cogent suggestions.[31]

Inasmuch as Williams's praise of Hoover until 1970 was muted, other members of the New Left school seem not to have followed the master's lead in this instance. The subject did not attract many leftist writers, and from the existing evidence one detects no trace of softness toward the Quaker president on the part of Williams's disciples. Hoover's emphasis upon voluntarism in promoting the ends of government, one New Leftist explained, amounted only to the "mailed fist in the velvet glove." The article hints at Hoover's friendliness toward labor unionism and concedes that much of the New Deal stemmed from Republican antidepression remedies. But this faint praise is offset by charging Hoover with fostering monopolies and cartels. We also learn that the president tried to convert agriculture into "a centrally cartelized industry." Hence, the author concludes, Hoover began the precedent, followed by Roosevelt, of creating a "corporate economy of fascism." A footnote awkwardly explains that neither major party tried to create a one-party system in totalitarian form simply because maintaining two parties agreed on the same goals better served the purposes of the would-be American fascists. In this article Hoover remains the "bumbling reactionary" whose image was overblackened by the liberal historians in order to accentuate the accomplishments of their favorite, the second Roosevelt.[32]

Here the image of Hoover rested until Williams, in an expanded book review, startled the historical guild by an outright rehabilitation. Williams now contended that Hoover understood that traditional Republican dollar diplomacy must be destroyed by positive action rather than by mere empty rhetoric. Even as secretary of commerce, Hoover had begun such action by opposing foreign loans to states who would use the money for military build-ups and unwise foreign adventures. To the amazement of many of Williams's readers, who regarded Hoover as a prime architect of informal American imperialism, they now learned that he had promoted foreign trade to provide mutual advantage for both buyer and seller. Hoover in his generation stood almost alone in his keen awareness of the global picture of Uncle Sam as a greedy imperialist. This role Hoover sought to correct by "non-imperial and anti-imperial action." [33]

Williams's review provoked a great deal of wonder and discussion, since Herbert Hoover seemed to be the strangest kind of a hero for Bill Williams, who had so long inveighed against pushing the frontiers of American industrial capitalism beyond our borders. "The hope of our commerce," said Secretary Hoover in 1921, "lies in the establishment of American firms abroad, distributing American goods under American direction." [34] In equal measure Hoover had supported the quest of United States oil tycoons for new overseas fields. Nor had he cared very much about the monopolization of overseas oil reserves, so long as that monopoly was held by Americans.[35] Scarcely a year before Williams's review appeared, one of his followers had singled Hoover out as the prime mover in expanding the Open Door policy in order to displace the colonial trade of England and France.[36] "We must," said Hoover during his 1928 campaign, "find a market for our surpluses." Moreover, it was Hoover's Commerce Department which had distributed the public relations propaganda of the monopolistic public utilities in wholesale lots.[37]

Who was more consistently paranoiac on the communist menace than Herbert Hoover? As Williams himself had previously disclosed, in 1918 the great humanitarian had refused to feed the starving Soviet Union unless Lenin would take the suicidal step of halting all military operations against the White Russians.[38] About the same time, the Food Administrator, after dismissing Bolshevism as "utter foolishness," still urged President Wilson to crush Russian Marxism before it could spread.[39] A decade later, Hoover accused his opponent Alfred E. Smith of advocating "state socialism," albeit the New York governor's campaign was managed by a member of the Du Pont Company complex.[40] The Kremlin,

Hoover was certain in 1932, was behind the Bonus marchers, whom he had dispersed with an undue show of force.[41] Nor did the long time expresident ever concede that communism was here to stay, for he cheerily predicted that the Marxists would never make a "go of it" in Asia.[42] Hoover, to the end, upheld his decision not to recognize the USSR and he deplored the loss of China which, he declared, had spread human slavery from 200 million to 800 million souls.[43]

Other factors in Hoover's career seem utterly at odds with Williams's own new-Marxist orientation. In 1924 Hoover had championed Japanese exclusion from the immigration quotas, arguing that the separation of races was justified because a mixture of bloods, he said, runs contrary to biological facts.[44] The very idea of equality, the Quaker president once noted, was "part of the claptrap of the French Revolution." [45] For all of these reasons Williams's depiction of Hoover as an advanced progressive is not convincing. It would seem that Hofstadter took a much more accurate measure of the man when he emphasized Hoover's passion for setting the clock back to return to "conditions, real or imagined, of the past." [46]

What then were Williams's motives in refurbishing Hoover's reputation? Probably the best answer lies in the attraction that the president's foreign policy holds for men of the New Left persuasion. To understand this attraction it is necessary to examine the persevering attempt of the radicals to rescue the pre-Pearl Harbor isolationists from the dustbins of history. At a time when conventional historians wrote off the America Firsters as myopic xenophobes, Williams insisted that the liberals in the isolationist coalition were deserving of reappraisal. Their criticism of the extravagant use of American power, Williams noted as early as 1959, "was insightful and fundamental." He added that the liberal isolationists saw clearly that while the United States could not democratize the rest of the world, it was dutybound to help uplift the disadvantaged nations. Williams singled out for special praise the bête noire of the liberal internationalists, Senator William E. Borah.[47] Other revisionists in the mold of Williams emphasize the liberal reformist ideas of the interwar isolationists. Their program is said to have special relevance today, since they insisted on American freedom of action in each foreign crisis. This, of course, is another way of saying that the United States must disengage itself from its string of post-1945 alliances on the grounds that these agreements might draw us into war.[48] Much of this cordiality toward the isolationists of yesteryear has come because, like their fathers in the depression decade, present-day Americans face the task of self-rehabilitation and social regeneration. This challenge, the revisionists insist, must take precedence over bailing out foreign nations from their troubles.[49] At a time of widespread fear of the military-industrial complex, it is easy to sympathize with Senator Gerald P. Nye and his followers, who tried to curb the munitions cartel which had allegedly lured the United States into World War I. "The three ideas [current in the 1930s] of freedom of action, non-intervention and abhorrence of war have," one observer notes, "a potent relevance for our view of American foreign relations today." [50]

This newlyfound appreciation of the classical isolationists is not confined to the New Left school. Robert W. Tucker has recently reminded us that while isolationism never meant "quitting the world," it did mean a stringent rein on the kind of self-assumed global responsibility that led to the awful agony of Vietnam. It is therefore, writes Tucker, worthy of study and possible emulation.[51] The isolationists, another recent writer holds, might well point out the path to the kind of qualified internationalism which the United States must henceforth pursue.[52] Such a policy would prove congruent to the present facts of international life, since the missile revolution in weaponry makes full defense possible without the need of alliance territory. The wheel has now come full circle, since we are back to the assumptions of the Hoover era, with national defense resting upon our own soil.[53]

In light of the foregoing, it is easy to comprehend Williams's nostalgic longing for the kind of limited internationalism that Hoover always advocated. The Hoover-Taft blueprint for a "Fortress America" appears much more inviting today than when it was broached during the late Truman years. Similarly, many of Hoover's pronouncements during his White House years have been rendered *au courant* by the seismic shift in values triggered by the Vietnamese nightmare. Historians now read with an approving eye Hoover's cautions against foreign entanglements, his hostility to overspending on defense, his emphasis upon the dangers of imperialism, and his dread of the "eternal malign forces" of the outside world.[54] To younger writers, who reached their maturity in the volatile world of nuclear tensions, restraint in the use of force makes good sense. Even Arthur Schlesinger, Jr., whose historical reputation rests upon a laudatory treatment of Franklin Roosevelt, now follows Herbert Hoover in conceding that the United States must henceforth lead the world by good example.[55] To a generation wearied of the task of global peacekeeping, Hoover's contention that American internationalism be confined to sincere cooperation with moral movements devoted to furthering the processes of peace holds great appeal. Moreover, with the intelligentsia in full-scale revolt against nuclear overkill, the Quaker president's stout efforts for disarmament draw fresh admiration.

In addition, some of Hoover's prophecies have come true. He correctly reasoned that the Japanese could never subdue China and that if they remained on the continent long enough they would be either absorbed or expelled. There has also been praise for Hoover's rugged determination never to preserve peace in foreign climes by waging war.[56] Hoover's pledge that the United States has no hates, wishes no more territorial possessions, harbors no military threats, and refuses to act as Big Brother to the world sound poignant today.[57] These words are especially welcome to the present community of dissent, for they embody that community's articles of faith.

Will the New Left school once more follow Williams's lead with a detailed reassessment of Hoover's place in history? It is still too early to be certain, but it is an educated guess that they will. New Deal specialists within the school have indicted Roosevelt for, in the name of reform, fastening industrial capitalism on the country all the more firmly.[58] Just as the liberal historians denigrated Hoover in order to make FDR's fame all the more lustrous, so it seems likely that Hoover will be built up in order to cut his successor down to size. This task may even prove congenial to the radical revisionists, for they could argue that Hoover at least was honestly procapitalist. Moreover, he pursued a foreign policy which appears enticing as the United States gropes once more for a sensible mean between a barren isolationism and an exaggerated concern for minor global convulsions.

A Reevaluation of Herbert Hoover's Foreign Policy

JOAN HOFF WILSON

California State University, Sacramento

Joan Hoff Wilson was born in Butte, Montana in 1937. She received her B.A. from the University of Montana, her M.A. from Cornell University, and her Ph.D. from the University of California, Berkeley. She is a former Woodrow Wilson Fellow and Fulbright Fellow and currently is Associate Professor of History at California State University, Sacramento. Her first book, American Business and Foreign Policy, 1921–1933 (Lexington: University of Kentucky Press, 1971) received honorable mention in the 1967 Frederick Jackson Turner award competition and received first place in the 1972 Stuart L. Bernath Prize competition sponsored by the Society for Historians of American Foreign Relations.

Wilson assesses Hoover's presidential foreign policies in light of his earlier record as secretary of commerce. She labels Hoover an "independent internationalist" whose "personal philosophy prevented him from endorsing any limitless open-ended" international concept in both political and economic policies. Furthermore, Wilson praises Hoover because his placing greater emphasis on internal self-sufficiency than did most diplomatists tempered his advocacy of the Open Door policy.

It is impossible to discuss Hoover's foreign policy as president without referring to his years as secretary of commerce. This is because it was during those years from 1921 to 1928 that most of his major foreign policy ideas were first given practical implementation. As with his domestic policies, Hoover hoped that the presidency would allow him to perfect ideas and carry out more successfully certain diplomatic ideas he had long held. Some of his first views on foreign policy, for example, were the result of his travels abroad as a young international engineer around the turn of the century.[1] Most of them, however, came out of his experiences during World War I, beginning in 1914 with his Belgium relief activities.[2]

Hoover's activities in the field of foreign affairs, like those of so many of his Republican and Democrat contemporaries, can be characterized by the term "independent internationalism." [3] The implicit assumption of independent internationalism was that the United States should cooperate in world affairs when it could not or did not want to solve a particular problem through unilateral actions. Independent internationalism was a realistic diplomatic method followed by many nations. But it was not systematically practiced by the United States until after World War I because it required the heightened appreciation of the concept of collective security that resulted from the unsuccessful fight for ratification of the League of Nations.

In practicing independent internationalism as a diplomatic method Hoover followed cooperative guidelines similar to those he had in the field of domestic policy, and in neither area did he subscribe to a "return to normalcy." For example, just as he believed that the unity, cooperation, and sacrifice demanded by the war had hastened the formation of new domestic relationships, he also thought the war had promoted domestic economic and political cooperation on a greater scale than ever before. Similarly, it had promoted unprecedented international economic interdependence. On 25 May 1921 the *Wall Street Journal* quoted the new secretary of commerce as saying that "international conditions . . . will become normal, not as the term was understood before the war, but normal in sympathy with vastly changed conditions consequent upon the war. . . ."

At the same time, however, Hoover came back from Europe in 1919 committed more strongly than ever to the uniqueness of the American system at home and to the mission of the United States abroad. In both cases he attributed this singularness to the moral, political, and economic superiority of Americans, and he was convinced that the economic strength of the United States was vital to the economic health of the entire world. Therefore he frankly recommended "Americanism" to Europeans as the solution for their postwar problems. This meant the practice of the traditional virtues of thrift, public and "neighborly service tempered by self-interest, efficiency," and the "maximum exertion of every individual within his physical ability." [4] In retrospect it is possible to argue that Hoover did not emphasize domestic economic development at home exclusively out of nationalistic self-interest based on American chauvinism, but out of a sincere concern for world prosperity. However, it is also now possible to see that his belief in the uniqueness of America and his concern for maintaining its domestic well-being had a moderating effect on the brand of internationalism he espoused after World War I, especially on his tariff and loan policies—both of which reflected his desire to see America become as prosperous and economically self-sufficient as possible through internal development. For example, at the very beginning of his career as secretary of commerce he had defensively asserted that if the United States had to, it could, "after a long term of years re-establish its material prosperity and comfort without European trade." Later, during the Great Depression, he also pointed out that "the potential and redeeming strength of the United States" was that "we are economically more self-contained than any other great nation." By this he meant that in 1930 American exports amounted to only 6 to 10 percent of its total productivity. Because "we consume an average of about 90 percent of our own production of commodities," Hoover argued, Americans could boost domestic consumption so that 97 percent of all domestic agricultural and manufacturing products, regardless of economic conditions in Europe, could be sold within the continental United States and its territories.[5]

But his insistence upon America's potential economic independence did not become a major factor in his economic foreign policy until after 1933 because it was countered throughout the 1920s by his other strong postwar belief in the idea that "no nation can morally or physically survive continued isolation" in light of the "economic interdependence of the world." [6] For Hoover, economic self-sufficiency was a luxury the United States happened to enjoy to a greater degree than other nations, until the depression made its maintenance an absolute necessity. Nonetheless, even in the 1920s, his concern for preserving what economic self-containment the United States did have forced him to try to reconcile his international experiences with his nationalist beliefs as he proceeded to draft a comprehensive plan for the reconstruction of war-torn Europe. And he very nearly succeeded.

Since the postwar idea that democratic nations were moving in the direction of greater economic interdependence and cooperation initially dominated Hoover's economic foreign policy, he viewed world peace as more of an economic than a political problem. Furthermore, the unusual prosperity of the war years had turned the United States into a creditor nation for the first time in its history.

No single individual in business or government circles completely understood the complex ramifications of this dramatic and rapid change in the world economic position of the United States or of the general economic maladjustments between nations in the post-war period. Hoover at least saw that economic reform at home, in addition to reconstruction of foreign economic systems, was necessary for future world stability.

Therefore his comprehensive postwar economic plan called for a more equitable American trade balance (although he did not advocate a low tariff, he did think that the United States should begin to increase its imports of nonstrategic goods and should become less dependent upon both agriculture and manufacturing exports than in the past); foreign loan supervision (he advocated controls not only to help guarantee that private American loans would constructively contribute to world productivity and prosperity, but also because they would counter the attractiveness of high foreign interest rates, thus preserving American capital for needed internal development); economic "associationalism" and self-regulating corporatism based on voluntary decentralization and cooperation (which would preserve both a sense of social responsibility and individualism); domestic monetary controls (these were aimed at stabilizing prices and wages through the actions of the Federal Reserve Board and through indirect government regulation of business cycles); and finally the creation of a mutually beneficial world community among industrial nations under American leadership, based on voluntary cooperation among commercial and financial interests involved in international business.[7]

Hoover and other internationally oriented policy makers insisted that this new world community or "commercial league of nations" be based on the principle of equal economic opportunity, that is, the Open Door policy. In Hoover's case, equal economic opportunity on an international scale was an obvious counterpart to the equal opportunity he wanted for Americans at home and to his desire to see the country maintain as much economic self-sufficiency or independence as possible. However, as an independent internationalist, Hoover advocated only a selective application of the Open Door policy. Thus, he espoused it most eagerly in areas where the United States faced serious economic competition, such as the Far East and the Middle East, but he almost never encouraged it where the opposite was true, in the Philippines, the Caribbean, and Central America.

From Hoover's personal, ideological point of view, the Open

Door policy presented just the right blend of nationalist self-interest with internationalist altruism. In theory, it meant a harmonious "world economy" where peaceful cooperative economic expansion substituted for political and military confrontations. In practice, equal economic opportunity in world trade and finance benefited the strongest competitor and Hoover was convinced of the postwar ability of the United States to compete successfully if granted the same opportunities as all other nations to buy, sell, invest. In the long run, the principle of unrestricted equal economic opportunity undermined the creation of a mutually beneficial world community of industrial nations, although it did insure American financial and commercial domination after 1920.[8] Because Hoover's personal philosophy prevented him from endorsing any limitless, open-ended concept and because he placed much greater emphasis on achieving internal economic self-sufficiency than most diplomatists, his advocacy of the Open Door policy was more tempered than that of his contemporaries or later generations of Americans. This, in part, explains his current popularity among New Left historians discussed below.

For one thing, this emphasis on obtaining domestic self-sufficiency limited Hoover's expansionist views after World War I by making him appreciate the need to coordinate economic and political policies abroad, so that the one did not work to further domestic development while the other retarded it. It also inclined him toward a noninterventionist or noncoercive military policy. This was especially true in the area of political foreign policy, where he insisted on persuasive and cooperative tactics rather than competitive or forceful ones. While his economic foreign policy was much more combative and competitive, even here he usually assumed a characteristically middle position with limited objectives that fell between the extremes of internationalism and nationalism. While he was not a pacifist, he did believe that no new economic or political world community could be achieved through the use of force and that military action abroad usually created more domestic problems than it solved. So in his foreign as well as his domestic policies Hoover assumed a middleman role of the "buffer" and tried to shape public opinion along moderate lines through the use of educational publicity that appealed to a combination of altruism and self-interest. Failing in this, however, he almost always remained true to his own beliefs regardless of public opinion.[9]

Because of his carefully thought out economic and ideological views, Hoover was particularly well equipped as an independent internationalist to begin to formulate modern American foreign policy both during and after World War I. Although he did not start his official career as a diplomatist until he became a member of President Wilson's War Council in March 1918, he had been unofficially and privately engaged in work of a diplomatic nature beginning with his experiences as a promotional agent for the Panama-Pacific Exposition in 1912. During and immediately following the war, he served as chairman of the Commission for the Relief of Belgium (1914–1920), as Food Administrator (1917–1920), as a member of the War Trade Council (1917–1920), as chairman of the United States Grain Corporation (1917–1919), as alternating chairman of the Inter-Allied Food Council (1917–1918), as chairman of the Sugar Equalization Board (1918–1919), and as director-general of the American Relief Administration in Europe (1918–1920).[10]

Because he was committed theoretically to the ideal of economic self-sufficiency for the United States, as Food Administrator, Hoover opposed any postwar program that "even looks like inter-allied control of our economic resources" and thwarted all Allied efforts to turn the Food Council into a reconstruction and relief agency. Instead, he favored the creation of a new organization which would insure independent American control over its own food, raw materials, and shipping. This was in keeping with the advice he later gave Woodrow Wilson. As a member of the Supreme Economic Council and the President's Committee of Economic Advisers for the Peace Conference, Hoover advised against American participation in the various economic and military commissions established under the Treaty of Versailles, and against the John Maynard Keynes plan for cooperative reconstruction financing of Europe based on multigovernment guaranteed bonds. At the same time, he and John Foster Dulles cautioned the president that he should not appear to be opposing general economic cooperation and strongly urged the creation of an International Economic Council to carry on the work of the Supreme Economic Council until the League of Nations was operational. When this failed to materialize by the time he was coordinating relief for Europe in 1919, Hoover suggested establishing "some sort of an economic committee" so that all domestic efforts connected with the "granting of private and public credits and in the supplying of raw materials and food to various countries of Europe" could be coordinated. Not surprisingly, therefore, at the Chicago Foreign Trade Financing Conference in 1920, he supported the idea of organizing a domestic corporation "through which credits could flow, with proper checks against speculative,

wasteful and bad loans." Along with international financiers like
Norman H. Davis, Paul M. Warburg, Benjamin Strong, and
Thomas W. Lamont, Hoover wanted to see the powers of the War
Finance Corporation extended to handle immediate credit advances
to European countries in desperate need of raw materials and manufactured goods. But unlike these men, he did not want the United
States government to "resort to direct loans . . . to foreign governments to promote commerce" following the war. Predicting the
emergence of a "new Economic Era," Hoover recognized that traditional individual competition had to give way to more cooperation if America was to retain and expand foreign markets. At the
same time, he wanted this done in a manner which would preserve
the principles of "private property and individual initiative to the
extent that this was possible." [11]

In other words, Hoover was clearly committed to the private
financing of Europe's reconstruction following World War I—financing which was to be based, as it was in his domestic economic
policies, on the principles of voluntary cooperation and self-regulation among private, multinational corporations with a minimum of
state intervention. Such an economic approach would not only lessen
the chance of future wars based on state-directed economic competition, but it would also allow the United States to take the lead
in organizing loose economic coordination between the major European nations along the same voluntary and cooperative lines.
Only economic cooperation at home and economic coordination
abroad, according to Hoover, would allow the combination of immediate self-interest and future self-sufficiency for the United States
with postwar European recovery and harmonious global trading
conditions. (When American financiers proved incapable of cooperatively regulating themselves while privately financing the reconstruction of Europe, Hoover, as secretary of commerce, recommended government controls, but immediately upon returning from
Europe in 1919 he first turned his attention to the ratification controversy.)

Following the war Hoover became a critical, but nonetheless
strong, supporter of both the League of Nations and of the Versailles peace settlement. As a new member of the League to Enforce
Peace, he initially took a very strong stand against reservations,
saying on 28 October 1919, that if "we attempt now to revise the
Treaty we shall tread a road through European chaos." By the end
of the debate over ratification, however, he asked Wilson to accept

all of the Republican reservations, since even the "undesirable" ones "do not seem to me to imperil the great principle of the League of Nations to prevent war." At the same time, Hoover pointed out the dangers as well as the advantages of the peace settlement by concentrating not on the "moral idealism of the League" but on the "issues of self-interest," which he thought could best be used to appeal to the American people.[12] This was in keeping with his own ideological conviction that altruism alone was not usually sufficient to motivate support for an abstract cause—a concept the Wilsonians in general and Wilson in particular found irritating.

Despite his personal reservations about the League turning into an "armed alliance" or a "super-government" and all the economic imperfections of the treaty, Hoover always insisted that "time and encouragement is [sic] needed to develop the Treaty constructively —and it cannot develop without the League." So he supported United States entrance into the League on the grounds that Americans could no longer enjoy the "pretense of an insularity that we do not possess" and that such a peacekeeping agency could "minimize war" by marshalling public opinion and moral and economic sanctions against aggressive nations. Finally, he justified the League as a means for "joining the moral forces of the world to reduce the dangers of growing armies, navies, national antagonism . . . [and] the spread of Bolshevism." [13] "No one," he asserted to Warren G. Harding on 2 August 1920, "except the former enemy and Bolsheviki and their sympathizers advocate abandonment of the Treaty."

Hoover remained suspicious, however, of Harding's commitment to the League during the presidential campaign of 1920. So, in the fall, he joined thirty other prominent Republicans in signing the October Declaration. This document attempted to assure the American people that a vote for the Republican party in November would be a vote for entrance into the League. Hoover was personally convinced that the "sincerity, integrity and statesmanship of the Republican party" was at stake on the League issue. After Harding won the election and denounced the League, Hoover continued to insist that the 1920 election was "distinctly in favor of the participation of the country in some form of international agreement for the maintenance of peace." Even after all hope for American entrance faded in the course of the decade, as secretary of commerce, he unsuccessfully continued to press for close cooperation with the new international body. As president, Hoover finally succeeded in establishing "systematic cooperation with the League in all of its

nonpolitical functions, including military and naval conferences,"
one being the first on-site investigation, in 1933, of a controversy
between two Latin American nations.[14]

His position during the ratification controversy after World
War I was characteristic of his desire to adopt a middle course between extremes—in this case between the "ideal of isolationism"
and "moral domination" of the world through internationalism.
"Many of us want neither extreme," he said at Johns Hopkins University on 23 February 1920. This middle position rested on a foreign policy principle to which Hoover remained true the rest of his
life: the idea that limited moral and political involvement with the
world, accompanied by controlled economic expansion, was valid
and could be distinguished from the less desirable extremes of overly
righteous internationalism (associated with the Wilsonian position)
or the extreme nationalism of irreconcilables like Hiram Johnson
and William E. Borah. During the fight over ratification before
1920, however, he had not developed or articulated this particular
brand of independent internationalism clearly enough to influence
foreign policy appreciably by uniting the one segment of American
society with which he was most identified; namely, the business
interests of the country.

Because of his business expertise, it is not surprising to find that
Hoover was extremely active in the area of economic foreign policy,
both as secretary of commerce and president. While he was not always successful in promulgating his ideas and policies in this field,
it is his economic foreign policy which has attracted the attention of
historians in recent years, because of his vast understanding of postwar economic problems. For example, Hoover clearly understood
that United States foreign policy following World War I was complicated because the country had become a creditor nation for the
first time in its history. It is now relatively easy to see that this
fact, along with certain prewar problems exacerbated during the
years 1914–1918, "completely altered the equilibrium of international payments."

These economic maladjustments between nations were largely the
result of overproduction in agriculture, increased competition for
dwindling foreign markets, especially among the older industrialized
nations, and the failure of the United States to adapt its commercial
policies to its new creditor status. What the First World War did,
then, was to accelerate an existing international balance-of-payments
problem with allied war debts and German reparations. It also

created the opportunity for the United States to replace British domination in world trade and finance. Many business and government leaders reasoned that the United States had both the moral and economic right to seize such an opportunity because of its unique world mission. Hoover was one of them. But unlike most, he had a comprehensive plan for dealing with the postwar balance-of-payment problems. Only those aspects of the plan involving co-ordination of tariff, foreign loan and Allied debt, and commercial policies of the United States will be discused here.[15]

Hoover's tariff views were significant at the time, not only because he occupied influential national offices between 1921 and 1933, but also because he was an internationally prominent business spokesmen who simultaneously supported what appeared to be contradictory positions on tariff policy. That is, Hoover took a nationalist position by favoring high protective duties, espeically on farm products, while at the same time he supported an internationalist position by advocating the principle of flexibility, an increase in the investigatory powers of the Federal Tariff Commission, and the expansion of American trade through the negotiation of commercial treaties with unconditional most-favored-nation clauses.[16]

Because the tariff was only one part of his multifaceted plans for the reconstruction of the war-torn world, Hoover maintained there was no contradiction in his tariff views. Tariff policy never became an end in itself for Hoover as it did with certain protectionist groups, like the Boston Home Market Club, and some agricultural interests. He always realized that, by itself, it could accomplish little in the way of transforming "the whole superorganization of our economic life" at home and abroad. Its effectiveness depended upon how well it was integrated into a general plan for worldwide economic reconstruction and reform, based on equality of opportunity and under American leadership.

Moreover, Hoover believed that the volume of imports to the United States depended more upon the internal prosperity of this country than on high or low customs duties. But he did not opt for low duties, because he was convinced by Commerce Department data that the protective system was one of maintaining a high standard of living, domestic prosperity, and some semblance of economic autonomy, since high tariff duties helped to control imports and to expand the domestic market for greater consumption of American agricultural and manufactured goods. He also was convinced that an indiscriminate lowering of the tariff would not increase American imports enough to help European nations pay their debts to this country or to help sick industries, agriculture, and textiles export their surpluses.

All nations, Hoover said in 1930, proceed on the "basis that domestic prosperity will result [from import duties] and that the protective principle is in itself the largest encouragement to foreign trade through the creation of buying [power] of their own citizens." With equal conviction, he publicly asserted again and again between 1921 and 1933 that "the American tariff did not strangle the buying power of foreign nations" because trade was no longer a matter of a one-to-one relationship between two nations, but "polyangular" among many nations. "World trade," he said in 1928, "has become more of the nature of a common pool into which all nations pour goods or credits and from which they retake goods and credit." It is worth noting, however, that at least on one occasion as secretary of commerce, Hoover privately confessed to a group of businessmen that only time and experience would prove whether his theories about the value of a high tariff were right or wrong and the same applied to those who wanted to lower duties. Publicly, however, he insisted that "there is no practical force in the contention that we cannot have a protective tariff and a growing foreign trade. We have both today." [17]

What Hoover and his economic advisers ignored, in the course of the 1920s, were the broader questions of whether or not the United States was "importing as much as the surplus on her balance of payments on current account required"; and the degree to which increased American exports were responsible for the overall decline in the exports of western European nations following the war. Also, Hoover personally made too much of what was called "invisible exports" in his defense of high import duties.[18]

For all of these reasons, as secretary of commerce and as a depression president, Hoover defended the high tariff policy of the Republican party. But he did not do so out of blind faith in protectionism, even after the depression began. For example, he was convinced by 1930, on the basis of Commerce Department reports and no little amount of chauvinism, that high American rates would not harm world trade even in time of depression. What Hoover did not see was that once the United States ceased to export capital as a result of the Great Depression, the high American tariff became a major obstacle to the adjustment of payments between nations, not simply a symptom of the international balance-of-payment problems that he had correctly perceived it to be up to

1929. What Hoover's nationalist nature also did not allow him to see between 1921 and 1933 was that high American duties were in fact "artificial restraints" of trade and often "deprived foreign producers of a 'fair price' for their goods," as did the international cartels and Soviet-controlled marketing agencies which he so vehemently attacked.

Therefore, he never appreciated the logical insistence, by countries like England and France, that their preferential tariff systems and national commodity monopolies were no more discriminatory than the protective American tariff. In part this was because he regarded dependence on foreign sources of raw materials as more important to American internal prosperity than dependence on overseas markets. The former was threatened by international cartels and commodity monopolies more than the latter was affected by retaliation against high American tariff duties. Accordingly, Hoover unequivocably proclaimed, in 1926, that the United States could more easily survive a loss of agricultural and manufactured exports than the loss of strategic raw material imports.

Finally, he did not consider the Smoot-Hawley tariff a depression issue. When he originally called for tariff revision in the spring of 1920, it was to obtain higher rates exclusively for agricultural products—as a complement to his Farm Board legislation—not to ameliorate depressed conditions generally. Political expediency demanded that he revise the tariff as early as possible in his first year as president. So Hoover ended up supporting high rates and flexible provisions in the name of party unity, aid for farmers, and because of his long-standing nationalist concern for preserving the American standard of living. He did so over the opposition of business internationalists of both parties, over a thousand economists, almost 40 percent of the Republican newspapers across the country, and twenty-four nations—all of whom formally complained about Smoot-Hawley legislation.

Although he never claimed the Smoot-Hawley bill was perfect, he signed it on 17 June 1930, much to the joy of the protectionists in the country, even though his reasons for supporting the tariff were not the same as theirs. In fact, he thought he could make both the Federal Tariff Commission and the flexible provisions work scientifically in the interest of internationalism, i. e., increasing imports where other presidents had failed. During the 1928 campaign, the tariff had been regarded by many as "the touchstone for the foreign policy of the Hoover administration," and Hoover said on 15 October 1928 that it was "one of the most important economic issues of this campaign." And indeed his stand on tariff policy in 1930 was indicative of how he would, as president, try to combine nationalism with internationalism in his foreign policy.

There were two other economic foreign policy issues which played important roles in Hoover's postwar reconstruction plans. They were the related issues of foreign loans and Allied debts. The two major questions which had to be answered by Washington officials about these private loans and public debts were: should the former be controlled by the federal government and should the latter be cancelled as the financial contribution of the United States to the Allied cause during the First World War?

There had been no systematic attempt to supervise private foreign loans until Hoover came on the scene as secretary of commerce in 1921. His failure to establish such supervision should not diminish the significance of his attempt and the understanding of economic foreign policy upon which it was based.[19] Since American financial sources were not unlimited, Hoover thought that loans should be restricted both at home and abroad according to "their security, their reproductive character, and their methods of promotion." By "reproductive" he meant that loans should be earmarked for projects which would improve living standards, increase consumer consumption, and contribute to social stability. Therefore he thought that loans used for military expenditures, for balancing spendthrift budgets, or for bolstering inflated currencies represented a waste of American surplus capital and "generally would be disastrous," because such loans would not increase productivity or contribute to the "economic rehabilitation of the world" and might involve the United States in the domestic affairs of unstable foreign nations. Thus to avoid unnecessary foreign entanglement and to insure that American bankers did not succumb to the temptation of high foreign interest rates and neglect needed capital investment at home, Hoover fought, in vain, for foreign loan supervision as secretary of commerce. (He was particularly worried in 1922 about the shortage of domestic capital for improving the country's railroad system.)[20]

Although the State Department proved the major stumbling block to Hoover's loan control program, members of the Senate can be added to the list of government officials who indirectly helped to undermine his plans for supervision. In 1925 and again in 1927 a subcommittee of the Senate Foreign Relations Committee conducted hearings on the role the government was playing in guaranteeing foreign economic investments. These hearings stimulated public criticism about placing the military power of the United States behind foreign economic transactions and about the practice of assuming internal financial functions in parts of Central America and the Caribbean. To the degree that these activities were misconstrued to be part of Hoover's desire to see all loans "approved," the hearings increased the pressure upon, and in some cases further encouraged, government officials outside of the Commerce Department to soft-pedal loan control.

This was ironic, because Hoover had issued more warnings against loans to Latin America than for any other part of the world and was on record in opposing the use of armed intervention or any other means of coercion, including the threat of nonrecognition, against foreign governments with whom the United States carried on economic relations, with the exception of Russia. As secretary of commerce the main reason he discouraged a venture he thought economically unsound was his unwillingness to back with armed force the foreign business his department encouraged and promoted. Indeed, this had been a fundamental point of disagreement between Hoover, on the one hand, and Secretary of State Charles Evans Hughes and the international bankers on the other, from the beginning of the decade. The latter felt it was the duty of the government to protect all American loans and investments abroad, while Hoover wanted to insure the economic soundness of such transactions to minimize the possibility of the United States being called upon to intervene. His failure meant, in essence, that America's economic empire expanded in an open-ended fashion after 1920, with increasingly less concern for the productivity of foreign investments and with little political foresight or coordination, except where ideological considerations perverted common sense, as was the case with Soviet Russia.

In the absence of effective national or international controls, public and private loans were able to obscure the economic instability created by American insistence on debt collection and high tariffs. They allowed foreign nations to meet their immediate debt payments and to purchase unprecedented amounts of goods from the United States, but there was no guarantee these loans could themselves be repaid in the future. Only strong loan control, in conjunction with a tariff policy designed to increase imports on the part of the United States, and cancellation of the outstanding intergovernmental debts, would have changed the world financial situation before 1929. While Hoover's views on these intergovernmental debts were not as internationalist in the early twenties as they became in the early thirties, he was ultimately more successful in exercising a moderating influence over nationalist tendencies within government and business circles than he did on the tariff and loan issues.[21]

In 1922, as a member of the World War Foreign Debt Commission, Hoover initially supported writing off the pre-Armistice debts in order to strengthen "our moral position" and enhance the "probabilities of payment." When told by his colleagues on the commission that Congress would never accept such a proposal, he then recommended that the United States forego collecting interest payments and spread the repayment of the principal over an undetermined number of years based on each debtor's capacity to pay. Again, the plan was considered unacceptable to other members of the commission, who insisted that Congress would never approve a debt-funding agreement which did not at least "preserve the appearance of repayment of both principal and interest." Beginning in 1923, debt-funding agreements were negotiated by the commission which did indeed give the "appearance of repayment," while in fact they reduced the combined outstanding indebtedness of the Allied nations by approximately 43 percent. In practice, this was a form of partial cancellation, but it was not accepted in name by Congress and other government officials, who were convinced that popular opinion would not tolerate the admission of cancellation.

For similar reasons, Hoover always referred to these reductions as "concessions," never as cancellations, because there had been no "cancellation of the capital sum of any debt." Throughout the decade, he privately remained willing to sacrifice interest payments for short periods of time as long as the funding agreements were not based "on deferment of the payment of the principal," for that would "steadily undermine the whole probability of repayment." Publicly, however, he encouraged the anticancellation forces in the country and refused to admit there was any legal or economic connection between German reparations and American war debts. While secretary of commerce, his irritation over the reluctance of the debtor nations to comply with what he considered very generous debt-funding agreements made him a leading critic of those "Americans who loved Europe more and America less . . . [and the like] our international bankers agitated for cancellation night and day." In 1929 he did verbally offer to exchange most of the remaining English war debt for Bermuda, British Honduras, and the island of Trinidad, but Prime Minister Ramsay MacDonald refused to consider his proposal. After the depression began, Hoover's opposition to cancellation became more rigid in the face of French and British propaganda calling for repudiation of all intergovernmental debts, but his international responsibilities as president finally forced him to modify his earlier nationalist position.

By the spring of 1931 the financial situation in Germany was deteriorating at an alarming rate. Hoover's personal record of the events leading to the proclamation of his moratorium on all intergovernmental debts clearly indicates that he conferred almost daily during May and June with the United States ambassador to Germany, Frederic M. Sackett, Secretary of State Henry L. Stimson, Secretary of the Treasury Andrew Mellon, and Undersecretary of the Treasury Ogden L. Mills, Senator and House of Morgan partner Dwight Morrow, and Chairman of the Federal Reserve Board Eugene Meyer about this impending economic crisis in Germany. Beginning on 11 May, Hoover suggested to Secretaries Stimson and Mellon that since both the funding agreements with the United States and German reparation payments were "predicated upon capacity to pay in normal times," possibly the depression had now made such payment impossible. He still insisted, however, that "there was no relationship between reparations and the debts due the American government," but within weeks his actions were to belie these words. The two secretaries apparently made no concrete replies to this suggestion, but Hoover was aware that they differed with each other and with himself on the war-debt question. Mellon was as firm an anticancellationist as Stimson was a cancellationist, and Hoover's position was characteristically somewhere in the middle. The upshot of subsequent conferences was Hoover's proposal on 20 June of a one-year moratorium on the war debts in return for reciprocal action by the Allies with respect to reparation payments.

This June 1931 moratorium fell far short of solving Europe's financial difficulties. For one thing, it came too late to prevent a general banking panic in Germany and soon enormous sums of short-term credits were frozen—the very thing that Hoover had hoped his moratorium would prevent. So he immediately had to arrange a "stabilization" or "standstill" conference in London to prevent further withdrawal of short-term credit from Germany. After considerable haggling with the French and the House of Morgan, a "standstill" agreement went into effect in September 1931.

Both actions are significant because they represent Hoover's belated recognition in practice, if not in theory, of the relationship between the war debts and reparations. He continued, nevertheless, to deny this relationship in public, never realizing apparently that this position on the part of the United States had retarded the development of international monetary equilibrium for over a decade. Unfortunately for his contemporary reputation as a "super-businessman" with an impeccable understanding of the world's political economy, Hoover's moratorium program did not restore international confidence in the face of the deepening depression. At best the moratorium and the "standstill" agreement stabilizing short-term credit to Germany only temporarily delayed the inevitable, that is, repudiation of both the inter-Allied debt and the reparation payments which took place at Lausanne in the summer of 1932. Reparations, therefore, represented the last problem of economic foreign policy facing Hoover in his remaining months as president.

Having been one of the most vocal critics of the reparations section of the Versailles Peace Treaty, Hoover thought throughout the 1920s that the reparations arrangement was "entirely unworkable." He even privately acknowledged at the beginning of 1923 that European "continental stability cannot be secured unless there is a settlement of interlocked debts, reparations and disarmament." But it was not until 1931 that he was forced by the worldwide depression to formulate and try to implement such a coordinated settlement.

Until that time his actions with respect to reparations had been relegated, as were those of Secretaries Hughes, Kellogg, Stimson, and Mellon, to supporting the Dawes and Young Plans of 1924 and 1929. Officially the United States government did not participate in the 1924 and 1929 meetings which produced these payment schedules, but, in fact, government officials appointed the American experts to both special commissions. The government also used its influence to get J. P. Morgan and Company to sponsor the American share of the loan necessary to put the Dawes Plan into operation. And in 1930 the Young Plan loan, in which the Morgan firm, the First National Bank of New York, and the First National Bank of Chicago were the principal sponsors, also had the moral, if not the legal, endorsement of the United States government. The Dawes and Young plan loans were, in essence, the government's unofficial alternatives to the periodic threat of German default on reparation payments. As such they generated much false hope among Americans, for in actuality they represented the inescapable fact that the success of the funding agreements signed with the

United States depended upon the payment of reparations to the Allies. But this was never admitted or explained to the public.

After issuing his moratorium, Hoover worked frantically to prevent permanent cancellation of German reparation payments as well as the inter-Allied debts. Privately, there was no longer any attempt made by financiers and politicians in the United States to insist that debts and reparations were not linked. It was also privately acknowledged by these same business and government leaders that drastic reductions in both types of payments were inevitable. But the decade-long refusal of American officials to take a candid position on the debts resulting from the war and to mold intelligent congressional and public opinion on the subject placed Hoover in a different position, which was further complicated by the impending presidential elections. Thus, like the Allied debt problem, Hoover seems to have had no hope that the public could be satisfactorily reeducated to accept a reversal in policy.

The president and his advisers employed two standard tactics in the face of the growing threat of debt cancellation. The first consisted of the unsuccessful attempt to have European nations concentrate on the relationship between reparations and land armaments at international conferences. This tactic failed at the Geneva and Lausanne conferences in the early 1930s. The other course, simultaneously pursued by the Hoover administration, had been initiated earlier by Secretary Hughes—the use of private financial experts to supplement normal diplomatic communication about economic problems. In this case, Thomas W. Lamont was the unofficial liaison who tried before the opening of the Lausanne Conference in June 1932 to present an economic alternative to complete cancellation and, at the same time, to impress foreign leaders with the delicate position of the Republicans in an election year. Hoover and other party leaders were convinced that the United States could not negotiate new debt settlements with the Allies nor extend the moratorium before the nation went to the polls in November. To do so would allow the Democrats to hang a "cancellation tag" on the Republican party. Despite Lamont's efforts, the Allies repudiated all intergovernmental debts arising from World War I.

Hoover's last and most original attempt to salvage the debt and reparations debacle came after his defeat for reelection. During the winter months of 1932–1933, he tried to obtain the cooperation of President-elect Roosevelt in reviving the Debt Funding Commission. A year earlier, the Democratic Congress had refused to approve such action, and so Hoover thought Roosevelt's endorsement was necessary, if the commission was to be recreated. More significantly, Hoover also wanted Roosevelt to help him appoint a nonpartisan delegation to the forthcoming London Economic Conference and to agree to coordinate all future discussions with European nations about disarmament, debts, and other economic and monetary problems, which included a commitment to an international gold standard. To achieve coordination, the president proposed the creation of an "interlocking directorate" selected by himself and Roosevelt from the delegation to the Geneva Disarmament and London Economic Conferences. With these suggestions, Hoover implicitly acknowledged the reciprocal relations between the major economic problems confronting the world and hinted that a comprehensive settlement was now the only solution.

Obviously, Hoover's emphasis on the importance of the London Conference and on the coordinated economic discussions represented his belief, by 1932, that the causes of the depression were foreign, not domestic, and therefore, international financial measures were necessary for recovery in the United States. He sought Roosevelt's concurrence on this theoretical point in vain, for to do so would have drastically limited FDR's options in dealing with the depression. At the same time, Hoover tried to obtain Roosevelt's consent to diplomatic methods that would insure a continuation of the broadly internationalist position on debts and reparations which had evolved in the last years of his administration. Since the summer of 1932 this plan had included lowering England's war-debt payments in return for British trade concessions and return to the gold standard.

Hoover was rightly convinced that no such comprehensive agreement could be reached before 4 March 1933, unless the president-elect made it abundantly clear to Congress and Europe that there would be no basic change in economic foreign policy after his inauguration. By this time Hoover was also convinced that the American gold standard could only be maintained through international cooperation, but Europe and (as it turned out) Roosevelt did not share his stubborn commitment to the gold standard. This was particularly true of the British, who had no intention of bargaining away for war-debt concessions the advantage devaluation of the pound had given them over the United States in the depressed world markets. And so Hoover's belated attempt to forge a comprehensive international economic agreement at the end of his term in office failed and along with it his attempt to bring Roosevelt over to his point of view on domestic and foreign matters.[22]

While it has taken Americans several decades to begin to appreciate some of the more complex aspects of Hoover's economic foreign policy, revisionist historians have long held a favorable view of his political foreign policies. This is not simply because of his relief work during and after the First World War or even because of his pro-League stand during the battle over ratification. It also rests on the position he took in favor of such issues as disarmament, the Kellogg-Briand Pact, the World Court, and against the use of force generally speaking in world affairs, especially in Latin America and the Far East.[23]

The basic reason behind Hoover's refusal to sanction the use of force in revolutionary situations in Latin America or during the Manchurian crisis of 1931–32 was his belief that no economic world community under American leadership could be permanently established by such means. He was no less a chauvinist in 1932 than he had been in 1919, but he was also no less committed to the *peaceful* promotion of American capitalism and democracy abroad. He had never pursued an open-ended, devil-take-the-hindmost course in foreign or domestic affairs. Consequently, even though he considered the Stimson Doctrine "one of the most important developments of American policy," he would not back it with force because it was "contrary to the policy and best judgment of the United States to build peace on military sanctions." [24] Today this position symbolizes what many consider the most advanced and modern features of Hoover's diplomacy: its noncoerciveness.

Perhaps the best example of his commitment to noncoerciveness can be seen in his attitude toward the Soviet Union. Contrary to standard interpretations and impressions, Hoover did not become a rampant Cold Warrior. In fact, despite his life-long verbal attack on communism, he did not affiliate with any anticommunist groups like the American Liberty League or China Lobby any more than he did with isolationist groups like the American First Committee. This was because he always recognized such organizations for what they were: irrationally extreme. He also refused to participate in the initial session of the House UnAmerican Activities Committee (HUAC) in March 1947, and three years later, during the McCarthy anticommunist hysteria, he refused to become chairman of Truman's bipartisan commission "to report on the question of the infiltration of communists in the Government." [25]

What is usually not understood about Hoover's attitude toward the Soviet Union is that it evolved from his strong opposition to Bolshevism in 1919, through his reluctance to trade with the new Soviet nation in the 1920s, to the financing of exports to the USSR in 1932–33 through the Reconstruction Finance Corporation, to an almost purely rhetorical opposition to communism as the economic viability of the Soviet Union became an indisputable fact after World War II. In 1929, as president he refused to engage in "red hunting" and actually expressed interest in a practical economic approach to the question of Russian recognition in order not to lose potential Soviet trade to America's foreign competitors. He had realized since the First World War that one could not kill an ideology by force; that the real ideological battlefield lay elsewhere— in the hearts and minds of men. "We cannot slay an idea of an ideology with machine guns," he once said. "Ideas live in men's minds in spite of military defeat. They live until they have proved themselves right or wrong." [26]

Given these views and his evolutionary brand of anticommunism, Hoover almost never suggested taking overtly hostile diplomatic or military actions against countries with unacceptable ideologies, like the USSR, or police-state tactics against internal dissenters. For example, instead of blaming the Bolsheviks for American economic unrest during the Red Scare of 1919–1920, he said, "we shall never remedy justifiable discontent until we eradicate the misery which ruthless individualism has imposed upon a minority," and he admonished Attorney General A. Mitchell Palmer that his "policemen could not overtake an economic force allowed to run riot in the country." Moreover, he usually preferred indirect, propagandistic actions against communism abroad, arguing that the United States had to "keep peace with dictatorships as well as with popular governments" and denouncing those who wanted to go to war to save democracy from communism or fascism.[27]

Hoover's noncoercive approach to foreign policy not only prevented him from supporting the Red Scare hysteria after World War I and from becoming a red-baiter of the McCarthy ilk in the 1950s, but as William Appleman Williams noted, it also turned him into "one of the most challenging critics of American foreign policy as it developed after 1890 along the lines of unlimited American intervention in world affairs." What this has come to mean, to members of both the New Left and the New Right today, is that Hoover recognized logical limits to which the power of the state could be used in domestic and foreign affairs. Without recognition of such limitations, he predicted that individual freedoms would be threatened at home by bureaucratic liberals who would so overextend America abroad that there would be no end to political and military intervention under their leadership. Because he realized "the dangers of relying on the national government to solve every problem" and perceived that "military intervention . . . was a measure of last resort rather than a routine instrument of policy," Hoover is gradually emerging as a major twentieth-century prophet to groups at opposite ends of the political spectrum. Even the assortment of his socialist and libertarian defenders are cogently pointing out that it is no longer historically accurate to lump Hoover's attempts "to evolve a more rational and moderate foreign policy" and to point out the dangers of corporate statism as designed by the New Dealers with the simplistic notions of "neo-isolationism" or "laissez-faire individualism." [28]

It is as though Americans had to experience the increasingly elitist and unrealistic leadership of political and corporate liberalism before they could begin to realize the value of Hoover's philosophy of voluntary cooperation, decentralization, antiinterventionism. Consequently, there is a good deal of talk today in political and historical circles about a "new" Hoover, largely because the "old" Hoover had been misunderstood for so long by apologists and critics alike.[29] In actuality, this rediscovery of Hoover is not as new as it first appears, especially in the field of foreign affairs where revisionist historians have for some time respected his views. In some instances they were personally encouraged and aided by Hoover after he left office in 1933.

Exactly how much influence Hoover exerted over revisionist scholarship is not yet fully known. There is evidence, however, indicating that several of his friends, such as John W. Blodgett, Jr., and members of the Pew family of Philadelphia, financed early revisionist writing before and after the Second World War.[30] Much more research needs to be done to reconstruct the entire picture and Hoover's exact position and function within it. At the present time it appears as though he played his favorite role of "hidden catalyst," supplying some documents in his possession to revisionist historians while withholding other material on events dating back to his presidency and the Manchurian crisis. This is not to say that there was complete agreement between historians like Charles A. Beard, Charles C. Tansill, and Henry Elmer Barnes, but they did agree that American foreign policy in the Far East had been ill-conceived during the late 1930s and early 1940s and that a number of diplomatic mistakes had been made during World War II—especially at the onset of the Cold War.

It is perhaps one of the ironies of history that Herbert Clark Hoover was once associated with the economic and ideological school of revisionist historical thought that has contributed in part to the rise today of the New Left criticism of American foreign policy. This is, nonetheless, understandable, for Hoover raised the very questions about the New Deal and interventionist foreign policy in the 1930s, which many antiestablishment historians (both Marxists and non-Marxists) have also asked. These remain the significant and lasting questions about twentieth-century domestic and foreign affairs: what is the relative importance of collective versus elitist or individual action in modern technological society, and in what ways and for what reasons and for what ends should the immense power of a managerial, corporate state be employed?

It is not that Hoover's answers and actions proved absolutely correct in retrospect—far from it. But he did clearly predict that unlimited expansion at home and abroad would create an American empire based on rigid ideological motivation and coercive military tactics which would ultimately destroy the system of voluntary cooperation at both the international and domestic levels that he tried so hard to create after World War I. Although he failed in establishing his dream for America and the world, it is time, as William Appleman Williams has said, that we stop holding him "responsible for the ideas and actions of other American leaders who did not follow his example." [31] At least Hoover knew what the right questions were. This fact alone places him ahead of most of his presidential predecessors or successors in this century.

Notes

Bibliographic Note

Reevaluations in this volume stand in contrast to the standard interpretations which evolved in the decades following Hoover's defeat in 1932. Frederick Lewis Allen, at the depth of the depression, set the historiographic stage for much of the negative view of the 1920s and the Hoover presidency. His sketch of the decade's shallowness, in *Only Yesterday* (New York: Harper & Bros., 1931), was consistent with his superficial description of Hoover's antidepression efforts as coming "to conspicuous failure." Only Walter Lippmann, in his now celebrated 1935 article describing the Hoover presidency as a precursor to the New Deal, broke with the perspective of the Hoover presidency which continued to prevail into the 1940s. In the excitement of the New Deal and America's involvement in World War II, Hoover appeared an anachronism. Following the war and the death of Franklin Roosevelt at the height of his "glory," historians formally settled into two clearly opposed sides. Although more objective than Allen in appreciating Hoover's efforts as president, simplistic chastisement seemed the order of the day. Karl Schriftgeiser, in *This Was Normalcy* (Boston: Little, Brown and Co., 1948), merely lumped Hoover with a Republican party consistently found wanting. Dixon Wecter, in his *The Age of the Great Depression, 1929–1941* (New York: Macmillan Co., 1948), presented Hoover as having "shivered on the brink" of depression. Richard Hofstadter, in his important *The American Political Tradition and the Men Who Made It* (New York: Alfred A. Knopf, Inc., 1948), viewed Hoover much as did Schriftgeiser and Wecter. He did at least note in Hoover's presidency more initiative than any predecessor had "brought to bear to meet a depression." More to Hofstadter's credit, he reminded his readers that Franklin Roosevelt's reputation was enhanced by his death "in the midst of things" and that "it would be fatal to rest content with his [Roosevelt's] belief in personal benevolence, personal arrangements, the suffering of good intentions, and month-to-month improvisation. . . ."

Herbert Hoover had his apologists, varying in worth from Eugene Lyons's early sophomoric biography to Edgar Robinson's later scholarly work, *The Roosevelt Leadership, 1933–1945* (Philadelphia: J. B. Lippincott, 1955). Robinson based his work in the context of Hoover's greatness, but invited criticism by accepting $25,000 from a Philadelphia businessman to write a book "without fear."

Broadus Mitchell, despite his socialist persuasion, admitted in his *Depression Decade* (New York: Holt, Rinehart and Winston, 1947), that "Hoover's still waters ran deeper than he has been given credit for. Relative to the period and the party, Hoover was experimental and adaptable." And, much later, Carl Degler, in a perceptive article, "The Ordeal of Herbert Hoover," published in the *Yale Review*, 52 (Summer 1963), anticipated much of the reassessment expressed at the conference. Finally, no Hoover bookshelf is complete without the president's own memoirs and several books written by such close friends as Ray L. Wilbur, Arthur M. Hyde, Walter H. Newton, William S. Meyers, and John T. Flynn.

However, despite the Hoover apologetics, the consensus history of the postwar period, and the New Conservatism of the 1950s, the public still largely viewed Hoover as an anachronism if they thought of him at all. Arthur Schlesinger's combative *The Crisis of the Old Order, 1919–1933* (Boston: Houghton Mifflin Co., 1955), was eagerly devoured by students and the general public alike. In it, the author administered faint praise to Hoover by calling him a "good" man but judged his presidency quite inferior to that of FDR's. Kenneth Galbraith's *The Great Crash, 1929* (Boston: Houghton Mifflin Company, 1955) continued the liberal refrain by denigrating Hoover's anticrash efforts. Harris Gaylord Warren, in the first worthwhile book devoted exclusively to the Hoover presidency, *Herbert Hoover and the Great Depression* (New York: Oxford University Press, 1959), elevated Hoover to the position of "the greatest Republican of his generation." But such recent authors as John D. Hicks, in his *The Republican Ascendancy, 1921–33* (New York: Harper and Bros., 1960), and Albert U. Romasco, in *The Poverty of Abundance* (New York: Oxford University Press, 1965), have been loath to give him even that accolade. Gene Smith's *The Shattered Dream* (New York: Morrow, 1970), while sympathetic to Hoover as president, is journalistic and lacks meaningful analysis. Joseph Huthmacher and Warren Sussman are editors of an important book, *Herbert Hoover and the Crisis of American Capitalism* (Cambridge, Mass.: Harvard University Press, 1973), which is based on new Hoover materials. It, however, pertains to the sweep of Hoover's economic thought and activities in the 1920s and only tangentially relates to his presidency. Craig Lloyd's *Aggressive Introvert, Herbert Hoover and Public Relations Management, 1912–1933* (Columbus: Ohio State University Press, 1973) is a very revealing book.

A mixture of historiographic perspectives has influenced the post-

World War II reevaluation of Hoover as president. The Progressive-Conflict historians peaked at the century's mid-point as their assessments of the New Deal came in. Distressed by the awesomeness of the Great Depression, they frequently viewed Franklin Roosevelt's response to it in near-messianic terms. In the process they exposed Hoover to such overkill that the corrective Consensus school of the 1950s and the 1960s, with all its New Conservatism, could not substantially change the anti-Hoover bias so firmly established by the history profession. Only recently have historians begun to correct the bias in research peripherally related to the Hoover presidency. Most notable have been the writings of Joan Hoff Wilson, Ellis Hawley, Jordan Schwarz, and William Appleman Williams. The first three increased the tempo of specialization in research on Hoover as president and present their latest findings in this book. They seem motivated more by the complexity of their subject than by a desire to correct Progressive historiography. William Appleman Williams, architect of New Left history, has made many serious contributions on the subject of Hoover and his policies. Although no specialist on the Hoover presidency or period, his ideas have had deep impact. (See below, p. 192.) Without question, his New Left perspective has contributed substantially to changing the bias and rehabilitating the Thirty-First President. Selig Adler and Albert Romasco (see IV-1 and II-1) particularly allude to Williams's work.

Most early literature on Hoover dealt with the domestic situation. Nonetheless, there were some early studies that treated Hoover's foreign policy. Robert H. Ferrell, in his *American Diplomacy in the Great Depression: Hoover-Stimson Foreign Policy, 1929–1933* (New Haven: Yale University Press, 1957), along with his biography of Henry Stimson, *Frank B. Kellogg and Henry L. Stimson* (New York: Cooper Square Publishers, Inc., 1963), measures Hoover and his secretary of state as men comparable in foreign matters, yet different in temper. The well-meaning caution of both men is Ferrell's interpretation. Most scholars investigating the interwar period have tended to remain with the standard political interpretation that stressed isolationism—the avoidance of future political commitments in future crises—and which generally ignores the economic issues. Best examples are L. Ethan Ellis, *Republican Foreign Policy, 1921–1933* (New Brunswick: Rutgers University Press, 1968); Selig Adler, *The Uncertain Giant, 1921–1941: American Foreign Policy Between the Wars* (New York: Macmillan Company, 1965); Robert James Maddox, *William E. Borah and American Foreign Policy* (Baton Rouge: Louisiana State University Press, 1969); Akira Iriye, *After Imperialism: The Search for a New Order in the Far East, 1921–1931* (Cambridge, Mass.: Harvard University Press, 1965).

Any substantial treatment of Hoover's economic foreign policy—so important in light of his reputation as an internationalist secretary of commerce and as a "businessman's businessman"—was missing until the 1960s. Again it was William Appleman Williams who in his early writings first drew attention to Hoover's economic philosophy: *American-Russian Relations, 1781–1947* (New York: Holt, Rinehart and Winston, 1952); "The Legend of Isolationism in the 1920's," *Science and Society* (Winter 1954); *The Tragedy of American Diplomacy* (Cleveland: World Publishing Co., 1959); *The Contours of American History* (Cleveland: World Publishing Co., 1961). His probings stirred a wave of new writing on the whole Republican era. For example, see Robert Freeman Smith's article, "American Foreign Relations, 1920–1942," in Barton Bernstein, ed., *Towards a New Past: Dissenting Essays in American History* (New York: Pantheon Books, 1968); Joan Hoff Wilson, *American Business and Foreign Policy, 1921–1933* (Lexington: University of Kentucky Press, 1971); Carl P. Parrini, *Heir to Empire: United States Economic Diplomacy, 1916–1923* (Pittsburgh: University of Pittsburgh Press, 1969); Murray Rothbard, "The Hoover Myth," *Studies on the Left*, 6 (1966). For criticism of Hoover's Commerce years, see Joseph Brandes, *Herbert Hoover and Economic Diplomacy: Department of Commerce Policy, 1921–1928* (Pittsburgh: University of Pittsburgh Press, 1962). One of the most articulate critics of economic revisionism is Robert James Maddox, "Another Look at the Legend of Isolationism in the 1920's," *Mid-America*, 53 (January 1971).

Textual Notes

The following abbreviations are used in citations in the various papers:

HHP   Herbert Hoover Papers, Hoover Presidential Library, West Branch, Iowa

PCP   Pre-Commerce Papers, Hoover Presidential Library, West Branch, Iowa

COF   Commerce Official File, Hoover Presidential Library, West Branch, Iowa

PPF   Presidential Personal File, Hoover Presidential Library, West Branch, Iowa

PNF   Presidential Name File, Hoover Presidential Library, West Branch, Iowa

PSF   Presidential Subject File, Hoover Presidential Library, West Branch, Iowa

PS   Public Statement, Hoover Presidential Library, West Branch, Iowa

PPP   Post-Presidential Papers, Hoover Presidential Library, West Branch, Iowa

HIA   Hoover Institute Archives, Stanford University, Stanford, California

NA   National Archives, Washington, D.C.

LC   Library of Congress, Washington, D.C.

Introduction

1. The following are important interpretations of the 1928 presidential campaign and have been used for this general interpretation. Further specific documentation is used only regarding specific quotations or very significant interpretations. Donald R. McCoy, "To The White House: Herbert Hoover, August, 1927–March, 1929" (see I-1); David Burner, *The Politics of Provincialism: The Democratic Party in Transition, 1918–1932* (New York: Alfred A. Knopf, Inc., 1968), Ch. VII; Lawrence H. Fuchs, "Election of 1928," in Arthur M. Schlesinger, Jr. and Fred L. Israel (eds.) *History of American Presidential Elections, 1789–1968* (New York: Chelsea House, 1971), Vol. III, p. 2647; Kent Schofield, "The Public Image of Herbert Hoover in the 1928 Campaign," *Mid-America*, 51 (October 1969): 278–93; Matthew and Hannah Josephson, *Al Smith, Hero of the Cities* (Boston: Houghton Mifflin Co., 1969), Ch. XIV, "The 1928 Campaign"; Harris Gaylord Warren, *Herbert Hoover and the Great Depression* (New York: Oxford University Press, 1959), Ch. 3; Edmund A. Moore, *A Catholic Runs for President: The Campaign of 1928* (New York: Ronald Press Co., 1956); Herbert

Clark Hoover, *The Memoirs of Herbert Hoover, the Cabinet and the Presidency, 1920–1935*, Vol. II, and *The Memoirs of Herbert Hoover: The Great Depression, 1929–1941*, Vol. III (New York: Macmillan Co., 1951).

2. See Craig Lloyd, *Aggressive Introvert, Herbert Hoover and Public Relations Management, 1912–1933* (Columbus: Ohio State University Press, 1973), for significance of public relations role in Hoover's public administration.

3. Fuchs, "The Election of 1928," discusses the dichotomous nature of America in 1928; Burner, *The Politics of Provincialism*, emphasizes Smith's accentuation of his Catholicism, his Tammany association, and his East-side mannerisms.

4. *New York Times*, 5 March 1929.

5. In regard to the following paragraphs covering the Hoover presidency prior to the October crash, the ensuing are important interpretations and have been used in this synthesis and will not be referred to subsequently except for direct quotation or for specific interpretation: David Burner, "Before the Crash: Hoover's First Eight Months in the Presidency" (see I-2); Ellis W. Hawley, "Herbert Hoover and American Corporatism, 1929–1933" (see II-3); Warren, *Herbert Hoover and the Great Depression*, Ch. 17; Donald R. McCoy, *Coming of Age* (Baltimore: Penguin, 1973), Ch. 6; Joan Hoff Wilson, *Herbert Clark Hoover: Forgotten Progressive* (Boston: Little, Brown & Co., in press), Ch. 5.

6. Herbert Hoover memorandum (handwritten), undated, Box 911, PSF, HHP.

7. M. L. Requa, "Memorandum to Lawrence Richey," 27 May 1929, Box 251, PSF, HHP.

8. See Edgar Eugene Robinson and Paul Carroll Edwards (eds.), *The Memoirs of Ray Lyman Wilbur, 1875–1949* (Stanford: Stanford University Press, 1960), Ch. 29.

9. Hawley, "Herbert Hoover and American Corporatism, 1929–1933" (see II-3), p. 102.

10. The following important works on the Agriculture Marketing Act have been utilized in this and subsequent discussion of the Act: Murray R. Benedict, *Farm Policies of the United States, 1790–1950* (New York: Twentieth Century Fund, 1953), Ch. 11; Gilbert Courtland Fite, *George N. Peek and the Fight for Farm Parity* (Norman, Oklahoma: University of Oklahoma Press, 1954), Ch. XIV; Theodore Saloutos and John D. Hicks, *Agriculture Discontent in the Middle West, 1900–1934* (Madison: University of Wisconsin Press, 1951).

11. For works on economic aspects of the depression, see George Henry Soule, *Prosperity Decade, From War to Depression: 1917–1929* (New York: Holt, Rinehart and Winston, 1947); Broadus Mitchell, *Depression Decade* (New York: Holt, Rinehart and Winston, 1952); Albert U. Romasco, *The Poverty of Abundance: Hoover, The Nation, The Depression* (New York: Oxford University Press, 1965).

12. John Kenneth Galbraith, *The Great Crash, 1929* (Boston: Houghton Mifflin Co., 1954), p. 45; Chandler, *America's Greatest Depression 1929–1941*, Ch. 2; McCoy, *Coming of Age*, p. 182.

13. Albert U. Romasco argues in his essay in this volume, "Herbert Hoover's Policies For Dealing With the Great Depression: The End of The Old Order or the Beginning of the New?" (see II-1), that there was considerable precedent for Hoover's policies in the responses of Presidents Theodore Roosevelt, Woodrow Wilson, and Warren Harding to the economic crises of 1907, 1914, and 1920–21, respectively.

14. Memorandum, "Data Regarding $825,000,000 Public Works Programs Already Reported by Governors in Response to President Hoover's Request," 26 December 1929, Box 83, PSF, HHP.

15. Warren, *Herbert Hoover and the Great Depression*, p. 67.

16. Lewis Strauss phone call to White House, 13 December 1929, Box 83, PSF, HHP.

17. James J. Davis to Herbert Hoover, 23 November 1929, *ibid.*

18. J. Joseph Huthmacher, *Senator Robert F. Wagner and the Rise of Urban Liberalism* (New York: Atheneum, 1968), Ch. 6.

19. Craig Lloyd, *Aggressive Introvert*, p. 157. Lloyd refers to the stabilization conferences in November and December of 1929 as "celebrity" conferences and notes the president's efforts, through them, to coordinate national newspapers and magazine publicity and thus to "carry his ideas to the larger constituencies represented by their members."

20. E. D. Durand to Robert P. Lamont, undated (probably April 1930), Box 84, PSF, HHP.

21. Edward T. Clark to Calvin Coolidge, 6 November 1930, Box 3; Edward T. Clark Papers, LC.

22. Arthur Woods to Herbert Hoover, 21 November 1930, Box 337, PSF, HHP; Lloyd, *Aggressive Introvert*, p. 159; Warren, *Herbert Hoover and the Great Depression*, p. 194.

23. Edward T. Clark to Calvin Coolidge, 6 November 1930, Box 3, Clark Papers, LC.

24. *New York Times*, 5 November 1930.

25. Julius Barnes to Herbert Hoover, 31 March 1930, Box 123, PSF, HHP.

26. Alexander Legge to C. C. Lewis, 2 January 1931, Box 908, *ibid.*

27. Alexander Legge to Herbert Hoover, 6 March 1930, *ibid.*

28. Herbert Hoover to Walter Newton, 21 March 1931; Walter Newton to Hoover, 23 March 1931, Box 124, *ibid.*

29. Herbert Hoover to William D. Mitchell, 11 April 1932, Mitchell to Hoover, 25 April 1932, *ibid.*

30. Herbert Hoover to Dan W. Turner, 6 July 1932, Box 125, *ibid.*

31. J. Joseph Huthmacher, *Senator Robert F. Wagner*, p. 85.

32. Herbert Stein, "Pre-Revolutionary Fiscal Policy: The Regime of Herbert Hoover," *Journal of Law and Economics* 9 (October 1966): 210.

33. Herbert Hoover to William D. Mitchell, 26 August 1931, Box 152, PSF, HHP.

34. Herbert Stein, "Pre-Revolutionary Fiscal Policy," *passim.*

35. William D. Mitchell to Herbert Hoover, 23 March 1932, Box 75, PSF, HHP. Attorney General Mitchell sent President Hoover two memorandums supporting the Norris-LaGuardia Act, the second one marked "confidential," suggesting that the president sign it, for if he were to veto it, the courts might be forced by an overwhelming overriding of the veto to an inordinate liberal interpretation of the Act.

36. Herbert Hoover to Herbert S. Crocker, 13 May 1932, Box 83, *ibid.*

37. Walter Newton to Lawrence Richey, 3 March 1932, Box 917, *ibid.*

38. Charles D. Hilles to Herbert Hoover, 26 August 1931, Box 104, *ibid.*

39. Important sources on the election of 1932 and the interregnum are: Alfred B. Rollins, "The View From the State House: FDR" (see III-1); Frank

Freidel, "The Interregnum Struggle Between Hoover and Roosevelt" (see III-2); Arthur M. Schlesinger, Jr., *The Crisis of the Old Order, 1919–1933* (Boston: Houghton Mifflin Co., 1957); Frank Freidel, "The Election of 1932," in Schlesinger, Jr. and Israel (eds.), *History of American Presidential Elections, 1798–1968;* Hoover, *Memoirs,* II and III; Schwarz, *The Interregnum of Despair;* Warren, *Herbert Hoover and the Great Depression.*

40. See Lloyd, *Aggressive Introvert,* p. 162, for important analysis, i.e., "When Hoover came to the presidency, it was the 'practical idealist' that had been underscored by the publicists. Not projected nearly so much were his more deeply rooted 'idealist' tendency and the almost religious intensity with which he valued 'individualism' and its political corollaries, 'local initiative and responsibility.' "

41. Herbert Hoover to Franklin D. Roosevelt, 18 February 1933, Box 927A, PSF, HHP.

42. Frank Freidel discussion at the Hoover "Conversation in the Discipline," Geneseo, New York, 28 April 1973.

43. Robert H. Ferrell, *American Diplomacy in the Great Depression: Hoover-Stimson Foreign Policy, 1929–1933* (New Haven: Yale University Press, 1957); Herbert Feis, *The Diplomacy of the Dollar: First Era, 1919–1932* (Baltimore: Johns Hopkins Press, 1950); Joseph Marion Jones, Jr., *Tariff Retaliation: Repercussions of the Hawley-Smoot Bill* (Philadelphia: University of Pennsylvania Press, 1934); H. G. Moulton and Leo Pasvolsky, *War Debts and World Prosperity* (Washington: The Brookings Institution, 1932).

44. See Adler, *The Uncertain Giant,* Ch. 5; Alexander DeConde, *Herbert Hoover's Latin American Policy* (Stanford: Stanford University Press, 1951); Julius William Pratt, *A History of United States Foreign Policy,* 3rd ed. (Englewood Cliffs, N.J.: Prentice-Hall, Inc., 1972), pp. 350–51; Arthur P. Whitaker, *The Western Hemisphere Idea: Its Rise and Decline* (Ithaca: Cornell University Press, 1954), p. 135; Samuel Flagg Bemis, *The Latin American Policy of the United States* (New York: Harcourt, Brace and Co., 1943), p. 221. A careful, balanced evaluation is in Bryce Wood, *The Making of the Good Neighbor Policy* (New York: Columbia University Press, 1961), pp. 123–28.

45. Hans Schmidt, *The United States Occupation of Haiti, 1915–1934* (New Brunswick: Rutgers University Press, 1971), pp. 200–201, 205–8, 222.

46. Benjamin B. Wallace, "How the United States 'Led the League' in 1931," *American Political Science Review* (1945): 101–16; Paul H. Clyde, "Diplomacy of Secretary Stimson and Manchuria, 1931," *Mississippi Valley Historical Review* (1948): 187–202; Armin Rappaport, *Henry L. Stimson and Japan, 1931–33* (Chicago: University of Chicago Press, 1963). Both Stimson and Hoover saw this episode as crucial in American foreign policy. See Stimson, *The Far Eastern Crisis* (New York: Harper and Bros., 1936) and Hoover, *Memoirs,* II, Chapter XLVIII.

47. Richard N. Current, *Secretary Stimson: A Study in Statecraft* (New Brunswick: Rutgers University Press, 1954), is a careful criticism of the secretary and raises the question of a possible dual Hoover/Stimson Doctrine in the crisis, which appears favorable to Hoover. To the contrary, Elting Elmore Morison, in his later study, *Turmoil and Tradition: A Study of the Life and Times of Henry L. Stimson* (Boston: Houghton-Mifflin Co., 1960), is very pro-Stimson to the disparagement of Hoover.

To the White House: Herbert Hoover, August 1927–March 1929
Donald R. McCoy

1. Donald Richard McCoy, *Calvin Coolidge: The Quiet President* (New York: Macmillan Co., 1967), p. 384.

2. Smith to McNary, 17 August 1927, Charles L. McNary Papers, LC.

3. Roy Victor Peel and Thomas C. Donnelly, *The 1928 Campaign: An Analysis* (New York: R. R. Smith, Inc., 1931), pp. 7–9.

4. Lawrence H. Fuchs, "Election of 1928," in Arthur M. Schlesinger, Jr., and Fred L. Israel, eds., *History of American Presidential Elections, 1789–1968* (New York: Chelsea House, 1971), III, p. 2647. See Kent Schofield, "The Public Image of Herbert Hoover in the 1928 Campaign," *Mid-America*, 51 (October 1969): 278–93, and Richard Hofstadter, *The American Political Tradition and the Men Who Made It* (New York: Alfred A. Knopf, Inc., 1948), pp. 284–92, for discussions of Hoover's attractiveness.

5. Claude M. Fuess, *Calvin Coolidge: The Man from Vermont* (Boston: Little, Brown and Co., 1940), p. 425.

6. McCoy, *Calvin Coolidge*, pp. 309–10, 319, 324, 332; William Allen White, *A Puritan in Babylon: The Story of Calvin Coolidge* (New York: Macmillan Co., 1938), p. 400.

7. George Hillman Mayer, *The Republican Party, 1854–1964* (New York: Oxford University Press, 1964), pp. 402–3; Harris Gaylord Warren, *Herbert Hoover and the Great Depression* (New York: Oxford University Press, 1959), p. 31; Akerson to George H. Adams, 12 October 1926, Personal File, George Akerson Papers, Hoover Library; Herbert Clark Hoover, *The Memoirs of Herbert Hoover: The Cabinet and the Presidency, 1920–1933*, Vol. II (New York: Macmillan Co., 1952), p. 190.

8. Hoover, *Memoirs*, II, pp. 190–92; Mayer, *Republican Party*, p. 404; *New York Times*, 4 January, 27 January, and 11 April 1928; Eugene Lyons, *Herbert Hoover: A Biography* (Garden City, N.Y.: Doubleday and Co., 1964), pp. 174–75; White, *Puritan in Babylon*, p. 375. That the Hoover campaign was operating, however cautiously, in August 1927 is documented in the Political File of the Akerson Papers; see, for example, Ashmun Brown to Akerson, 14 August 1927, Akerson to Brown, 22 August 1927, and Walter H. Newton to Akerson, 15 August 1927. The appointment of a seasoned Ohio politician, Walter F. Brown, as assistant secretary of commerce on 2 November 1927 was a move to bolster further Hoover's campaign strength.

9. Peel and Donnelly, *The 1928 Campaign*, pp. 5–7; Akerson to R. W. Bailey, 8 December 1927, Political File, Akerson Papers; Warren, *Herbert Hoover*, pp. 31–32; Mayer, *Republican Party*, p. 404; *Congressional Record*, 31 January 1928, p. 2253.

10. Hoover, *Memoirs*, II, pp. 190–91; *New York Times*, 13 February 1928.

11. Of the 1,089 delegates to the 1928 Republican National Convention, 502 were chosen by election. That is undoubtedly an additional reason why Hoover entered the primaries. Peel and Donnelly, *The 1928 Campaign*, pp. 13, 18.

12. *Ibid.*, p. 20.

13. *Ibid.*, p. 14, pp. 173–74; Mayer, *Republican Party*, p. 404.

14. McCoy, *Calvin Coolidge*, pp. 388, 390; *New York Times*, 21 April 1928; James E. Watson, *As I Knew Them* (Indianapolis: Bobbs-Merrill Co., 1936), pp.

255–56. Hoover must still have had some nagging doubts about Coolidge. In May he visited the president to tell him that he had 400 delegates behind his nomination, but that he was "in a position to influence most of them to vote for" Coolidge. The president replied, "If you have 400 delegates, you better keep them." Hoover, *Memoirs,* II, p. 193.

15. Hoover, *Memoirs,* II, p. 194; *New York Times,* 13 June 1928.

16. *Official Report of the Proceedings of the Nineteenth Republican National Convention* (New York: The Tenny Press, 1928), *passim* but especially pp. 112–31.

17. *Ibid.,* pp. 177–221, 250–51.

18. *Ibid.,* pp. 225–26.

19. *Ibid.,* p. 227.

20. For example, one leading textbook gives five-and-one-half paragraphs to Smith and one-and-a-half to Hoover in its coverage of the 1928 campaign; Samuel Eliot Morison, Henry Steele Commager, and William E. Leuchtenburg, *The Growth of the American Republic,* Sixth Ed. (New York: Oxford University Press, 1969), II, pp. 439–42. Fuchs, "Election of 1928," gives at least twice as much attention to Smith as to Hoover, pp. 2592–2609.

21. *Proceedings of the Nineteenth Republican National Convention,* p. 288; Vaughn Davis Bornet, *Labor Politics in a Democratic Republic: Moderation, Division, and Disruption in the Presidential Election of 1928* (Washington: Spartan Books, 1964), *passim* and especially p. 294.

22. Fuchs, "Election of 1928," pp. 2592–94. For details, see David Burner, *The Politics of Provincialism: The Democratic Party in Transition, 1918–1932* (New York: Alfred A. Knopf, Inc., 1968).

23. Peel and Donnelly, *The 1928 Campaign,* pp. 30–35; Edmund A. Moore, *A Catholic Runs for President: The Campaign of 1928* (New York: Ronald Press Co., 1956), pp. 121–26.

24. Fuchs, "Election of 1928," pp. 2611–24; U.S. Bureau of the Census, *Historical Statistics of the United States: Colonial Times to 1957* (Washington: Government Printing Office, 1960), p. 682.

25. Although Hoover refused to inject personality into the campaign, some of his political and personal associates saw Smith as a vulgarian or a saloon-style fighter, a view apparently shared by many voters. See Akerson Papers, Personal File, Henry J. Allen to Akerson, 19 June 1928; Ray Lyman Wilbur to Hoover, 31 October 1928, Pre-Presidential Papers, HHP; Moore, *A Catholic Runs for President, passim.*

26. Peel and Donnelly, *The 1928 Campaign,* pp. 37–38, 47–48, 51, 72–86. For an example of the nominee's supervision of campaign operatons, see Hoover to Henry J. Allen, 13 September 1928, Pre-Presidential Papers, HHP.

27. Warren, *Herbert Hoover,* pp. 42–43; Preston Wolfe Oral History Interview, Hoover Library, pp. 10–13; Marian C. McKenna, *Borah* (Ann Arbor: University of Michigan Press, 1961), p. 253; Donald Richard McCoy, *Landon of Kansas* (Lincoln: University of Nebraska Press, 1967), pp. 52–54.

28. *New York Times,* 3, 8, 11, 14, 17, 18, 19 July 1928.

29. *Ibid.,* 5, 15, 22 August; 13, 16, 23, 30 September; 4 October; and 3 November 1928.

30. Cf. Coolidge's 1920 and 1924 campaigns, McCoy, *Calvin Coolidge,* 128, 254–55; *New York Times,* 22 August 1928.

31. Warren, *Herbert Hoover,* pp. 42–43; Peel and Donnelly, *The 1928 Cam-*

paign, passim; Hoover, *Memoirs,* II, pp. 192, 197, 199, 205–7; Misrepresentations and Countermisrepresentations Files, Pre-Presidential Papers, HHP.

32. Hoover, *Memoirs,* II, p. 198; Mayer, *Republican Party,* p. 407; *New York Times,* 3 July 1928; Henry J. Allen, Mabel Walker Willebrandt, and Printed Materials Files, Pre-Presidential Papers, HHP.

33. *New York Times,* 12 August 1928; *Proceedings of the Nineteenth Republican National Convention,* pp. 279–97.

34. *New York Times,* 18 and 23 September 1928.

35. *Ibid.,* 22 August, 18 and 30 September 1928. For additional material on the Republican party and the attacks on Smith, see Hoover, *Memoirs,* II, p. 208; Moore, *A Catholic Runs for President,* pp. 146–57, 175–94; Mabel Walker Willebrandt File, especially Willebrandt to Hubert Work, 27 September 1928, Pre-Presidential Papers, HHP.

36. *New York Times,* 7, 16 October 1928.

37. *Ibid.,* 23 October 1928.

38. *Ibid.,* 3 November 1928.

39. Peel and Donnelly, *The 1928 Campaign,* p. vii; Bureau of the Census, *Historical Statistics,* pp. 682, 684; John D. Hicks, *The Republican Ascendancy, 1921–33* (New York: Harper and Bros., 1960), p. 213.

40. Bureau of the Census, *Historical Statistics,* p. 691.

41. Howard H. Quint and Robert H. Ferrell (eds.), *The Talkative President: The Off-the-Record Press Conferences of Calvin Coolidge* (Amherst: University of Massachusetts Press, 1964), p. 253; Hoover, *Memoirs,* II, pp. 210–11.

42. *New York Times,* 20 November 1928, 7 January 1929; Hoover, *Memoirs,* II, pp. 211–15.

43. *New York Times,* 16 November 1928, 7, 8 January 1929; Latin American Trip, especially Lawrence Richy File and Calendar File, January–March 1929, Pre-Presidential Papers, HHP.

44. Hoover, *Memoirs,* II, pp. 217–19.

45. McCoy, *Calvin Coolidge,* p. 379; *New York Times,* 9, 17 January 1929. Regarding Hoover's sensitivity to Coolidge, see telegram from Hoover to Coolidge, 28 January 1929, Pre-Presidential Papers, HHP.

46. *New York Times,* 23 January, 8, 19 February 1929; Calendar File, January–March 1929, Pre-Presidential Papers, HHP.

47. *New York Times,* 5 March 1929; Herbert Clark Hoover, *The State Papers and Other Public Writings of Herbert Hoover,* edited by William Starr Myers (Garden City, N.Y.: Doubleday Doran and Co., 1934), I, pp. 3–12.

Before the Crash: Hoover's First Eight Months in the Presidency
David B. Burner

1. *New York Times,* 10 May 1928.

2. Hoover gave the revealing title, *The New Day: Campaign Speeches of Herbert Hoover, 1928* to a collection of his campaign addresses (Stanford: Stanford University Press, 1928), p. 5. The title is in harmony with a tradition encompassing Theodore Roosevelt's New Nationalism or Wilson's published volume of speeches, *The New Freedom.* It also brings to mind such optimistic titles of the Progressive Era as *The Changing of the Old Order* or *The Promise of American Life.*

3. Hoover, *The New Day,* p. 16.

4. John L. McNab, "What Hoover Means to the West," *Sunset*, 61 (October 1928): 12.

5. *New York Times*, 1 August 1928.

6. *New York World*, 29 August 1928.

7. Kent M. Schofield, "The Figure of Herbert Hoover in the 1928 Campaign" (Ph.D. dissertation, University of California at Riverside, 1966), p. 90.

8. Willis J. Abbot, *Watching the World Go By* (Boston: Little, Brown and Co., 1933), p. 345; cf. *Christian Science Monitor*, 27 November 1932.

9. W. C. Durant of General Motors crashed the gates of the White House around 10:00 p.m. one night in April allegedly to chastise Hoover for reading the riot act to the Federal Reserve Board. The White House appointment book of 3 April 1929 records a meeting with Wall Street Bulls, HHP.

10. Herbert Clark Hoover, *The Memoirs of Herbert Hoover: The Cabinet and the Presidency, 1920–1933*, Vol. II (New York: Macmillan Co., 1952), p. 223.

11. *Ibid.*, p. 216.

12. Private memorandum, "Mississippi Flood," Commerce Series, HHP. See also Bruce A. Lohof, "Hoover and the Mississippi Valley Flood of 1927" (Ph.D. dissertation, Syracuse University, 1968), and Lohof, "Herbert Hoover's Mississippi Valley Land Reform Memorandum: A Document," *Arkansas Historical Quarterly* 29 (Summer 1970): 112–18.

13. The A F of L story is from Cyrus Stuart Ching, *Review and Reflection* (New York: B. C. Forbes, 1953), p. 28. During the 1928 campaign Franklin Roosevelt, among others, had played on conservative fears. He wrote to the Thom McAnn shoe king. Ward Melville, complaining that "Mr. Hoover has always shown a most disquieting desire to investigate everything and to appoint commissions and send out statistical inquiries on every conceivable subject under Heaven. He has also shown in his own Department a most alarming desire to issue regulations and to tell business men generally how to conduct their affairs." 21 September 1928, Governor's file, Franklin D. Roosevelt Papers, Franklin D. Roosevelt Library, Hyde Park, N.Y.

14. *On Growing Up* (New York: William Morrow and Co., 1959), p. 5.

15. White House Press Release, 14 March 1929, PS, HHP.

16. Press Conference of 26 March, PS, HHP; Hoover's southern policies were quite involved but clearly not anti-Negro. Donald Lisio of Coe College is working on this subject. On patronage in particular, see Arthur Krock, "Hoover Brings Change to Southern Politics," *New York Times*, 14 April 1929. On his sensitivity to most minorities, note, for example, his not untypical letter to his attorney general recommending that the makeup of the new Parole Board take into account the proportion of blacks and women in the prison population. 14 May 1930, "Colored Question, 1930B," Box 100, A, PSF, HHP.

17. Box 14, Press Relations, PSF, HHP; *The Nation* spoke of the "admirable" new arrangements with Washington correspondents (128 [3 April 1929]: 386).

18. Press Conference of 12 March and White House Press Release, 15 March 1929, HHP; *The Nation* 128 (27 March 1929): 359.

19. 29 March 1929, PS, HHP; *Commercial and Financial Chronicle*, 6 April 1929.

20. The final recommendation is contained in Hoover's first annual message to Congress, 3 December 1929. But see the public statements of 2 July and 23 July. PS, HHP.

21. Hoover, said George Akerson speaking for the president, did not intend

to engage in any "Red Hunt" when so many vital issues were before the country. *New York World,* 27 June 1929; *Time,* 11 (8 July 1929): 14; *New Republic,* 59 (10 July 1929): 19.

22. Hoover to W. D. Mitchell, 23 April 1929; Jane Addams to Lawrence Richey, 29 May 1929; Mitchell to Hoover, 23 August 1929; Addams to Hoover, 28 September 1929. "Amnesty, 1929," Box 62, PSF, HHP.

23. Hoover to Mitchell, 18 October 1930. The president remembered an investigation under Woodrow Wilson, which had found improper judicial procedures in the Moorey case.

24. *New York Times,* 24 April 1929; Clement H. Congdon to Hoover, 23 April 1929, Box 16, HHP; David Burner, *The Politics of Provincialism: The Democratic Party in Transition, 1918–1932* (New York: Alfred A. Knopf, Inc., 1968), p. 205.

25. Boxes 100–102, HHP.

26. U.S. Department of the Interior, *Annual Report* (Washington: Government Printing Office, 1930), pp. 1024–30.

27. *New York World,* 9 May 1928.

28. White House Press Release, 14 December 1929; "Communism—1929, Aug.-Dec.," Box 108, HHP.

29. 24 March 1920, Speech File, no. 53, HHP.

30. Mitchell to Wilbur, 24 June 1929, File 1–249, pt. I, Interior Department, NA.

31. Taylor/Gates Collection, File 200, HHP.

32. Hoover's management of public relations is the subject of Craig Lloyd's keen *Aggressive Introvert, Herbert Hoover and Public Relations Management, 1912–1933* (Columbus: Ohio State University Press, 1973).

33. Hunt, "The Cooperative Committee and Conference System," a paper read before the Taylor Society of New York on 14 December 1926, Box 161, COF, HHP.

34. Theodore Goldsmith Joslin, *Hoover Off the Record* (Garden City, N.Y.: Doubleday, Doran and Co., 1934), p. 50.

35. By 1932, for instance, thirty-seven states had made use of the "Standard State Zoning Enabling Act," prepared by the Advisory Committee on City Planning and Zoning of the Department of Commerce. See also pp. 101–147 of John M. Gries and James Ford (eds.), *President's Conference on Homebuilding and Home Ownership* (Washington: Government Printing Office, 1932), Vol. XI.

36. Hoover to Couzzens, 6 March 1929, Box 97, HHP.

37. Introduction, I, 5.

38. *Memphis Commercial Appeal,* 4 December 1929.

39. Hoover to J. Clawson Roop, 16 October 1929, Box 84, HHP.

40. "Better Homes," Box 72, HHP.

41. Press Release, 25 April 1929, Interior Department, NA.

42. "Housing Objectives and Programs," Vol. XI, *President's Conference on Homebuilding and Home Ownership.*

43. Introduction, U.S. National Advisory Committee on Education, *Report* (Washington: Government Printing Office, 1930), I, 5.

44. "Proposed Department of Health, Education and Welfare," Box 171; "Interior-1930-C," Box 6; HHP.

45. *Saturday Evening Post,* 196 (31 May 1924): 27.

46. Speech File, no. 1205, HHP.
47. *The Forum,* 56 (6 February 1924): 9; Box 165, HHP.
48. 15 December 1924, Wilbur Papers, Hoover Library.
49. Hoover to Scott Leavit, 29 March 1930, File 5–3, pt. I, Interior Department, NA.
50. See miscellaneous correspondence in Box 72, HHP. In an article that I believe oversimplifies the Hoover government's Indian policies, Kenneth Phelp argues that Rhoads gave little effective support for the program of John Collier. "Herbert Hoover's New Era: A False Dawn for the American Indian, 1929–1932," *Rocky Mountain Social Science Journal* 9 (April 1972): 53–60.
51. See Barry D. Karl, "Presidential Planning and Social Science Research: Mr. Hoover's Experts," *Perspectives in American History* 3 (1969): 347–409.
52. Year-by-year figures can be found in the U.S. Department of the Interior, *Annual Report* (Washington: Government Printing Office).
53. Report of C. J. Rhoads to Senator William King, 18 January 1933, Taylor/Gates Collection, Hoover Library.
54. Donald C. Swain, *Federal Conservation Policy, 1921–1933* (Berkeley: University of California Press, 1963), p. 165.
55. Wilbur to A. J. Eager, 29 March 1929, File 2–37, Box 684, RG48, NA. On 20 April 1929, Secretary of Agriculture Hyde reduced the number of ducks and geese allowed hunters. "Game Protection, 1929–1930," Box 162, HHP.
56. File 2–37, Box 684, RG48, NA.
57. Box 3, Wilbur Papers.
58. An account unsympathetic to Hoover is Gerald D. Nash, *United States Oil Policy, 1890–1964* (Pittsburgh: University of Pittsburgh Press, 1968). Nash exaggerates local resentments at the March closing of oil lands.
59. *New York World,* 28 August 1929.
60. Beverly Moeller emphasizes the role of Phillip Swing. *Phil Swing and Boulder Dam* (Berkeley: University of California Press, 1971).
61. Press Release, 21 October 1929, Department of the Interior, NA.
62. *New Republic* 129 (16 November 1929): 509.
63. *New York World,* 7 September 1929.
64. *Judge,* 2 December 1929.

Herbert Hoover's Policies for Dealing with the Great Depression:
the End of the Old Order or the Beginning of the New?
Albert U. Romasco

1. Charles A. Beard, "Written History as an Act of Faith," *American Historical Review* 39 (January 1934): 220.
2. William Starr Myers and Walter H. Newton, *The Hoover Administration, A Documented Narrative* (New York: C. Scribner's Sons, 1936), p. 516.
3. *Ibid.,* pp. 516–21.
4. *Ibid.,* p. 520.
5. *Ibid.,* p. 3.
6. *Ibid.,* pp. 4, 12, 25–30, 52–59, 122.
7. *Ibid.,* pp. 88–94, 143–44, 163, 171–73.
8. *Ibid.,* pp. 122, 142, 368.
9. *Ibid.,* p. 370.
10. *Ibid.,* p. 276.

11. John Thomas Flynn, *The Roosevelt Myth* (New York: Devin-Adair Co., 1948), pp. 165, 206.

12. Edgar Eugene Robinson, *The Roosevelt Leadership 1933–1945* (Philadelphia: J. J. Lippincott, 1955), pp. 36–37.

13. *Ibid.*, p. 400.

14. *Ibid.*, p. 376.

15. Earnest Kidder Lindley, *The Roosevelt Revolution: First Phase* (New York: Viking Press, 1933), pp. 15, 272; Raymond Moley, *After Seven Years* (New York: Harper and Bros., 1939), p. 11; Rexford Tugwell, *The Democratic Roosevelt* (Garden City, N.Y.: Doubleday, 1957), p. 197; Robert Emmet Sherwood, *Roosevelt and Hopkins* (New York: Harper and Bros., 1950 edition), I, pp. 46–48.

16. Basil Rauch, *The History of the New Deal 1933–1938* (New York: Creative Age Press, Inc., 1944), pp. 15, 18; Dixon Wecter, *The Age of the Great Depression, 1929–1941* (New York: Macmillan Co., 1948), p. 44; Richard Hofstadter, *The American Political Tradition and the Men Who Made It* (New York: Alfred A. Knopf, Inc., 1948), pp. 282, 289–90, 302; John D. Hicks, *The Republican Ascendancy 1921–1933* (New York: Oxford University Press, 1960), pp. 216–17.

17. John Kenneth Galbraith, *The Great Crash 1929* (Boston: Houghton Mifflin Co., 1954), pp. 181–88.

18. Arthur M. Schlesinger, Jr., *The Crisis of the Old Order 1919–1933* (Boston: Houghton Mifflin Co., 1957), pp. 246–47.

19. Walter Lippmann, "The Permanent New Deal," *The Yale Review* 24 (1935), reprinted in Richard M. Abrams and Lawrence W. Levine (eds.), *The Shaping of Twentieth-Century America* (Boston: Little, Brown Co., 1965), p. 430.

20. Abrams and Levine, *Shaping of Twentieth-Century America*, p. 436.

21. Broadus Mitchell, *Depression Decade* (New York: Holt, Rinehart and Winston, 1947), pp. 38, 57, 77, 80–81, 86, 114–16, 306, 341, 404–405.

22. *Ibid.*, p. 89.

23. *Ibid.*, pp. 88, 145, 190.

24. Carl N. Degler, "The Ordeal of Herbert Hoover," *The Yale Review* 52 (1963), reprinted in Abrams and Levine (eds.), *The Shaping of Twentieth-Century America* (Boston: Little, Brown Co., 1971 edition), p. 358.

25. Abrams and Levine, *Shaping of Twentieth-Century America*, 1971 edition, p. 359.

26. *Ibid.*, p. 363.

27. *Ibid.*, p. 364.

28. William Appleman Williams, *The Contours of American History* (Chicago: Quadrangle, 1966), p. 438.

29. *Ibid.*

30. *Ibid.*, pp. 428, 437–38.

31. Milton Friedman and Anna Jacobson Schwartz, *A Monetary History of the United States 1867–1960* (Princeton: Princeton University Press, 1963), p. 307.

32. My treatment of this episode draws heavily from material presented in Theodore Roosevelt, *The Letters of Theodore Roosevelt*, edited by Elting E. Morison *et al.* (Cambridge: Harvard University Press, 1952), V, pp. 822–49.

33. *Ibid.*, pp. 848–49.

34. *Ibid.*, p. 826.

35. Theodore Roosevelt to Cortelyou, 24 October 1907, text printed in the *New York Times*, 27 October 1907.

36. Roosevelt, *Letters of Theodore Roosevelt*, p. 822.

37. *Ibid.*, pp. 830–31.

38. *Ibid.*, pp. 848–849; U.S. Department of the Treasury, *Response of the Secretary of the Treasury to Senate Resolution No. 33 of Dec. 12, 1907* (Washington: Government Printing Office, 1908), pp. 7–11.

39. My material on Wilson is drawn primarily from Arthur Link, *Wilson, The Struggle for Neutrality, 1914–1915* (Princeton: Princeton University Press, 1960).

40. *Ibid.*, p. 76; Ray Stannard Baker, *Woodrow Wilson Life and Letters* (Garden City, N.Y.: Doubleday, Page and Co., 1935), V, p. 97.

41. Link, *Struggle for Neutrality*, p. 76; William Gibbs McAdoo, *Crowded Years, The Reminiscences of William G. McAdoo* (Boston: Houghton Mifflin Co., 1931), pp. 290–93.

42. Link, *Struggle for Neutrality*, p. 77.

43. *Ibid.*, p. 78.

44. *Ibid.*, p. 79.

45. *Ibid.*, pp. 81–90; Alexander Dana Noyes, *The War Period of American Finance 1908–1925* (New York: G. P. Putnam's Sons, 1926), pp. 97, 113 ff.

46. My treatment of the 1920–1921 depression relies heavily upon material drawn from Robert K. Murray, *The Harding Era: Warren G. Harding and His Administration* (Minneapolis: University of Minnesota Press, 1969).

47. *Ibid.*, p. 170.

48. *Ibid.*, p. 183.

49. *Ibid.*, pp. 172–74, 184, 190, 195–98.

50. *Ibid.*, pp. 201, 203, 206–10.

51. *Ibid.*, p. 84.

52. *Ibid.*, pp. 231–32.

53. Philip Klein, *The Burden of Unemployment* (New York: Russell Sage Foundation, 1923), pp. 57–59.

54. Among those who have accepted and perpetuated this claim without modification, I include myself in *The Poverty of Abundance: Hoover, the Nation, the Depression* (New York: Oxford University Press, 1965).

55. *Ibid.*, pp. 187–94.

56. For a more detailed treatment, see *ibid.*, Chapter 4.

57. *Ibid.*, pp. 142, 171–72.

58. *Ibid.*, pp. 121–24.

59. *Ibid.*, pp. 222, 227–29.

60. For a discussion of the themes of change and continuity and their interplay during the Great Depression, see Richard S. Kirkendall, "The New Deal As Watershed: The Recent Literature," *Journal of American History* 54 (March 1968): 839–52.

Hoover and Congress: Politics, Personality, and Perspective in the Presidency
Jordan A. Schwarz

1. Jordan A. Schwarz, *The Interregnum of Despair: Hoover, Congress and the Depression* (Urbana: University of Illinois Press, 1970), pp. 32–41; quoted in *Washington Post*, 5, 6 March 1931.

2. See Container 1-E/104, HHP; Herbert Hoover, *Hoover After Dinner* (New York: C. Scribner's Sons, 1933), p. 61; Herbert Clark Hoover, *The State Papers and Other Public Writings of Herbert Hoover,* edited by William Starr Myers (Garden City, N.Y.: Doubleday, Doran and Co., 1934), I, p. 565.

3. Schwarz, *Interregnum*, pp. 78–81, 88–90, 94–95.

4. The classic statement of Hoover's ideas prior to his presidency is Herbert Clark Hoover, *American Individualism* (Garden City, N.Y.: Doubleday, Page and Co., 1922). Some readers may find it too vague and general. His concepts are elaborated in the *State Papers*, in two volumes. Special attention should be given to his 15 June 1931 address at the dinner of the Indiana Republican Editorial Association. The best description of his ideas is found in Albert U. Romasco, *The Poverty of Abundance: Hoover, the Nation, the Depression* (New York: Oxford University Press, 1965), pp. 10–23.

5. Edward Tracy Clark to Calvin Coolidge, 14 November 1932, Clark Papers. L. C. Clark was a former secretary to President Coolidge. Asked by Hoover to serve in a similar capacity, Clark declined in favor of a private law practice in Washington. Still, he dropped into the White House often during the Hoover years, informally advising Hoover and his staff. During August 1932 he briefly helped out in the White House while others vacationed. Clark enjoyed easy access to prominent Republicans and his frequent letters to Coolidge during the Hoover years are rich with insights into GOP thinking in the White House and on Capitol Hill.

6. Ogden L. Mills to Ogden M. Reid, 21 October 1927, Ogden Mills Papers, LC.

7. Quoted in James MacGregor Burns, *Roosevelt: The Lion and the Fox* (New York: Harcourt, Brace, 1956), pp. 156–57.

8. Edward Mandell House, *The Intimate Papers of Colonel House*, edited by Charles Seymour (Boston: Houghton Mifflin Co., 1928), IV, p. 268; James E. Watson, *As I Knew Them* (Indianapolis: Bobbs Merrill, 1936), p. 279; Frank Kent to Bernard Baruch, 13 May 1929, Bernard Baruch Papers, Princeton University; Diary, 18 June 1931, Henry L. Stimson Papers, Yale University; Baruch to Kent, 15 May 1929, Baruch Papers.

9. Diary, 1 November 1930, Stimson Papers, see also 11 November 1930 and 22 July 1932.

10. See introduction by Theodore Joslin in *Hoover After Dinner*, pp. vi–viii.

11. "The Reminiscences of Louis J. Taber," p. 227, Oral History Research Office, Columbia University (hereafter cited as OHRO).

12. Alex Legge to Bernard Baruch, 19 March 1921, Baruch Papers; "Conversation with Senator Borah . . ." Scrapbook 2, Arthur Vandenberg Papers, University of Michigan.

Hoover's loyal subordinate, Harvey H. Bundy, assistant secretary of state, who served with him in the war, also noted "how comparatively inept he was in running a political show [in the presidency] compared to the enormous skill as an administrator I'd seen in the Food Administration." "The Reminiscences of Harvey H. Bundy," pp. 76–77, 112–13, OHRO.

13. "The Reminiscences of Robert L. O'Brien," p. 76, "The Reminiscences of William Stiles Bennet," p. 164, OHRO; Theodore Goldsmith Joslin, *Hoover Off the Record* (Garden City, N.Y.: Doubleday, Doran and Co., 1934), pp. 13, 18.

14. Joslin, *Hoover Off the Record*, pp. 20, 144; Diary, 18 June 1931, 25 November, 28 December 1930, 28 April 1931, Stimson Papers; see Box 4, Lawrence Richey Papers, Herbert Hoover Presidential Library.

15. Watson, *As I Knew Them*, p. 259; Charles L. McNary to John H. McNary, 7 March 1930, Charles L. McNary Papers, LC; "Just One More of Those Little Hoover Mistakes," Scrapbook 3, Vandenberg Papers; Hiram Johnson to Chas. K.

McClatchy, 26 February 1930, Hiram Johnson Papers, University of California, Berkeley.

16. Herbert Clark Hoover, *The Memoirs of Herbert Hoover: The Great Depression, 1929–1941*, Vol. III (New York: Macmillan Co., 1951), p. 103; J. F. Essary in *Baltimore Evening Sun*, 1 March 1931; Herbert Clark Hoover, *The Memoirs of Herbert Hoover: The Cabinet and the Presidency, 1920–1933*, Vol. II (New York: Macmillan Co., 1953), p. 220; Joslin, *Hoover Off the Record*, p. 163; Diary, 18 June 1931, Stimson Papers.

17. "The Reminiscences of Stanley Washburn," p. 191, OHRO.

18. Herbert Clark Hoover, *The Memoirs of Herbert Hoover: Years of Adventure*, Vol. I (New York: Macmillan Co., 1951), p. 248; Josephus Daniels, *The Cabinet Diaries of Josephus Daniels, 1913–1921*, edited by E. David Cronon (Lincoln: University of Nebraska Press, 1963), p. 148; Seward W. Livermore, *Politics is Adjourned: Woodrow Wilson and the War Congress, 1916–1918* (Middletown, Conn.: Wesleyan University Press, 1966), pp. 41, 49–52, 68, 170–71, 173, 292; Ellen Maury Slayden, *Washington Wife: Journal of Ellen Maury Slayden from 1897–1919* (New York: Harper and Brothers, 1962), pp. 308–9, 323.

19. Robert K. Murray, *The Harding Era: Warren G. Harding and His Administration* (Minneapolis: University of Minnesota Press, 1969), p. 98; Schwarz, *Interregnum*, pp. 45–47. Democrat Breckenridge Long sought to persuade Hoover to become a Democrat in early 1920, but Hoover railed against both parties and exhibited "a disdain for political organizations . . . which is likely to lead him to trouble." Diary, 7 February 1920, Breckenridge Long Papers, LC.

20. Murray, *Harding*, pp. 194–95, 314–16, 422–23; Francis Russell, *The Shadow of Blooming Grove: Warren G. Harding in His Times* (New York: McGraw-Hill Book Company, 1968), p. 433. On executive-legislative conflict over foreign policy, see Melvyn Leffler, "The Origins of Republican War Debt Policy, 1921–1923: A Case Study of the Open Door Interpretation," *Journal of American History*, 59 (December 1972): 585–601.

21. Murray, *Harding*, pp. 231–34; Carolyn Grin, "The Unemployment Conference of 1921: An Experiment in National Economic Planning," *Mid-America*, 55 (April 1973): 83–107.

22. Ellis W. Hawley, "Secretary Hoover and the Bituminous Coal Problem, 1921–1928," *Business History Review*, 42 (Autumn 1968): 247–70.

23. Hoover, *Memoirs*, II, pp. 103–05.

24. Robert H. Zieger, *Republicans and Labor, 1919–1929* (Lexington: University of Kentucky Press, 1969), p. 204.

25. Hawley, "Herbert Hoover and the Expansion of the Commerce Department: The Anti-Bureaucrat as Bureaucratic Empire-Builder," paper given at Organization of American Historians Convention, Los Angeles, 17 April 1970.

26. James H. Shideler, *Farm Crisis, 1919–1923* (Berkeley: University of California Press, 1957), pp. 160–62; Gary H. Koerselman, "Herbert Hoover and the Farm Crisis of the Twenties: A Study of the Commerce Department's Efforts to Solve the Agricultural Depression, 1921–1928" (Ph.D. dissertation, Northern Illinois University, 1971), pp. 292–368, *passim*.

27. For Congress in the Coolidge years, see Donald R. McCoy, *Calvin Coolidge: The Quiet President* (New York: Macmillan Co., 1967), pp. 193–236, 273–86, 301–35.

28. Harris Gaylord Warren, *Herbert Hoover and the Great Depression* (New

York: Oxford University Press, 1959), pp. 84–97, 130, 171–2; Schwarz, *Interregnum*, pp. 6–11; Richard L. Watson, Jr., "The Defeat of Judge Parker: A Study in Pressure Groups and Politics," *Mississippi Valley Historical Review,* 50 (September 1963): 213–14.

29. Hoover, *Memoirs*, III, p. 101; Joslin, *Hoover Off the Record*, p. 22–23, 119, 216; William Starr Myers, "Looking Toward 1932," *American Political Science Review,* 25 (November 1931): 929–30; Marian C. McKenna, *Borah* (Ann Arbor: University of Michigan Press, 1961), p. 268.

30. Schwarz, *Interregnum*, pp. 79–98; Joslin, *Hoover Off the Record*, p. 191.

31. Schwarz, *Interregnum*, pp. 59–71, 100–103, 114–17.

32. *Ibid.*, pp. 106–41.

33. Clark to Coolidge, 6 May 1932, Clark Papers; Herbert Stein, *The Fiscal Revolution in America* (Chicago: University of Chicago Press, 1969), pp. 26–30, 36, 471; see Box 1-E/80, HHP.

34. Grin, "The Unemployment Conference of 1921," p. 107; Schwarz, *Interregnum*, pp. 142–78.

35. Schwarz, *Interregnum*, pp. 205–29; Charles A. Beard, "Representative Government under Fire," *Yale Review* 22 (1932): 35–51; Henry Hazlitt, "Without Benefit of Congress," *Scribner's Magazine* 92 (1932): 13–18; "Unbalanced Government," *Saturday Evening Post* (18 February 1933): 20; "What's Wrong with Congress," *Colliers* (28 January 1933): 46; "Do We Need a Dictator?" *Nation* 136 (1 March 1933): 22; Thomas Amlie to Max W. Heck, 1 June 1932, Thomas Amlie Papers, Wisconsin State Historical Society; Rep. Ralph Lozier to Charles E. Prettyman, Jr., 26 May 1932, Ralph Lozier Papers, University of Missouri; Newton Baker to Walter Lippmann, 13 May 1932, Newton Baker Papers, LC.

36. Charles L. McNary to John H. McNary, 25 January, 20 March 1933, McNary Papers. Clark described Hoover's legislative technique as demanding "not cooperation but compliance. . . ." Clark to Coolidge, 27 May 1932, Clark Papers.

Herbert Hoover and American Corporatism, 1929–1933
Ellis W. Hawley

1. Compare Robert Huddleston Wiebe, *The Search for Order* (New York: Macmillan Co., 1967); Rowland Berthoff, *An Unsettled People* (New York: Harper and Row, 1971); and Ronald Radosh and Murray Rothband (eds.), *A New History of Leviathan* (New York: Dutton 1972). See also Louis Galambos, "The Emerging Organizational Synthesis in Modern American History," *Business History Review* 44 (Autumn 1970): 279–90.

2. See, for example, Kenneth Barkin, "Populism in Germany and America," in Herbert Bass, ed., *The State of American History* (Chicago: Quadrangle Books, 1970), pp. 373–404; Heinrich Winkler *et al.*, *Die Grosse Krise in America* (Gottingen: Vandenhoeck and Ruprecht, 1973); and John Garraty, "The New Deal, National Socialism, and the Great Depression," *American Historical Review*, 78 (October 1973): 907–44. For broader trends in this field, see also Cyril Black, *The Dynamics of Modernization* (New York: Harper and Row, 1966), pp. 175–99.

3. See, for example, Radosh *et al.*, *Leviathan*, pp. 146–87; Grant McConnell, *Private Power and American Democracy* (New York: Alfred A. Knopf, Inc., 1966); Andrew Shonfield, *Modern Capitalism* (London: Oxford University Press,

208 Notes to Pages 102–5

1965), 308–14; James Weinstein, *The Corporate Ideal in the Liberal State* (Boston: Beacon Press, 1969); and William Appleman Williams, *The Contours of American History* (Cleveland: World Publishing Co., 1961).

4. One of the best short discussions of corporatism is in Eugene Golob, *The Isms* (New York: Harper, 1954), pp. 541–97. As he points out, corporatism was never necessarily linked with fascism. Nor was it, in theory anyway, incompatible with democracy. Compare also the developments described in Matthew Elbow, *French Corporative Theory* (New York: Columbia University Press, 1953), Ralph Henry Bowen, *German Theories of the Corporative State* (New York: Whittlesey House, 1947), and Robert Alexander Brady, *Business as a System of Power* (New York: Columbia University Press 1943), pp. 21–188, with those described in Wiebe, *Search for Order*, Weinstein, *Corporate Ideal*, Samuel Hays, *Response to Industrialization* (Chicago: University of Chicago Press, 1957), Louis Galambos, *Competition and Cooperation* (Baltimore: Johns Hopkins Press, 1966), and Edwin T. Layton, Jr., *The Revolt of the Engineers* (Cleveland: Press of Case Western Reserve, 1971).

5. See McConnell, *Private Power*, pp. 54–70. For American attempts to provide a philosophical base, see Herbert Hoover's Penn College Commencement Address, PS 496, HHP; Owen D. Young's "Dedication Address," in *Harvard Business Review* 5 (July 1927): 385–94; Edwin Parker's *Self-Regulation by Business* (Washington: Chamber of Commerce of the United States, 1927); and Glen Frank, "Self-Governing Industry," *Century*, 98 (June 1910): 225–36.

6. See the discussion in McConnell, *Private Power*, pp. 4–5, 64–70, 268–81, and in Peri Arnold, "Herbert Hoover and the Department of Commerce" (Ph.D. dissertation, University of Chicago, 1972), pp. 211–22.

7. See especially Herbert Hoover, *American Individualism* (Garden City, N.Y.: Doubleday, Page and Co., 1922), pp. 41–47, 54–56, 63–72; Hoover, "We Can Cooperate and Yet Compete," *Nation's Business* 14 (June 1926): 11–14; and Hoover, *The New Day: Campaign Speeches of Herbert Hoover, 1928* (Stanford: Stanford University Press 1928), pp. 9–44, 196–204.

8. Hoover, *New Day*, pp. 22–23; Hoover, *Larger Purposes of Department of Commerce* (Washington: Government Printing Office, 1928).

9. Hoover, Inaugural Address, 4 March 1929; Message to Congress, 16 April 1929; "What Business May Expect from President Hoover," 9 March 1929, PS 977, 984, 1011, HHP.

10. The tension involved in particular areas of policy is described below, but for examples of documents reflecting the dialectic see Hoover's "Address to the American Federation of Labor," 6 October 1930, PS 1385, HHP; Hoover's "Memorandum on Farm Board Organization," 13 July 1929, Farm Matters File, PSF, HHP; and Hoover's "Address to the Chamber of Commerce," 1 May 1930, PS 1279, HHP. It was also an old theme with Hoover. See, for example, *American Individualism*, pp. 41–44, and his Penn College Address, 12 June 1925, PS 496, HHP.

11. Hoover to W. O. Thompson, 30 December 1929, PS 1197, HHP; E. E. Hunt, "Looking to the Future," Box 19, E. E. Hunt Papers, HIA; Barry D. Karl, "Presidential Planning and Social Science Research," in Donald Fleming and Bernard Bailyn (eds.), *Perspectives in American History* (Cambridge, Mass.: Harvard University Press, 1969), pp. 351–52, 362–63.

12. Karl, "Presidential Planning," pp. 362–65; Alva Johnston, "Mr. Hoover's Commissions Open New Era," *New York Herald Tribune*, 30 January, 1 Febru-

ary 1930; Hoover, Press Statement, 2 July 1929, PS 1071-A, HHP. In early 1930, Hoover also planned to follow up recovery from the panic of 1929 with a full-dress study of economic stabilization. See his address to the Chamber of Commerce, 1 May 1930, PS 1279, HHP.

13. See, for example, E. E. Hunt, "National Planning Board," 2 July 1926, Box 18, Hunt Papers, HIA.

14. "Industry Conference," Commerce Dept. File, PSF, HHP; Hoover to Lamont, 17 May 1929, AFL File, PSF, HHP; Barnes, "Notes for an Autobiography," 5 January 1943, File 2, Drawer 7, Henry Elmer Barnes Papers, St. Louis County Historical Society, Duluth, Minnesota; Hunt to Arch Shaw, 17 March 1931, Box 37, Hunt Papers, HIA.

15. Hoover to J. L. O'Brian, 30 August 1929, Justice Dept. File, PSF, HHP; Rush Butler to George Akerson, 20 April 1929, Antitrust File, PSF, HHP; Galambos, *Competition and Cooperation*, pp. 143–47. B. C. Forbes of *Forbes Magazine* also believed that Hoover would take an "active part" in setting up the type of interbusiness planning agencies being advocated by such systematizers as Benjamin Javits and Manny Straus. See "Minutes of Conference on Industrial Coordination," 5 March 1929, Unemployment File, PSF, HHP.

16. Mitchell to R. L. Wilbur, 29 March 1929; Hoover, Press Statement, 2 April 1929, both in Oil File, PSF, HHP; Herbert Clark Hoover, *The Memoirs of Herbert Hoover: The Cabinet and The Presidency, 1920–1933*, Vol. II (New York: Macmillan Co., 1951), p. 238.

17. Hoover to O'Brian, 30 August 1929, Justice Dept. File, PSF, HHP; Hoover, *Memoirs*, II, p. 302.

18. Trade association lawyer Felix Levy, in particular, was threatening to turn over evidence of lax enforcement to the press, and leaders of the National Civic Federation were urging action, both to protect legitimate cooperation and with the idea of getting more groups interested in "modernizing" the law. Even before these pressures developed, however, Hoover had decided that Donovan's enforcement of the Sherman Act had been "very bad." See Hoover's "Memorandum on Reasons Why Donovan Was Not Taken into the Cabinet," Donovan File, PNF, HHP; Levy to Mitchell, 4 April 1929, File 60-o, Justice Department Archives, RG60, NA; Robert Himmelberg, "Relaxation of the Federal Anti-Trust Policy as a Goal of the Business Community, 1918–1933" (Ph.D. dissertation, Pennsylvania State University, 1963), pp. 176–81.

19. Himmelberg, "Relaxation of Anti-Trust," pp. 189–98; *Business Week* (19 February 1930): 22–24; O'Brian to Benjamin Kirsh, 22 October 1929, File 60-o, RG 60, NA. The major groups involved were the Bolt and Nut Institute, the Sugar Institute, the Wool Institute, and the Asphalt Shingle and Roofing Institute.

20. O'Brian to Mitchell, 16 January 1931, File 60-57-32, RG 60, NA; "Federal Trade Practice Conferences," 14 June 1930, FTC File, PSF, HHP; *Business Week* (16 April 1930): 25; (18 October 1930): 13–14.

21. Hoover to Coolidge, 22 September 1926, FTC File, COF, HHP; Abram Myers to Hoover, 2 May 1931, FTC File, PSF, HHP.

22. Lawrence Richey to Louis Flye, 16 September 1930; Myers to Hoover, 2 May 1931; Hoover to Myers, 4 May 1931, all in FTC File, PSF, HHP.

23. Hoover, "Address to the AFL," 6 October 1930; "State of the Union Message," 2 December 1930, PS 1385, 1429, HHP.

24. Hoover to J. J. Davis, 21 July, 13 August 1930, Coal File, PSF, HHP. For

the nature of the coal problem and Hoover's earlier struggle with it, see my "Secretary Hoover and the Bituminous Coal Problem, 1921–28," *Business History Review* 42 (Autumn 1968): 253–70.

25. Wilson Compton to Hoover, 2, 5 April 1930, National Timber Conservation Board File, PSF, HHP. For Hoover's earlier difficulties with conflicting factions in the industry, see Arnold, "Hoover and Department of Commerce," pp. 158–71.

26. Mark Requa, "Colorado Springs Petroleum Conference," 13 June 1929; Hoover to Wilbur, 15 December 1930, both in Oil File, PSF, HHP; William Olbrich, "The Hoover Administration and the Oil Crisis," unpublished ms., author's files.

27. For Hoover's plan and its origins, see James H. Shideler, "Herbert Hoover and the Federal Farm Board Project, 1921–25," *Mississippi Valley Historical Review* 42 (March 1956): 710–29.

28. Albert U. Romasco, *The Poverty of Abundance: Hoover, the Nation, the Depression* (New York: Oxford University Press, 1956), p. 23.

29. Hoover, "Memorandum on Farm Board Organization," 13 July 1929; Carl Williams to Hoover, 10 July 1930, both in Farm Matters File, PSF, HHP; Hoover, "Message to Congress," 16 April 1929, PS 1011, HHP.

30. Hoover, "Memoranda on Farm Board Organization and on Possible Procedure," 13 July 1929; Hoover to Alexander Legge, 15 March 1930; Legge to John Richardson, 1 April 1930, all in Farm Matters File, PSF, HHP.

31. The 1921 activities are described in Carolyn Grin, "The Unemployment Conference of 1921: An Experiment in National Cooperative Planning," *Mid-America* 55 (April 1973): 83–107.

32. Romasco, *Poverty*, pp. 27–31, 48–54; Press Release, 21 November 1929, Business Conference File, PSF, HHP; "Activities of the National Business Survey Conference," 23 January 1930; "The National Building Survey Conference," 21 January 1930, both in Chamber of Commerce File, PSF, HHP.

33. Hoover, "Addresses to Chamber of Commerce," 5 December 1929, 1 May 1930, PS 1178, 1279, HHP; Press Release, 22 November 1929, Business Conferences File, PSF, HHP; U.S. Chamber of Commerce, *Business Conditions and Outlook* (7 December 1929).

34. Hoover, *New Day*, pp. 22–23; Hoover to David Lawrence, 29 December 1927, American Businessman File, COF, HHP.

35. For examples of such "advice," see the *Commercial and Financial Chronicle* 132 (20 June 1931): 4524; 133 (12 September 1931): 1670–71; *New York Times*, 25 January 1931, II, p. 19; Frank A. Fetter, *The Masquerade of Monopoly* (New York: Harcourt, Brace and Co., 1931); *Barron's* 11 (29 June 1931): 3, 8; J. K. Davis to Hoover, 29 October 1930, Oil File, PSF, HHP Newton Baker, in *Review of Reviews* 84 (September 1931): 57–59. For discussion of those who deplored Hoover's "artificial" intervention with "natural laws," see also Romasco, *Poverty*, pp. 79–84, and *Business Week* (13 May 1931): 56. For the antitrust view that the depression was due to "combinations," "chain organizations," and "price or cost fixing associations," see Senate Resolution 46, 72 Cong., 1 Sess., 9 December 1931, copy in Box 2, Tray 9, George Norris Papers, LC.

36. See, for example, W. H. Denney to Hoover, 25 May 1931, Business File, PSF, HHP; C. F. Abbott to Hoover, 17 October 1930, Abbott File, President's Secretary File (PSec), HHP; Gerard Swope to Hoover, 2 October 1930; Wallace

Donham, "The Unemployment Emergency," 6 February 1931; Darwin Meserole to Hoover, 24 November 1930, all in Unemployment File, PSF, HHP.

37. William Scroggs, "Anti-Trust Laws Under Fire," *Outlook and Independent* 156 (3 December 1930): 545; *Business Week* (7 May 1930): 14; (19 November 1930): 27; McGraw-Hill Co., *American Business Management Speaks Out* (1931); Philip Cabot, "Vices of Free Competition," *Yale Review* 21 (September 1931): 38–55; James H. Williams, "Reign of Error," *Atlantic Monthly* 147 (June 1931): 787–96.

38. See, for example, Oswald Garrison Villard, in *Nation* 131 (3 September 1930): 237–39; John Ryan, in *Commonweal* 12 (3 September 1930): 436–38; George Soule, in *New Republic* 56 (11 March 1931): 88–91; Rexford Tugwell, in *Political Science Quarterly* 46 (June 1931): 188–224; "Program of the Progressive Conference," 11–12 March 1931, Norris Papers, LC.

39. The arguments of cartelizers frequently stressed the notion that social health depended upon protecting capital and organizational commitments in a "basic" or "vital" industry. Labor held that all else depended upon the payment of "just" or "socially efficient" wages. Small merchants insisted that liquidating them would mean the end of "economic democracy," "local self-government," and all else that was really healthy in American society. And farm leaders argued that both economic and social well-being depended upon preserving an industry that was "fundamental" to all others and a social group that provided American society with most of its virtues. The latter two arguments, in particular, resembled the glorification of the peasant, artisan, and small shopkeeper that was characteristic of the corporatist-oriented "middle-class socialism" in Germany. See, for example, Cornelius Kelley, in New York University, *National Conference on the Relation of Law and Business* (1931), pp. 109–14; *Monthly Labor Review* 33 (November 1931): 1044–47; Frederick K. Hardy, "The Special Taxation of Chain Stores" (Ph.D. dissertation, University of Wisconsin, 1934), pp. 95–115; Louis B. Schmidt, "Role and Techniques of Agrarian Pressure Groups," *Agricultural History* 30 (April 1956): 55–57; Arthur Schweitzer, *Big Business in the Third Reich* (Bloomington: Indiana University Press, 1964), pp. 70–83, 115–17.

40. Stuart Chase, "A Ten Year Plan for America," *Harper's Magazine* 163 (June 1931): 1–10; Charles A. Beard, "A 'Five Year Plan' for America," *Forum* 86 (July 1931): 1–11; George Soule, "National Planning," *New Republic* 66 (4 March 1931): 61–65.

41. See, for example, Maurice Mendelson and Henry Baker, "The Industrialization of Russia." *Current History* 33 (January 1931): 481–92; Lewis Lorwin, in *New Republic* 66 (29 April 1931): 294–97; *Christian Century* 48 (11 March 1931): 334–36.

42. *Bulletin of the Taylor Society* 16 (April 1931): 82–83.

43. *New Republic* 69, Pt. 2 (13 January 1932); Isador Lubin, "The New Lead from Capitol Hill," *Survey* 67 (1 March 1932): 573–77; *Congressional Digest,* 11 (April 1932): 103; U.S. Senate, Committee on Manufactures, *Establishment of a National Economic Council* (72 Cong., 1 Sess., 1932).

44. Himmelberg, "Relaxation of Anti-Trust," pp. 224, 235–41; Elmer Davis, "Can Business Manage Itself?" *Harper's Magazine* 162 (March 1931): 385–96; George H. Bailey to Lamont, 14 September 1931, File 82448/48, RG 40, NA; Rush Butler, in New York University, *National Conference,* pp. 235–38.

45. Galambos, *Competition and Cooperation,* pp. 179–80; *New York Times,*

(27 October 1931): 3; (9 December 1931): 23; (11 December 1931): 29; New York University, *National Conference*.

46. *Business Week* (21 January 1931): 10.

47. Galambos, *Competition and Cooperation*, p. 177.

48. *Business Week* (14 May 1930): 22; R. H. Whitehead, "Plan for a National Industrial Council," 1 October 1931, File 83057, Commerce Dept. Archives, RG 40, NA; M. L. Requa, "Industrial Self-Regulation," Requa File, PPF, HHP; Benjamin Javits to Lamont, 15 October 1929, Box 14, Lamont Papers, RG 40, NA; Javits to Hoover, 18 December 1931, Unemployment File, PSF, HHP; Matthew Woll, Address over WOR, Business Stabilization File, PSF, HHP.

49. David Goldsmith Loth, *Swope of G. E.* (New York: Simon and Schuster, 1958), pp. 201–202; "Swope Address," reprinted in *Monthly Labor Review* 33 (November 1931): 1049–57.

50. *Literary Digest* 111 (3 October 1931): 8–9; Norman Thomas, in *Nation* 133 (7 October 1931): 357–59; H. A. Bullis to James Bell, 3 November 1931, Box 1, James Bell Papers, Minnesota Historical Society, St. Paul, Minn.; Swope, "Discussion of Stabilization of Industry," Swope File, PSec, HHP.

51. "Resolutions Adopted at Atlantic City," May 1931; Barnes to Hoover, 4 September 1931, both in Chamber of Commerce File, PSF, HHP.

52. Barnes to Hoover, 4 September 1931; "Report of the Committee on Continuity of Business and Employment," 4 October 1931, both in Chamber of Commerce File, PSF, HHP. The groups to be represented were the Chamber of Commerce, labor, agriculture, government (Department of Commerce), manufacturing, banking, railroads, utilities, distribution, law, engineering, and economics.

53. *Business Week* (30 December 1931): 14; Barnes to Hoover, 18 December 1931, Chamber of Commerce File, PSF, HHP.

54. The business community was still badly divided, and this was more apparent in other organizations than the Chamber. Large numbers of business leaders still feared that relaxing the antitrust laws would strengthen their rivals or open the way to labor "monopolies" and hostile governmental bureaucracies. See Himmelberg, "Relaxation of Anti-Trust," pp. 245–69, and A. W. Briggs, "Proposals Relating to the Antitrust Laws," 11 January 1932, Antitrust File, PSF, HHP.

55. "No President," Hoover told Barnes, "must ever admit he has been wrong." See Barnes, "Notes regarding the Panic of 1929–30," File 6, Drawer 6, Barnes Papers. For this pattern in Hoover's earlier life, see also Geoffrey Blainey, "Herbert Hoover's Forgotten Years," *Business Archives and History* 3 (February 1963): 70.

56. For the progressive development of this view, see Hoover's addresses of 2 October 1930, 2 December 1930, 15 June 1931, and 11 August 1932, PS 1382, 1429, 1587, 1939, HHP. See also Herbert Clark Hoover, *The Memoirs of Herbert Hoover: The Great Depression, 1929–1941*, Vol. III (New York: Macmillan Co.), pp. 197–202.

57. The terms appear in Hoover to Arch Shaw, 17 February 1933, Shaw File, PPF, HHP, and Hoover, "Acceptance Speech," 11 August 1932, PS 1939, HHP.

58. Hoover, Press Statements of 14, 19 August, 17 October 1930, PS 1359, 1363, 1389, HHP.

59. Hoover, "Message to Congress," 3 March 1931; Press Statements, 9 December 1930, 3 February 1931, 9 August 1931, PS 1503, 1436, 1474, HHP; Public Letter

of James C. Stone to F. J. Wilmer, 13 May 1931, Farm Matters File, PSF, HHP; U.S. Federal Farm Board, *Second Annual Report* (Washington: Government Printing Office, 1931).

60. Hoover, "Addresses," 12 February, 15 June 1931, PS 1484, 1587, HHP.

61. See, for example, R. J. Caldwell to Hoover, 30 April 1931, Box 2, Lamont Papers, RG 40, NA; J. W. Sparks to Mitchell, 9 April 1931, File 60–104–13, RG 60, NA; Oscar Sutro to Requa, 18 December 1931, Oil File, PSF, HHP; *Business Week* (9 July 1930): 12.

62. Louis Domeratzky, in *Foreign Affairs* 10 (October 1931): 34–53; William Mitchell, "Address," 16 May 1931, Justice Department File, PSF, HHP; Hoover, "Memorandum on the Swope Plan," 11 September 1931, Business Stabilization File, PSF, HHP.

63. Hoover, "State of the Union Message," 2 December 1930, PS 1429, HHP.

64. Drafts of such statements were prepared for him in late 1930, but no statements were made. See drafts dated 12 December 1930, Business File, PSF, HHP.

65. Julius Klein to Robert Blumenthal, 15 May 1931; Klein to Oscar Cooley, 7 November 1931; Lamont to John Crout, 27 May 1931, all in File 83057, RG 40, NA.

66. Hoover, "Memorandum on the Swope Plan," 11 September 1931; Hoover to Thomas Thacher, 12 September 1931; Thacher to Hoover, 1 October 1931; Hoover to Hebert, 11 September, 2 October 1931; Hebert to Hoover, 15, 18 September 1931; Hebert, "Statement on the Subject of Stabilization of Industry," all in Business Stabilization File, PSF, HHP.

67. Hoover, *Memoirs*, III, pp. 334–35; Barnes to Hoover, 10 October, 30 November, 18 December 1931, Chamber of Commerce File, PSF, HHP.

68. Hoover, "State of the Union Message," 8 December 1931, PS 1729, HHP.

69. F. C. Croxton to Heads of Trade Association, 18 July 1931; Frederick Feiker to Klein, 16 September 1931; T. R. Taylor to Feiker, 16 September 1931, all in Business Stabilization File, PSF, HHP; Feiker to Klein, 30 June 1931, Box 83, Frederick Feiker Papers, Bureau of Foreign and Domestic Commerce Archives, RG 151, NA.

70. Committee on Planning to Feiker, 22 October 1931; "Notes for Use in Asheville Speech," 19 September 1931, Boxes 81, 84, Feiker Papers, RG 151, NA.

71. Feiker, "Address before the ATAE," 24 September 1931; Feiker, "An American Economic Plan," 30 October 1931, Boxes 81, 83, Feiker Papers, RG 151, NA; American Trade Association Executives, *Listening-In*, 10 October 1931, 17 November 1931; Feiker to Lamont, 24 September 1931, Box 1, Lamont Papers, RG 40, NA; Klein to Sheldon Cary, 2 October 1931, File 81288, RG 40, NA; Himmelberg, "Relaxation of Anti-Trust," pp. 212–16.

72. Galambos, *Competition and Cooperation*, p. 156; Himmelberg, "Relaxation of Anti-Trust," pp. 209–11; Lamont, "Remarks before Conference of Textile Industry," 25 January 1932, Box 6, Lamont Papers, RG 40, NA.

73. "Accomplishments of the BFDC," Box 2, Taylor-Gates Material, HHP; "Trade Association Activities and Department of Commerce Assistance," 30 October 1931; Feiker, "An Ideal Charter for Trade Associations," Boxes 78, 94, Feiker Papers, RG 151, HHP.

74. Ripley Bowman, "The U.S. Timber Conservation Board," File 87338, RG 40, NA; Hoover to Lamont, 11 November 1930, National Timber Conservation Bd. File, PSF, HHP.

75. "Review of Efforts of FOCB and Various State Authorities to Solve Problems of Oil Industry," 13 March 1931, PS 1511, HHP; Lamont, "Address before the API," 11 November 1931, File 82272/1, RG 40, NA; E. S. Rochester to Wilbur, 1 April 1932, Box 13, Wilbur Papers, HIA.

76. "Trade Practice Conference Rules for the Petroleum Industry," 12 June 1931; Mitchell to O'Brian, 21 July 1931, both in File 60–57–32, RG 60, NA; *New York Journal of Commerce*, 10 August 1931.

77. W. N. Doak to Hoover, 29, 31 August 1931, Coal File, PSF, HHP; O'Brian, "Proposed Plan of Bituminous Coal Operators," 7 January 1932; O'Brian to E. L. Greever, 26 January 1932; O'Brian to Mitchell, 27 January 1932, all in File 60–187–67, RG 60, NA; National Coal Association, *The Regional Sales Agency Plan* (1931); *Business Week* (15 July 1931): 7; (16 December 1931): 18.

78. Hoover, Press Statements, 1, 14, 19, August, 17 October 1930; 19 August, 6 October 1931; "Addresses," 24 September, 19 November 1930; 2 December 1931, PS 1351, 1359, 1363, 1389, 1643, 1675-A, 1377, 1419, 1725, HHP.

79. Harris Gaylord Warren, *Herbert Hoover and the Great Depression* (New York: Oxford University Press, 1967 ed.), pp. 73–74; "Expression of Pleasure on Approving Wagner-Graham Act," 10 February 1931, PS 1481, HHP; James Olson, "The End of Voluntarism," *Annals of Iowa* 41 (Fall 1972): 1107–13.

80. Secretary of Labor Doak supported the Davis-Kelley Bill for coal stabilization and Secretary of the Interior Wilbur endorsed the Nye Bill to legalize trade practice conference agreements, but Hoover endorsed neither. See *New York Times* (1 April 1932): 10, and Doak to Hoover, 17 February 1932, Coal File, PSF, HHP.

81. Hoover to Crocker, 21 May 1932, Unemployment File, PSF, HHP; Hoover, Press Statements, 25 March, 6 July 1932; Message to Congress, 11 July 1932, PS 1817, 1904, 1909, HHP.

82. "Statement by 122 Industrialists," 11 February 1932; "A Plea from Representatives of Independent Industrial Units," 11 February 1932; Hoover to Malcolm Whitman, 11 February 1932; Gordon Corbaley to Richey, 22 January 1932, all in Business File, PSF, HHP; Corbaley to Richey, 7 April 1932, Corbaley File, PSec, HHP.

83. Montague to Hoover, 15 March 1932; Hoover to Montague, 16 March 1932; both in Antitrust File, PSF, HHP; Galambos, *Competition and Cooperation*, pp. 183–84; Z. L. Potter to Lamont, 5, 17, 27 May 1932; Lamont to Potter, 12 May, 4 June 1932, File 83057, RG 40, NA.

84. Hoover to Daniel Willard, 20 May 1932; Hoover to Albert Cox, 10 June 1932; Hoover to Howard Coffin, 13 June 1932; Cox and others to Hoover, 10 June 1932; Coffin to Hoover, 12 June 1932, all in U.S. Council for National Defense File, PSF, HHP.

85. Romasco, *Poverty*, pp. 189–94; Warren, *Hoover*, pp. 143–47, 163–66; Hoover, "Address," 6 March 1932, PS 1803, HHP.

86. "Confidential History of the National Conference of Banking and Industrial Committees," Box 59, Ogden Mills Papers, LC; Romasco, *Poverty*, pp. 198–199.

87. Hoover, *Memoirs*, III, p. 40; Hoover to Franklin D. Roosevelt, 18 February 1933, Roosevelt File, PNF, HHP.

88. Hoover, "Acceptance Speech," 11 August 1932; "State of the Union Message," 6 December 1932; "Message to Congress on Vital Measures," 29 February 1933; "Endorsement of Share-the-Work Movement," 21 November 1932, PS 1939,

2078, 2128, 2061, HHP; Hoover to Edward Butler, 3 December 1932, James Rand File, PNF, HHP; Hoover to Shaw, 17 February 1933, Shaw File, PPF, HHP.

89. Galambos, *Competition and Cooperation,* p. 184; Hoover, "Address," 28 October 1932, PS 2019-A, HHP; Hoover to R. H. Hartley and Julius Meier, 11 July 1932, Antitrust File, PSF, HHP.

90. Eugene Lyons, *Herbert Hoover: A Biography* (Garden City, N.Y.: Doubleday and Co., 1964), p. 294.

91. Taylor to Roy Chapin, 6, 7 October 1932; Silas Strawn, "Progress Report on Anti-Trust Laws," both in File 82248/48, RG 40, NA; C. J. Junkin to Chapin, 20 January 1933, Box 103, Feiker Papers, RG 151, NA; Galambos, *Competition and Cooperation,* pp. 186–90.

92. See my *The New Deal and the Problem of Monopoly* (Princeton: Princeton University Press, 1966), pp. 35–52, 472–90.

93. For political reasons, both the New Dealers and the Hooverites tended to accentuate the differences, the former applying the label of "do-nothingism," the latter seeing the New Deal as a mixture of "socialist" and "fascist" ideas. Both images rest more on political invective than on dispassionate analysis, and the time seems long since past for laying both of them aside and recognizing both Hoover's activism and the limited aims of and changes wrought by the New Deal.

94. For arguments along this line, see Galambos, *Competition and Cooperation,* pp. 199–202; Olson, "End to Voluntarism," p. 1113; Otis L. Graham, Jr., "The Planning Ideal and American Reality," unpublished ms., author's files.

The View from the State House: FDR
Alfred B. Rollins

1. A. B. Rollins, "Was There Really a Man Named Roosevelt?" in George Athan Billias and Gerald N. Grob (eds.), *American History: Retrospect and Prospect* (New York: Free Press, 1971), p. 233.

2. Carl Degler, "The Ordeal of Herbert Hoover," *Yale Review* 52 (1963): 563–83.

3. Edgar Eugene Robinson, *The Roosevelt Leadership, 1933–1945* (Philadelphia: J. J. Lippincott, 1955).

4. Arthur M. Schlesinger, Jr., *The Age of Roosevelt: The Crisis of the Old Order, 1919–1933* (Boston: Houghton Mifflin Co., 1957), pp. 80–81.

5. Frank Freidel, *Franklin D. Roosevelt: The Ordeal* (Boston: Little, Brown and Co., 1954), p. 69; James MacGregor Burns, *Roosevelt: The Lion and the Fox* (New York: Harcourt, Brace, 1956), p. 144; Raymond Moley and Elliott A. Rosen, *The First New Deal* (New York: Harcourt, Brace and Co., 1966), p. 210.

6. Schlesinger, *Crisis,* p. 80 ff; Frank Freidel, *Franklin D. Roosevelt: The Apprenticeship* (Boston: Little, Brown and Co., 1952), p. 319; *The Ordeal,* pp. 7, 10, 56–69.

7. Burns, *Roosevelt,* p. 142 ff; Freidel, *The Ordeal,* pp. 56–69.

8. John D. Hicks, *The Republican Ascendancy, 1921–1933* (New York: Harper and Bros., 1960), pp. 32, 67, 126–27.

9. *New York Times,* 4 June 1927.

10. American Construction Council file, Group XIV, Franklin D. Roosevelt Papers, Roosevelt Library, Hyde Park, N.Y.

11. Freidel, *The Ordeal*, pp. 153–56; Schlesinger, *Crisis*, pp. 65, 374 ff; Hicks, *Republican Ascendancy*, p. 12; A. B. Rollins, "The Political Education of Franklin D. Roosevelt, 1909–1928" (Ph.D. dissertation, Harvard University, 1953), pp. 707–709.

12. Louis Howe to Roosevelt, n.d., Group XIV, Roosevelt Papers.

13. Georges St. Jean to Roosevelt, 31 August 1927, Group XI, Roosevelt Papers.

14. Freidel, *The Ordeal*, p. 226.

15. *New York Times*, 25 October 1928.

16. Roosevelt to Irving Hiett, 5 September, Roosevelt to William Loeb, 21 September, Roosevelt to Ward Melville, 21 September 1928, Group XVII, Roosevelt Papers; Rollins, "Political Education," pp. 854–55.

17. Moley, *First New Deal*, p. 22.

18. Jordan A. Schwarz, *The Interregnum of Despair: Hoover, Congress and the Depression* (Urbana: University of Illinois Press, 1970), p. 12.

19. *Ibid.*, pp. 23 ff, 38, 153.

20. Moley, *First New Deal*, p. 246; Schwarz, *Interregnum*, pp. 181–82, 198; Roosevelt to Royal Copeland, 23 February 1931, quoted in Schwarz, *Interregnum*, p. 71.

21. Franklin Delano Roosevelt, *The Public Papers and Addresses of Franklin D. Roosevelt*, edited by Samuel Rosenman (13 vols. New York: Russell and Russell, 1938–1950), I, pp. 373–76.

22. Roosevelt, *Public Papers*, I, pp. 448–449; Freidel, *The Triumph*, p. 139.

23. Roosevelt, *Public Papers*, I, p. 405.

24. Franklin Delano Roosevelt, *Public Papers of Franklin D. Roosevelt, Forty-Eighth Governor of the State of New York, 1931* (Albany: J. B. Lyon Co., 1937), pp. 734, 740–41; Roosevelt to Elizabeth Marbury, 9 June 1931, in Franklin Delano Roosevelt, *Personal Letters of Franklin D. Roosevelt, 1928–1945*, edited by Elliott Roosevelt (New York: Kraus Reprint Co., 1947), p. 195.

25. Schlesinger, *Crisis*, p. 121 ff.

26. Roosevelt, *Public Papers*, I, pp. 203–205.

27. *Ibid.*, 669–84.

28. *Ibid.*

29. *Ibid.*, pp. 742–56, 807–10; Burns, *Roosevelt*, p. 144.

The Interregnum Struggle Between Hoover and Roosevelt
Frank Freidel

1. For the details of the struggle, especially from the viewpoint of Roosevelt, see Frank Freidel, *Franklin D. Roosevelt: Launching the New Deal* (Boston: Little, Brown and Co., 1973), chs. 1–3, 7–8, 11.

2. Raymond Moley, *After Seven Years* (New York: Harper and Bros., 1939), 67–108, 138–61; Herbert Clark Hoover, *The Memoirs of Herbert Hoover: The Great Depression, 1929–1941*, Vol. III (New York: Macmillan Co., 1952), 167–75, 218–349, *et passim*. See also Moley and Rosen, *The First New Deal* (New York: Harcourt, Brace and Co., 1966), pp. 21–66; 127–64. Herbert Feis, *1933: Characters in a Crisis* (Boston: Little, Brown Co., 1966), pp. 3–91.

3. On Roosevelt's side of the early relationship, see Frank Freidel, *Roosevelt: The Ordeal* (Boston: Little, Brown and Co., 1954), pp. 56–58, and, quoting Hoover's letter of congratulation, p. 69. Roosevelt to Hugh Gibson, 2 January

1920; Hoover to Roosevelt, 13 July 1920, Container 1-G1981, HHP. There are also copies in the Franklin D. Roosevelt Library, Hyde Park, N.Y.

4. Hoover, "My Personal Relations with Mr. Roosevelt," Container 1-G1981, HHP. On this ms. are the pencilled notations "Sept. 26 '58" and, in Hoover's hand, "not used." The offending letter was Roosevelt to M. D. Wood, 11 October 1928, bearing a bad imitation of Roosevelt's signature, of the sort his "letter-writing factory" turned out by the thousands. Also in the Hoover mss. are several other similar Roosevelt letters of the 1928 campaign. Freidel, *Roosevelt: The Ordeal*, p. 226.

5. Freidel, *Roosevelt: The Triumph* (Boston: Little, Brown and Co., 1956), p. 324.

6. Hoover, "My Personal Relations with Mr. Roosevelt," Container 1-G1981, HHP.

7. Adolf A. Berle, Jr., memorandum, 7 November 1932, Adolf A. Berle Papers, University of Minnesota, Minneapolis.

8. Hoover, *Memoirs*, III, pp. 176–77.

9. P. Nichols comment on Sir Ronald Lindsay to Sir John Simon, 14 November 1932, Foreign Office 371/15914 C 9437. Public Record Office, covered by Crown-copyright and quoted by permission of the Controller of H. M. Stationery Office.

10. Herbert Clark Hoover, *The State Papers and Other Public Writings*, edited by William Starr Myers (Garden City, N.Y.: Doubleday, Doran and Co., 1934), II, pp. 483–86.

11. Rexford G. Tugwell diary, 20 December 1932, Roosevelt Library, Hyde Park, N.Y.; Moley, *After Seven Years*, p. 68.

12. Telephone conversation between Hoover and Roosevelt, 17 November 1932, Container 1-G1981, HHP; Stimson diary, 14, 16 November 1932, Henry L. Stimson Papers, Yale University, New Haven, Conn.

13. Hoover memorandum, 22 November 1932, Container 1-G1981, HHP.

14. Henry F. Misselwitz to Raymond Clapper, December, 1932, Raymond Clapper Papers, LC.

15. Stimson diary, 22 November 1932, Stimson Papers.

16. Stimson diary, 3, 4 January 1933, *ibid.;* FDR to Hoover, 4 January 1933; Hoover to FDR, 5 January 1933; transcript of telephone conversation between Hoover and FDR, 6 January 1933, 4:15 P.M., Container 1-G1981, HHP.

17. Hoover memorandum on conference of 20 January 1933 with Hoover long-hand emendations, Container 1-G1981, HHP; Stimson diary, 20 January 1933, Stimson Papers; Moley diary, 21 January 1933, Raymond Moley Papers, HIA.

18. Hoover to FDR, 18 February 1933. The original is in the President's Secretary's File, Roosevelt Papers; it appears in William Starr Myers and Walter H. Newton, *The Hoover Administration, A Documented Narrative* (New York: C. Scribner's Sons, 1936), pp. 338–40.

19. Hoover to David A. Reed, 20 February 1933 in Myers and Newton, *Hoover Administration*, p. 341.

20. *New York Times*, 14, 15 May 1935.

21. On Hoover's pressure on Glass, confidential source. Circumstantial evidence in the Hoover Papers points toward Mark Sullivan as the person who may have urged financial editors to call upon Roosevelt to pledge himself to a continued gold standard.

Hoover's Foreign Policy and the New Left
Selig Adler

1. Robert F. Smith, "American Foreign Relations 1920–1942," in Barton J. Bernstein (ed.), *Towards a New Past: Dissenting Essays in American History* (New York: Pantheon Books, 1969 ed.), pp. 232–62.

2. Herbert Clark Hoover, *The Memoirs of Herbert Hoover: The Cabinet and the Presidency, 1920–1933*, Vol. II (New York: Macmillan Co., 1952), pp. 338, 350, 352.

3. Wayne S. Cole, *An Interpretive History of American Foreign Relations* (Homewood, Ill.: Dorsey Press, 1968 ed.), pp. 493–94, 561. Selig Adler, *The Isolationist Impulse: Its Twentieth-Century Reaction* (New York: Abelard-Schuman, 1957), pp. 437–40.

4. Jules Davids, *America and the World of Our Time*, 3rd ed. (New York: Random House, 1970), p. 145; Julius William Pratt, *America's Colonial Experiment* (New York: Prentice-Hall, Inc., 1950), pp. 320–22; Selig Adler, *The Uncertain Giant 1921–1941: American Foreign Policy Between the Wars* (New York: Macmillan Co., 1965), pp. 107–108. See also Robert H. Ferrell, *American Diplomacy in the Great Depression: Hoover-Stimson Foreign Policy, 1929–1933* (New Haven: Yale University Press, 1957), *passim*. In the light of Robert H. Ferrell's article, "Repudiation of a Repudiation," *Journal of American History* 51 (March 1965): 669–73, it seems that Hoover was far from enthusiastic about the release of the Clark Memorandum.

5. Alexander DeConde, *Herbert Hoover's Latin-American Policy* (Stanford: Stanford University Press, 1951), *passim;* Julius William Pratt, *Cordell Hull* [*The American Secretaries of State and Their Diplomacy*] Vols. XII–XIII (New York: Cooper Square Publishers, 1964), XII, p. 140.

6. Joan Hoff Wilson, *American Business and Foreign Policy, 1920–1933* (Lexington: University of Kentucky Press, 1971), pp. 166, 177.

7. Pratt, *America's Colonial Experiment*, p. 322.

8. Hoover's reasons for his veto are objectively presented in Richard William Leopold, *The Growth of American Foreign Policy* (New York: Alfred A. Knopf, Inc., 1962), pp. 502–503. See also Pratt, *Hull*, XII, p. 232.

9. See, for instance, L. Ethan Ellis, *Republican Foreign Policy, 1921–1933* (New Brunswick, N.J.: Rutgers University Press, 1968), pp. 25–27.

10. Manfred Jonas, ed., *American Foreign Relations in the Twentieth Century* (New York: Crowell Publishing Co., 1967), p. 81.

11. Richard W. Van Alstyne, *American Crisis Diplomacy* (Stanford: Stanford University Press, 1952), pp. 31–32.

12. Julius William Pratt, *A History of United States Foreign Policy*, 3rd ed. (Englewood Cliffs: Prentice-Hall, 1972), pp. 323–24; Davids, *America and the World of Our Time*, p. 108.

13. Henry S. Commager, "Twelve Years of Roosevelt," *American Mercury* 60 (April 1945): 391–401.

14. Hoover, *Memoirs*, II, p. 366 ff.

15. Pratt, *A History of United States Foreign Policy*, 1st ed. (New York: Prentice-Hall, 1955), p. 585.

16. Richard Hofstadter, *The American Political Tradition and the Men Who Made It* (New York: Alfred A. Knopf, Inc., 1948), p. 305, fn. 13.

17. L. Ethan Ellis, *A Short History of American Diplomacy* (New York: Harper, 1951), p. 377.

18. Hofstadter, *American Political Tradition*, pp. 279–347.

19. *Ibid.*, p. 345.

20. Professor Current thus described himself to the present writer in August 1952.

21. Richard N. Current, "Henry L. Stimson," in Norman A. Graebner (ed.), *An Uncertain Tradition: American Secretaries of State in the Twentieth Century* (New York: McGraw-Hill, 1961), pp. 168–83.

22. Richard N. Current, *Secretary Stimson: A Study in Statecraft* (New Brunswick: Rutgers University Press, 1954), *passim;* Current, "The Stimson Doctrine and the Hoover Doctrine," *American Historical Review* 59 (April 1954): 513–42.

23. William Appleman Williams, *American-Russian Relations, 1781–1947* (New York: Holt Rinehart and Winston, 1952), pp. 219, 225–26, 228–29, 255.

24. William Appleman Williams, "The Legend of Isolationism in the 1920's," *Science and Society* 18 (Winter 1954): 1–20.

25. William Appleman Williams, *The Tragedy of American Diplomacy* (New York: Dell Publishing Co., 1962 ed.), pp. 108–109, 115, 125.

26. *Ibid.*, pp. 126–28, 147.

27. *Ibid.*, pp. 129, 131.

28. *Ibid.*, pp. 136–37.

29. *Ibid.*, pp. 164, 305.

30. William Appleman Williams, *The Contours of American History*, paperback ed. (Chicago: Quadrangle Books, 1966), pp. 429–30.

31. *Ibid.*, p. 414.

32. Murray Rothbard, "The Hoover Myth," *Studies on the Left* 6 (1966): 70–84.

33. William Appleman Williams, "What This Country Needs," *New York Review* (5 November 1970): 7 ff.

34. Carl P. Parrini, *Heir to Empire: United States Economic Diplomacy, 1916–1923* (Pittsburgh: University of Pittsburgh Press, 1969), p. 166.

35. Wilson, *American Business and Foreign Policy*, p. 186.

36. Parrini, *Heir to Empire, passim.*

37. Williams, *Tragedy of American Diplomacy*, p. 123; Hofstadter, *American Political Tradition*, p. 287.

38. Williams, *American-Russian Relations*, p. 170.

39. *Ibid.*, p. 160; Hofstadter, *American Political Tradition*, p. 292, fn. 5.

40. Hofstadter, *American Political Tradition*, p. 292.

41. Herbert Clark Hoover, *The Memoirs of Herbert Hoover: The Great Depression, 1929–1941*, Vol. III (New York: Macmillan Co., 1952), p. 361.

42. Davids, *America and the World of Our Time*, p. 473.

43. Hoover's speech of 9 February 1951 in Lawrence S. Kaplan (ed.), *Recent American Foreign Policy: Conflicting Interpretations* (Homewood, Ill.: Dorsey Press, 1972), pp. 12–15.

44. Wilson, *American Business and Foreign Policy*, p. 220.

45. Hofstadter, *American Political Tradition*, p. 293.

46. *Ibid.*, p. 308.

47. Williams, *Tragedy of American Diplomacy*, pp. 118–21.

48. Paterson, "Isolation Revisited," *Nation* 209 (1 September 1969): 166–69.

49. Henry S. Commager in the *New York Times,* 12 March 1967.
50. Paterson, "Isolationism Revisited."
51. Robert W. Tucker, "The Revival of Isolationism," *Buffalo Courier-Express,* 22 October 1972.
52. Wilson, *American Business and Foreign Poilcy,* p. 241.
53. Robert W. Tucker, "What This Country Needs Is a Touch of New Isolationism," *New York Times,* 21 June 1972.
54. Hoover, *Memoirs, II,* pp. 338, 350, 352; Adler, *The Uncertain Giant,* pp. 125–26.
55. Selig Adler, "The Ghost of Isolationism," *Foreign Service Journal* (November 1969): 34 ff.
56. Williams, "What This Country Needs . . ."
57. Wilson, *American Business and Foreign Policy,* p. 241; Williams, "What This Country Needs . . ."
58. Howard Zinn (ed.), *New Deal Thought* (Indianapolis: Bobbs-Merrill Co., Inc., 1966), Introduction.

A Reevaluation of Herbert Hoover's Foreign Policy
Joan Hoff Wilson

1. Businessmen, for example, considered Hoover an expert on Chinese relations. As an engineer he had come to basically negative conclusions about China's potential for trade, investment, resource development, industrialization, and democratization which influenced his foreign policy views about the Far East in the 1920s and early 1930s. Although he did somewhat modify his original pessimism about commercial possibilities for American traders in China, he never succumbed to the myth of the China market. See: Herbert Clark Hoover, *The Memoirs of Herbert Hoover: Years of Adventure,* Vol. I (New York: Macmillan Co., 1952), pp. 35–72; *The Memoirs of Herbert Hoover: The Cabinet and the Presidency,* Vol. II (New York: Macmillan Co., 1952), pp. 180–81; Charles Evans Hughes to Hoover, 25 June 1924, China File, COF, HHP; Ray Lyman Wilbur to Hoover, 26 January 1933, Foreign Affairs File-Far East, HHP. Other references to Hoover's knowledge of Chinese affairs can be found in Countries File-China, HHP.
2. The "Hoover relief organization" became, in the course of the war, a skeleton government which negotiated directly with military and civilian leaders on both sides (an activity that led Senator Henry Cabot Lodge to charge Hoover with violating the Logan Act); issued passports which were honored across enemy lines; developed "independent sources" of information and a code system based on American slang (these were later used to keep the peace delegation from the U.S. informed of political and economic conditions "over the whole of Europe"); defied the Allied food blockade of former enemy countries after the November armistice; reconstructed telegraph and railroad systems throughout postwar Europe and even mediated peace settlements between local warring factions that had not honored the cease fire of 11 November 1918. See: Hoover to Wilson, 28 March 1919, Correspondence with Wilson File, PCP, HHP; Eugene Lyons, *Herbert Hoover: A Biography* (Garden City, N.Y.: Doubleday and Co., 1964), pp. 86–87, 115; Gene Smith, *The Shattered Dream* (New York: Morrow, 1970), pp. 38–39; Lewis Lichtenstein Strauss, *Men and Decisions* (Garden City,

N.Y.: Doubleday and Co., 1962), pp. 38, 42, 46–47; Harold Wolfe, *Herbert Hoover* (New York: Exposition Press, 1956), pp. 60–65.

3. For a more detailed definition and application of independent internationalism see: Joan Hoff Wilson, *American Business and Foreign Policy, 1920–1933* (Lexington: University of Kentucky Press, 1971), pp. xxvi–xxvii, *passim*. While Hoover was not the only independent internationalist of his generation, he was a particularly good example because as one contemporary biographer noted: ". . . however international in experience, [Hoover] is in conduct nationalistic almost to a fault." William Hard, *Who's Hoover* (New York: Dodd, Mead and Co., 1928), p. 229.

4. Speech delivered at A.I.M.E. dinner, 16 September 1919, Hoover Speeches and Addresses, 1915–1923, HIA.

5. Draft of letter, 10 January 1922, Economic Recovery in Europe File and "Economic Prospects of 1924," Economic Situation in U.S. File—both in Personal File, COF, HHP; Hoover Public Statements, 16 May 1922, 2 October 1930, 15 June 1931, PS 228, 1382, 1587, HHP; Hoover, *The Future of Our Foreign Trade* (Washington: Government Printing Office, 1926), *passim*.

6. Statement in *Chicago Daily News*, 15 September 1920, Speeches and Addresses, HIA; Hoover Public Statements, 15 June 1931, PS 1587, HHP.

7. *Wall Street Journal* (25 April 1921): 2; Unemployment and Unemployment/Business Cycles Files, COF, HHP; Hoover to Hughes, 29 April 1922, Foreign Loans File, COF; Hoover, *The Memoirs of Herbert Hoover: The Great Depression*, Vol. III (New York: Macmillan Co., 1952), pp. 5–9; Joan Hoff Wilson, *Herbert Clark Hoover: Forgotten Progressive* (Boston: Little, Brown and Co., in press), chpts. 4, 6. Also see footnote no. 5 above.

8. Wesley Clair Mitchell, *Business Cycles* (New York: National Bureau of Economic Research, Inc., 1927), p. 424; *Wall Street Journal*, 25 May 1921; Wilson, *Business and Foreign Policy, passim*.

9. Wilson, *Hoover*, ch. 2, 3, 4, 6.

10. Because of his many wartime offices it was natural that Hoover quickly became a "sort of outpost adviser . . . on the political and emotional forces moving in the war as they might bear on the possibilities of bringing about peace." From 1915 on, the White House consulted with Hoover through Col. Edward M. House on major foreign policy questions. During the peace conference alone Hoover was a member of twenty committees and chairman of six. See: Joseph H. Davis, "Herbert Hoover, 1874–1964: Another Appraisal," *The South Atlantic Quarterly* 68 (Summer 1968): 298–99; Lyons, *Hoover*, p. 115; Hoover, *Memoirs*, I, p. 201; *idem, The Ordeal of Woodrow Wilson* (New York: McGraw-Hill, 1958), pp. 1–3, 83–84.

11. Hoover to Wilson, 24 October 1918 and Hoover to Joseph Cotton, 4 November 1918, in Suda Lorena Bane and Ralph Haswell Lutz (eds.), *The Organization of American Relief in Europe, 1918–1919* (Stanford: Stanford University Press, 1943), pp. 26–27, 32–33; Hoover to Wilson, 11 April, 27 June, 12 July 1919, Hoover to Lord Robert Cecil, 9 July 1919, Hoover memorandum on financial rehabilitation of Europe, 16 May 1919—all in Correspondence with Wilson File, PCP, HHP; confidential reports of President's Committee of Economic Advisers, April and May 1919, Davis and Lamont to Russell Leffingwell, 27 May 1919—all in Box 16a, Norman H. Davis Papers, LC; Warburg, "Some Phases of Financial Reconstruction," 6 December 1918, Box August 1918–1931, Paul M.

Warburg Papers, Yale University, New Haven, Conn.; Lamont to Leffingwell, 18 November 1919, U.S. Senate, 74th Cong., 2nd sess., *Special Committee on the Investigation of the Munitions Industry* (Washington: Government Printing Office, 1936), pp. 10472–73; Lester V. Chandler, *Benjamin Strong: Central Banker* (Washington: Brookings Institution, 1958), pp. 141, 144, 145, 147; Hoover, "Momentous Conference," *Journal of American Bankers' Association* 13 (January 1921): 462–63.

12. Ruhl Jacob Bartlett, *The League to Enforce Peace* (Chapel Hill: University of North Carolina Press, 1944), p. 150; Hoover to Wilson, 12 November 1919, Correspondence with Wilson File, PCP, HHP; statement in *Chicago Daily News*, 15 September 1920, Speeches and Addresses, HIA; Hoover, *Memoirs*, II, pp. 10–13. In particular Hoover, like most of the members of the President's Committee of Economic Advisers, saw an economic threat to the United States in the so-called "anti-Open Door" features of the treaty; namely the fact that no reasonable reparations sum had been set for Germany to pay, that restrictive mandate rights had been set up in oil-rich areas, and that numerous economic limitations had been placed on Germany. While in principle agreeing with collective security, Hoover feared that Article 10 might be used to preserve forcefully the arbitrary territorial boundaries established by the treaty. He also worried that the League would ultimately threaten "the very essential principle of nationalism upon which our patriotism and progress is founded." In the end he argued that the United States had to join the League to prevent these potential dangers from materializing.

13. Hoover to Wilson, 11 April 1919, and Hoover to William Allen White, 13 June 1924—both in Correspondence with Wilson File, PCP, HHP; Hoover to Warren Gregory, 30 March 1920, Box 7, Irving Fisher Papers, Yale University, New Haven, Conn. By 1931, during the Manchurian crisis, Hoover no longer believed in the efficacy of economic boycotts to prevent war, but he definitely did in 1919 and 1920 when he was defending the League, *contrary* to the impression conveyed in his memoirs.

14. Hoover to Warren G. Harding, 2 August 1920, Hoover Correspondence, Jan.–Aug., 1920, HIA; Hoover, *Ordeal of Wilson*, pp. 268, 282–83, 299 (fn. 3); Hoover, *Memoirs*, II, pp. 34–35, 330, 332, 337, 352, 378 (fn. 8); John Chalmers Vinson, *Referendum for Isolation* (Athens, Ohio: University of Ohio Press, 1961), pp. 119–20; Alexander DeConde, *Herbert Hoover's Latin American Policy* (Stanford: Stanford University Press, 1951), pp. 39–43.

15. Heinz Wolfgang Arndt, *The Economic Lessons of the Nineteen-Thirties* (London: Oxford University Press, 1944), pp. 10–14, 223, 228, 232, 283–87, 290, 292–95; Carl P. Parrini, *Heir to Empire: United States Economic Diplomacy, 1916–1923* (Pittsburgh: University of Pittsburgh Press, 1969), pp. 40–71; Hoover, statements and memoranda in Financial Cooperation between the U.S. and Europe Folder, No. 5, HIA; Hoover quoted in *Wall Street Journal* (25 April 1921): 2. Other aspects of his economic foreign policy not discussed here include his general promotion of foreign trade through an expanded Bureau of Foreign and Domestic Commerce, sponsorship of China Trade Acts in the 1920s, and development of oil policy.

16. Unless otherwise noted the following material on tariff policy is documented in Wilson, *Business and Foreign Policy*, pp. 87–100.

17. Herbert Clark Hoover, *The New Day: Campaign Speeches of Herbert Hoover, 1928* (Stanford: Stanford University Press, 1928), pp. 133, 136, 139; tran-

script of Hoover's address and question and answer session at a Businessman's Conference on Agriculture, 15 April 1927, McNary-Haugen Bill File, Personal File, COF, HHP.

18. Arndt, *Economic Lessons*, p. 287; Hoover, *New Day*, pp. 134–35; Benjamin Harrison Williams, *Economic Foreign Policy of the United States* (New York: McGraw-Hill Book Company, Inc., 1929), pp. 238–39.

19. Unless otherwise noted the following material on loan supervision is documented in Wilson, *Business and Foreign Policy*, pp. 105–22.

20. Hoover to Hughes, 29 April 1922, Foreign Loans File, COF, HHP.

21. Unless otherwise noted the following material on reparations and debts is documented in Wilson, *Business and Foreign Policy*, pp. 122–56.

22. For details on the relationship between Hoover and FDR during the interregnum period see: Frank Freidel, *Franklin D. Roosevelt: Launching the New Deal* (Boston: Little, Brown and Co., 1973), *passim.*

23. Robert Freeman Smith, "Republican Policy and the Pax Americana, 1921–1932," in William Appleman Williams (ed.), *From Colony to Empire* (New York: J. Wiley, 1972), pp. 291–92; *idem, The Tragedy of American Diplomacy*, 2nd rev. ed. (New York: Dell Publishing Co., 1972), pp. 112–67; Wilson, *Business and Foreign Policy*, pp. 58–63, 162–83, 199–241; *idem, Hoover*, chpt. 6; DeConde, *Herbert Hoover's Latin American Policy;* Richard N. Current, "The Stimson Doctrine and the Hoover Doctrine," *American Historical Review* 59 (April 1954): 513–42; *idem*, "Henry L. Stimson," in Norman A. Graebner (ed.), *An Uncertain Tradition: American Secretaries of State in the Twentieth Century* (New York: McGraw-Hill, 1961), pp. 168–83.

24. Hoover to Stimson, 13 January 1933, Manchurian Incident Folder, Ray Lyman Wilbur Papers, Hoover Library West Branch, Iowa; Hoover, 1930 statement on Kellogg-Briand Pact, Debts File-Speech Drafts, HHP.

25. Hoover to Wilbur, 17 January 1941, Hoover to Senator Gerald Nye, 27 May 1941, Hoover to Christian Herter, 15 March 1947—all in Hoover Correspondence, 1941–49, PPP, HHP; Hoover to Truman, 26 November 1950, Truman Correspondence, PPP, HHP.

26. Hoover to Wilson, 28 March 1919, Correspondence with Wilson File, PCP, HHP; press statement, 25 April 1919, Hoover Public Statements, PS 19, HHP; *Time*, 8 July 1929; *New Republic* (10 July 1929): 19; William Appleman Williams, *Tragedy*, p. 167; *idem, Colony to Empire*, p. 482; *idem, American-Russian Relations, 1781–1947* (Holt, Rinehart Winston, 1952), pp. 192–229; Herbert Clark Hoover, *Addresses Upon the American Road, 1933–1938* (New York: C. Scribner's Sons, 1937), p. 319. For details of Hoover's evolving views on the Soviet Union throughout his entire life see: Joan Hoff Wilson, *Ideology and Economics: American Relations with the Soviet Union, 1918–1933* (Columbia: University of Missouri Press, in press); *idem, Hoover*, chpts. 3, 6, 8.

27. Edwin T. Layton, Jr., *The Revolt of the Engineers* (Cleveland: Press of Case Western Reserve, 1971), p. 170; Hoover, *Addresses Upon the American Road*, p. 121. The major deviation he made from this personal foreign policy guideline for dealing with communism abroad came in December 1939 after the Soviet invasion of Finland when Hoover urged that the United States withdraw its ambassador from the USSR. William R. Castle, Jr., his personal friend and a career diplomat, privately convinced him, however, that such a break in relations would be as much a step in the direction of war as an economic embargo (which Hoover opposed) would be. See: Castle to Hoover, 7

December 1939 and Hoover to Castle, 11 December 1939, William R. Castle Papers, Hoover Library, West Branch, Iowa; Hoover to John Callan O'Laughlin, 3 December 1939, O'Laughlin Papers, LC.

28. William Appleman Williams, *Colony to Empire*, pp. 5, 482–83; *idem*, "What This Country Needs . . . ," *New York Review of Books* (5 November 1970): 7–11; Peregrine Worsthorne, "The New Establishment," *Spectator* (27 March 1971): 414–15; Ronald Radosh and Murray N. Rothbard (eds.), *A New History of Leviathan* (New York: Dutton, 1972), pp. 144–45.

29. The single historian who has deviated least in his evaluation of Hoover over the years and who has consistently defended Hoover's brand of enlightened conservatism in domestic and foreign affairs is William Appleman Williams. From his first book, *American-Russian Relations, 1781–1947* to his introductory and concluding remarks in *From Colony to Empire*, he has pointed out Hoover's perspicacious understanding of economic foreign policy and the limitations that his conservative temperament placed upon his use of state power at home and abroad. Moreover, he was one of the first historians to point out "the process of development in Hoover's thought." This has been particularly helpful in understanding Hoover's opposition to the Soviet Union—an opposition which became more and more an abstract philosophy over the years rather than an ideological guide to action. Now some of Williams's former students (such as Carl P. Parrini, Robert Freeman Smith and Robert VanMeter) and a number of younger historians (representing a variety of political points of view from Ronald Radosh, a socialist, to Murray Rothbard, a right-wing libertarian) are also investigating the importance of Hoover's ideas for his own and our times.

30. See the Charles A. Beard Papers at DePauw University, Chicago, Ill., the Henry Elmer Barnes Papers at the University of Wyoming, Laramie, Wyo., and the Charles C. Tansill Papers and Walter Trohan Papers at Hoover Library, West Branch, Iowa, for general references to Hoover's relationship with revisionist historians, and for more specific references see: John W. Blodgett, Jr. to Hoover, 15 December 1950, 5 November 1951, 4 March 1952, 2 February, and 10 May 1954, Blodgett Correspondence; Beard to Ray Lyman Wilbur, 9 October 1945, Wilbur to Hoover, 16 October 1945, Hoover to Beard, 16 October 1945, Ray Lyman Wilbur Correspondence; Barnes to Hoover, 12 May 1952, Castle Papers; Ray Henle to Hoover, 10 June 1958, Ray Henle Folder of Hoover Correspondence, 1945–1959—all in PPP, HHP; Richard Hofstadter, *The Progressive Historians: Turner, Beard, Parrington* (New York: Alfred A. Knopf, Inc., 1968), p. 340.

31. William Appleman Williams, rejoinder to letter to editor, *New York Review of Books* (28 January 1971): 46.